HAND BOOK OF DAIRY FORMULATIONS, PROCESSES AND MILK PROCESSING INDUSTRIES

LIST OF PUBLICATIONS/BOOKS PUBLISHED BY
ENGINEERS INDIA RESEARCH INSTITUTE 4449, NAI SARAK, MAIN ROAD, DELHI - 6 (INDIA)

CHEMICALS/DYES/PETRO CHEMICALS/LUBRICANT/ ELECTROPLATING

Name of Books	₹	US$
* Hand Book of Lubricants, Grease and Petrochemical Technology	750/-	75
* Small Medium & Large Scale Chemical Industries	375/-	40
* Industrial Chemicals Technology Hand Book	1100/-	110
* Project Ideas on All Chemicals & Allied Industries	1300/-	130
* Electroplating, Anodizing & Surface Finishing Technology	750/-	75
* Agro Chemical Industries (Insecticide & Pesticides)	900/-	90
* Technology of Synthetic Dyes, Pigments Intermediates	1100/-	110
* Petrochemicals, Lubricants, Greases & Petroleum Refining	900/-	90
* Modern Technology of Organic & Inorganic Chemicals	1400-	140

GUMS, ADHESIVES & SEALANTS

Name of Books	₹	US$
* Technology of Gums, Adhesives & Sealants with Formulations	950/-	95
* Hand Book of Adhesives with their Formulae	650/-	65
* Adhesives Technology & Formulations Hand Book	975/-	100

SMALL SCALE INDUSTRIES/ STATIONERY/PAPER/INKS/ CANDLES & EXPORT BUSINESS

Name of Books	₹	US$
* Start Your Own Export Business (How To Export)	350/-	35
* Start Your Own Small Business and Industry	350/-	35
* Candle Making Processes & Formulations Hand-Book	380/-	38
* Stationery, Paper Converting & Packaging Industries	400/-	40
* Profitable Businesses to Start for Entrepreneurs	400/-	40
* Modern Small and Cottage Scale Industries	650/-	65
* Profitable Small Cottage Tiny & Home Industries	650/-	65

OFFSET PRINTING, SCREEN PRINTING & PACKAGING PRINTING INKS

Name of Books	₹	US$
* Printing Processes Technologies & Industries	375/-	40
* Hand Book of Printing Technology (Offset, Screen, Flexo, Gravure, Inkjet & Digital)	975/-	100
* Hand Book of Offset Printing Tech.	500/-	50
* Screen Printing with Processes & Technology	350/-	35
* Hand Book of Packaging Industries	1300/-	130
* Hand Book of Packaging Technology	900/-	90
* Modern Inks Formulaes & Manufacturing Industries	325/-	33
* Modern Technology of Printing Inks.	1150/-	115
* Modern Packaging Technology for Food Products	600/-	60
* Hand Book of Food Packaging Technology	900/-	90
* Hand Book of Pre Press	800/-	80

WOOD, VENEER, FOREST BASED

Name of Books	₹	US$
* Modern Technology of Wood, Veneer, Plywood, Particle Board, Fibre Board, Bamboo and Forest Products	1600/-	160

PAINT, VARNISH, COATING AND LACQUERS

Name of Books	₹	US$
* Paint Pigment Varnish & Lacquer Manufacturing	450/-	45
* Paint Varnish Solvents & Coating Technology	800/-	80
* Technology of Coatings, Resins, Pigments & Inks Industries	975/-	100
* Paint, Pigment, Solvent, Coating, Emulsion, Paint Additives and Formulation	900/-	90
* Mfg. Tech. & Formulations H.B on Thinners, Putty, Wall & Industrial Finishes & Synthetic Resins	900/-	100

PLASTIC/POLYMER PROCESSING, COMPOUNDING, MOULDS, PET, RESINS & RUBBER INDUSTRIES

Name of Books	₹	US$
* Injection Moulding of Plastics	750/-	75
* Moulds Design & Processing Hand Book	495/-	50
* Plastic Processing & Packaging Industries	975/-	100
* Hand Book of Plastic Projects (Hi-Tech Plastic Projects)	1300/-	130
* Synthetic Resins Technology with Formulations	800/-	80
* Technology of PET Bottles, Preform & PET Recycling	850/-	85
* Plastic Compounding, Masterbatches, PET & Other Plastics	750/-	75
* Technology of PVC Compounding and Its Applications	900/-	90
* Hand Book of Polymer and Plastic Technology	950/-	90
* Plastic Water Recycling Technology	750/-	75
* Hand Book Plastic Materials & Processing Technology	750/-	75
* Technology of Plastic Films	650/-	65
* Rotational Moulding Technology	450/-	45
* Hand Book of Fiber Glass Moulding	450/-	50
* Technology of Reinforced Plastics	750/-	75
* Modern Technology of Extrusion and Extruded Products	800/-	80
* Technology of Synthetic Resins and Emulsion Polymers	975/-	100

BAKERY & CONFECTIONERY

Name of Books	₹	US$
* Hand Book of Bakery Industries	350/-	35
* Hand Book of Confectionery with Formulations	600/-	60
* Hand Book of Modern Bakery Prod.	750/-	75
* Modern Bakery Tech. & Fermented Cereal Products with Formulae	1250/-	130
* Breakfast, Dietary Food, Pasta, Cereal Product Technology	1150/-	115

REAL ESTATE/HOTEL

Name of Books	₹	US$
* Real Estate Plazas, Hotel, Hospital & Commercial Complexes	1300/-	130

BIO-TECHNOLOGY

Name of Books	₹	US$
* Model Technology of Bio-Proccessing	1475/-	150
* Technology of Bio-Fuel (Ethamel & Biodiesel	975/-	100

E-Mail: eiribooks@yahoo.com, eiriprojects@gmail.com

Website : www.eiriindia.org, www.eiribooksandprojectreports.com, www.eiri.in

HAND BOOK OF DAIRY FORMULATIONS, PROCESSES AND MILK PROCESSING INDUSTRIES

Written By :

EIRI Consultants and Engineers

ENGINEERS INDIA RESEARCH INSTITUTE

4449, Nai Sarak, Main Road, Delhi-110 006 (India)

Ph. : 91-11-23918117, 23916431, 45120361

Fax : 91-11-23916431, 23918117

✶ **E-Mail :** eiribooks@yahoo.com

✶ **Website :** www.eiriindia.org

Sole Distributor :

EIRI PROJECT CONSULTANTS & PUBLISHERS

4/54, Roop Nagar, Delhi-110007

Printed and Published by :

ENGINEERS INDIA RESEARCH INSTITUTE

4449, Nai Sarak, Main Road, Delhi-110 006 (India)
Ph. : 91-11-23918117, 23916431, 45120361
Fax : 91-11-23916431, 23918117
✶ **E-Mail :** eiribooks@yahoo.com
✶ **Website :** www.eiriindia.org

Distributed by :

EIRI PROJECT CONSULTANTS & PUBLISHERS
4/54, Roop Nagar, Delhi-110007

2nd Edition

ISBN : 9788186732106
Printed in New Delhi (India)

₹ 750

Printed and Published by Sudhir Gupta for
"Engineers India Research Institute", 4449, Nai Sarak, Main Road,
New Delhi-110 006 and Printed at Swastik Offset, Delhi

PREFACE

India is now emerging as a major grower in the International Dairy market. With the current liberalisation of Indian Economy it has opened a wide field for entrepreneurs from other countries to participate in development of Indian Dairy Industry. The Dairy Industry which is the second largest industry of India employs millions of persons in our country. There is tremendous scope of growth in dairy industry and we can bring white revolution in our country if this industry is properly organised.

The book which is in your hand covering, three parts of dairy industries which are fully covered with the technologies, formulations, processing alongwith the sources of different machineries (Indian/Overseas) and raw materials.

The book is indispensable for all entrepreneurs as well as well established industrialists who are in venture for the complete informations about dairy and dairy products including the packing of these kinds of products.

Director
ENGINEERS INDIA RESEARCH INSTITUTE
Nai Sarak, New Delhi.

CONTENTS

S. NO.	PARTICULARS	PAGE NO.

PART - 1

INTRODUCTION, MANUFACTURING, TECHNOLOGIES, PACKAGING, STATISTICAL FIGURES & FORMULATIONS OF VARIOUS MILK & MILK BASED PRODUCTS

PART - 2

PROJECT PROFILES ON
DAIRY & MILK PRODUCTS

PART - III
DIRECTORY SECTION

LIST OF PUBLICATIONS/BOOKS PUBLISHED BY

ENGINEERS INDIA RESEARCH INSTITUTE 4449, NAI SARAK, MAIN ROAD, DELHI - 6 (INDIA)

Name of Books	₹	US$
EXPORT ORIENTED INDUSTRIES/PROCEDURES		
* Hand Book of Export Oriented Industries	1300/-	130
SPICES & COLD STORAGE		
* Hand Book of Spices & Packaging with Formulaes	750/-	75
* Start Your Own Cold Storage Unit	750/-	75
TEXTILE AUXILIARIES & CHEMICALS		
* Textile Auxiliaries and Chemicals with Processes and Formulations	950/-	95
* Modern Technology of Bleaching Dyeing Printing and Finishing of Textiles	750/-	75
PHARMACEUTICALS & DRUGS		
* Pharmaceuticals and Drugs Technology with Formulations	950/-	95
LEATHER & LEATHER PRODUCTS		
* Hand Book of Leather & Leather Products Technology	850/-	85
BIOTECHNOLOGY/BIOFERTILIZERS		
* Hand Book of Biotechnology	900/	90
* Hand Book of Biofertilizers and Vermiculture	900/-	90
AYURVEDIC MEDICINES		
* Ayurvedic & Herbal Medicines with Formulaes	750/-	75
* Hand book of Ayurvedic Medicines with Formulation	900/-	90
RUBBER & RUBBER INDUSTRIES		
* Rubber Chemicals & Processing Industries	400/-	40
* Technology of Rubber & Rubber Goods Industries	900/-	90
* Modern Rubber Chemicals Compounds and Rubber Goods Technology	1500/-	150
MINERAL & MINERALS		
* Hand book of Minerals and Minerals based Industries	975/-	100
FISH FARMING		
* Hand Book of Fish Farming and Fishery Products	650/-	65
ORGANIC FARMING/FOOD		
* Hand Book of Organic Farming & Organic Foods with Vermi-Composting and Neem Products	1100/-	110
PULP & PAPER BASED TECHNOLOGY		
* Hand book of Pulp & Paper, Paper Board and Paper Based Technology	1150/-	115
STEEL / S.S./ NON FERROUS METALS		
* Modern Technology of Non Ferrous Metals and Metal Extraction	1100/-	100
* Processing Technology of Steels and Stainless Steels	1900/-	190

MULTIPLE PROJECT REPORTS IN CD-ROM AT ECONOMY COSTS

Title	₹
* 92 New Lucrative Project Reports in Cd	25,000/-
* 45 Infotech/IT, Hospitality, Hospital, College, School & Clubs	16,000/-
* 23 Profitable Construction Projects	16,000/-
* 56 Agro Based & Food Process Projects	16,000/-
* 52 Food, Dairy, Bakery, Confectionery & Snacks Foods	16,000/-
* 100 Profitable Plastic, Polymers & Allied Projects (100 Project Reports)	25,000/-
* 45 New Chemicals & Allied Reports	18,000/-
* 44 Textile, Garments, Hosiery & Allied	16,000/-
* 23 Dairy Farming (Buffaloe & Jersey Cows), Dairy Products and other Milk Processing Industries	16,000/-
* 42 Paper & Pulp, Paper Board and Paper Converting Industries	18,000/-
* 31 Essential Oils, Perfumes, Flavours & Aromatic Compounds	16,000/-
* 63 Profitable Packaging & Allied Projects	16,000/-
* 36 Profitable Printing & Allied Projects	16,000/-
* 28 Surgical & Disposable Medical Projects	16,000/-
* 99 Profitable Printing & Packaging Projects	25,000/-
* 42 Electroplating, Anodizing & Allied Proj.	16,000/-
* 31 Profitable Plantation, Cultivation & Farm	18,000/-
* 55 Profitable Projects from Agro and other Industrial Wastes	18,000/-
* 35 Gums, Adhesives, Sealants & Resins	18,000/-
* 43 Iron, Steel, Casting, Fabrication, Wire Drawing & Rolling Mills Projects	18,000/-
* 54 Paint, Varnish, Solvents, Lacquers, Enamels, Thinner & Powder Coating Proj.	18,000/-
* 26 Educational Projects (Schools, Colleges, Management/Training Institutes etc.)	16,000/-
* 12 Mosquitoes Preventive Projects (Coils, Mat, Liquids, Agarbatti, Nets, Spray etc.)	12,000/-
* 52 Cosmetics (Herbal & Synthetics) Technology Projects (52 Proj. Reports)	18,000/-
* 67 Rubber & Rubber Goods Industries	18,000/-
* 21 Bakery & Allied Project Reports	12,000/-
* 37 Aluminium & Aluminium Based Ind.	16,000/-
* 14 Potato & Potato Based Industries	12,000/-
* 50 Electrical, Electronic & Computer/IT Based Industries (50 Project Reports)	18,000/-
* 5 Power Plant Projects (Thermal, Hydro, Solar, Wind Energy & Lignite Coal Based)	16,000/-
* 35 New Profitable Industries (35 Reports)	16,000/-
* 10 Molasses Based Lucrative Projects	16,000/-
* 24 Fruits/Veg. & Allied Food Dehydration Proj.	16,000/-
* 24 Soap and Detergents	18,000/-
* 30 Chemicals, Mechanicals, Packaging and other Profitable Projects	16,000/-
* 43 Automobile and Automobile Based Projects	18,000/-
* 160 New Export Oriented Units & Most Profitable Projects (160 Project Reports)	30,000/-
* 5 Ginger and Ginger Based Industries	12,000/-
* 13 Fish Farming & Fishery Projects	16,000/-
* 9 Tea Plantation & Processing Industries	15,000/-
* 14 Roasted/Salted, Cashewnuts, Almonds, Namkeens and Spice Projects	15,000/-
* 28 Fruit Juice, Food Dehydration & Allied	16,000/-
* 6 Agarbatti and Allied Projects	15,000/-
* 23 Injection Moulded Plastic Projects	15,000/-
* 38 Biofertilizer, Biofuel, Enzyme, Organic Farming, Protein & Allied Projects	18,000/-
* 11 Infotech/IT Lucrative Projects	16,000/-
* 11 Solar & Solar Based Projects	15,000/-
* 42 Hospitality, Building Materials, Power, Steels, Alcohol & Other Food Products	18,000/-
* 10 Coconut & Coconut Bye Products	16,000/-
* 22 Alcohol, Beer, IMFL, Country Liquor, Wine & Other Related Projects	22,000/-
* Food Processing & Agro Proj.	30,000/-

1

MILK

Milk is the normal secretion of the mammary glands for the feeding of young mammals and it is the fundamental requirement of body to survive.

An infant needs mother's milk to fulfil the quench of the body-thrist to extract the basic nutrients of its body. This is the food, which is required since birth till the survival.

The composition of milk is rather complex and of Moisture, Fat, Minerals, Carbohydrates, Energy/Calories, Calcium, Phosphorus an d Iron. Though the percentage of these constituents vary in different types of milk. The figures mentioned below would highlight the percentage of these constituents in different kinds of milk derived from different cattles:

Sl. No.	Constituents	Milk derived from			
		Buffalo	Cow	Goat	Liquid Skimmed Milk
1.	Moisture (gm)	8.100	87.50	86.80	92.10
2.	Protein (gm)	4.30	3.20	3.30	2.50
3.	Fat (gm)	6.50	4.10	4.50	0.10
4.	Minerals (gm)	0.80	0.80	0.80	0.70
5.	Carbohydrates (gm)	5.00	4.40	4.60	4.60
6.	Energy/Calories (Kcal)	117.00	67.00	72.00	29.00
7.	Calcium (mg)	210.00	120.00	170.00	120.00
8.	Phosphorous (mg)	130.00	90.00	120.00	90.00
9.	Iron (mg)	0.20	0.20	0.30	0.20

All these constituents of milk are responsible our bodily needs, at different stages of life. As per Recommended Daily Allowance (RDA), one year old child needs around 1000 Kealories per day, a 3 year child needs around 3000 to 5000 Kealories a day. A normal child needs at least 3 servings of milk or milk poducts per day. The amount of milk/milk product consumed, yields the norishment to our body through milk exchange and Fat Exchange processes. These are nutritional needs of the body to keep the person healthy and fit.

Milk Exchange is the substitution of alternatives in the form of other items, besides milk products, to fulfil the nutritional needs of the body. In other words, the milk exchange is a serving of food equivalent to I cup milk, retaining its energy and nutritional contents. One milk exchange contains the substantial amounts of Carbohydrates and Proteins and about 80 Kealories of energy. Here the milk exchange programme and fat exchange programme shall be highlighted, enabling the reader to procure the awareness pertaining to Nutritional needs of the body. Since the milk exchange has already been defined, let us take fat exchange into consideration. Although it is most prevalent idea that the fat contents of any product are responsible for the formation of Cholesterol in the body. So it is utmost to take this aspect into consideration. Although the regular exercise and by burning fat, one can prevent the formation of Cholesterol in our body.

A whole milk adds 2 fat exchange, whereas I cup of fortified milk with 1% fat, adds 1/2 fat exchange. One cup of the fat fortified plain/unflavoured Yogurt made from 2% of fortified milk adds 1 fat exchange. A cup of milk contains 12 gm of carbohydrates and 1 gm of carbohydrates is worth 4 Kealories. 48 Kealories are derived from carbohydates and 32 Kealories are derived from protein. Cream and butter are not milk exchange because they contain little or no carbohydrates and insignificant amounts of other nutrients, important in milk. They simply contain fat and are responsible fot the fat exchange process.

This is the significance of milk pertaining to the human body, but the other living creatures other than human beings, who need the body nutrients for the infants' body, need no education in regard to this. It is the nature and the bodily needs which teach them every thing, as per the demand of the time. A human body has a brain which understands the logic and reacts accordingly, but an animal is almost brainless and is governed and nurtured by the nature as per the timely needs of the body. But above all, the milk is the basic and utmost need of any living creature, besides human beings. No matter the creatur is on the earth, under earth or in the sea.

The Breast milk of human or the human milk, which is sufficient enough to keep the infant healthy and fit to generate the body resistance to fight the diseases and illness, throughout the life, is no less than the nature's miracle. The human milk/breast milk of the human being is consisted of the following ingredients and the percentage:-

The human milk is consisted of 88.0 gm of moisture, 1.1 gm of Protein, 3.4 gm of Fat, 0.1 gm of Minerals, 7.4 gm of carbohydrates, 65 Kealories of energy, 28 mg of calcium, 11 mg of Phosphorus and insignificant amount of Iron. This is the drink which is responsible to form a dirm base of an infant till its death. The fundamental nutrients are extracted by an infant in the womb and after taking birth, the human milk is responsible to create the body resistance to curb and fight the different kind of diseases and sickness. Besides human beings, even the animals also need the mothers milk in any form or the other to form a solid base to erect the building of a strong and healthy survival. The food habits in India are confined to a little limited sphere of milk consumption, in the form of milk or its derivatives, but in the other parts of world also, it is the milk or the milk products which are consumed as a culture in their lives. Keeping in view the comparison, it is apparent, that India needs a lot of modification and the development in the field of Dairy. It may be in regard to the Cattled Breeding or the maintenance of the cattle providing us the milk. We must overcome the discrepancies pertaining to the quality and standards of the milk procured from the cattle. These setbacks are well apparent, although, not admitted. The present conditions of the milk yielding cattle are pathetic despite the Government trying to complement many a regulations.

Precisely, the cow is considered to be a holy creature among the animals, mythologically. But the present scenario is well descriptive to reveal the truth, in practical manner. The stray cattle, abandomed by the owners, are responsible for many a road hazards and accidents in the metro cities like Delhi. The eating habits of milk yielding animals, especially cow, are really pathetic and unhygienic.

The presently prevailing conditions reveal the poor quality of milk derived from such animals,, precisely cow, a holy6 creature, mythologically. It means that to procure the best quantity and quality of milk, fundamentally, the milk yielding animal has to be maintained well. Its food habits, the sheds etc., must be kept clean and hygienically intact to procure the best quantity and quality of the milk to keep the whole generation of the national to fight the odd future despite the age of advancement. Entering in the 21st century would require a lot of enlightenment and awareness with regard to present scenario, to cope up with the developing or developed countries. In this era of globalisation and liberalisation, we Indians have to mould ourselves to sustain in the International market, to fight the stage of competition inthe International market. It may concern the field of Exporters to abide by the buyers' specifications as per the International norms. If we do not improve the quality of our products, we may fail and left behind in the International market. To ascertain the quantity and the quality, we have to learn a lot, to cope up with the International market, to sustain ourselves. Not only this, if we do not improve, the Foreign Investors may conquer us and our freedom may be in danger. Besides this, as already highlighted, we may earn a lot of foreign exchange to nourish our country, otherwise for a better placement in the International Survival.

To fight the present scene of inflation, due to which, even the biggest capitalist like United States of States of America, is longing to have the Japanese collaboration to sustain in the International market. Why can't we become like Japanese, who sacrificed every thing in the Second World War, but still have a name in the International market to keep their survival safe.

2

INDIAN BUFFALOES

Buffaloes have been classified into two main categories namely riverine and swamp depending upon variation in their habitat and genome. The swamp buffaloes are stocky animals with marshy land habitats and have 48 chromosomes. They are found primarily in south east Asian countries but few animals are also available in north-eastern states of India. These animals are used for draught power in paddy fields and haulage and are also used for meat production. River buffaloes are massive in size mostly with curled horns and prefer to enter clear water and have 50 chromosomes. Though these two distinct breeds have been successfully interbred, yet they maintain a separate genetic identity.

World's buffalo population has undergone demographic change over a long period of time in different countries. Out of the total buffalo population of 147 millions about 142 millions are predominantly found in Asia and the pacific. The trend of global population change indicates almost 3 times faster rate of increase per annum (2.04) during 1950 to 1970 (0.64 per cent). The average rate of change from 1950 to 1992 being 1.47 per cent per annum.

India continues to be the leading most buffalo populated country having 78 million heads, most of which are riverine. Buffaloes in India are primarily maintained by farmers in more than 570 thousand villages in the herd size of 2 to 3 animals. Large herds are also available in milk shed areas of metropolitan and big cities where dairying is considerd as an industry and intensive system of management is followed. Besides, there are approximately 60-70 Govt. institutional farms for research and developmental activities in the country.

The picture with regard to buffalo **milk production** is very encouraging as is evident from the fact that about 95% of world buffalo milk (45.3 million tons) is produced in Asia and the Pacific, while 64.4 per cent is produced in India (FAO, 1992). From the data for trend in milk production from 1950 to 1992 it appears that milk production in the world increased by 4.26%. Except for Italy, all other buffalo owning countries in Europe have shown downfall milk production mainly due to the larger emphasis on buffaloes for meat production. However, significant improvement in lactation milk production have been reported for riverine buffaloes (mainly imported from India) in Bulgaria, Italy and Egypt. The all round increase in buffalo milk production is an indication of increasing importance and preference of Indian buffaloes over cattle in India as well as in other countries.

The percent of total bovines slaughtered in the world during the last decade has remained almost constant i.e. 17.1 to 17.4 per cent. However, in India the number of animals going to abattoir has doubled during the last 10 days whereas the overall increase in the world is just 0.22 per cent. Similarly, the total quantity of meat produced has increased at the rate of almost 15 per cent per annum in India which is much higher than the percent increase in Asia (6.6%) and the world (1.6%) per annum over the last 10 years.

The increasing trend of buffalo population is most of the Asian countries and in Brazil and Italy is indicative of the fact that buffalo will continue to play a vital role in the economy of the developing countries for the supply of milk, meat and draught power for lung time to come.

BREEDS

India posseses some of the best milch breeds of the world e.g. Murrah, Nili-RAVI and Surti. Some other breeds of this type found in India e.g. Meshing, Jaffarabadi and Bhadawari also have high potential for milk and fat production besides being used for work.

Buffaoles of different breeds have been classified into various group types depending upon their phenotypes and geographic locations. Cockril (1982) classified all buffaloes of river type into following two sub-groups.

1. The sub-group in which the *horns are curled* and set close to the head and are down swept e.g. Murrah Ravi, Mehsana, Jaffarabadi and Sambalpur.

2. The sub-group in which the **horns are sickle shaped and unswept** e.g. Bhadawari, Kalahandi, Kanara, Manda, Nagpuri, Pandharpuri, Surti, Tarai and Toda.

Indian buffaloes have also been classified on the basis of their well defined characters into five major groups (Acharya and Bhat, 1988 and Balaine, 1988). Indian buffaloes and classified below on the basis of their group type and breeding tract of each of the breed is also indicated.

Bıeeds buffaloes of Indian origin and their breeding tracts.

Group	*Breed*	*Breeding Tract*
Murrah type	Murrah	Rohtak, Jind, Hisar, Bhiwani, Sonepat District in Haryana.
	Nili Ravi	Ferozepur District in Punjab.
Gujarat	Surti	Kai ra and Baroda districts.
	Jaffarabadi	Kutch, Junagarh and Jamnagar districts.
	Mehsana	Mehsana, Sabarkantha andBanaskantha districts.
Uttar Pradesh	Bhadawari	Bhadawari estate and Bah tehsil in Agra, Gwalior and Etawah district.
	Tarai	Tarai region of Uttar Pradesh.
Central India	Nagpuri	Nagpur, Akola and Amraoti districts.
	Pandharpuri	South Maharashtra, West Andhra Pradesh and North Karnataka.
	Paralakhemundi	Ganjam, Koraput and Plateau region of Orissa.
	Kalahandi	Hilly region of Andhra Pradesh & Orissa.
	Sambalpur	Bilaspur district
South India	Toda	Nilgiri hills
	South Kanara	West Coast in Kerala

All riverine breeds are primarily good milk producers though majority of them are dual purpose animals exhibiting good meat and draught characteristics, however, their potentiality for meat remains unexplored and unexploited. Of the breeds listed above only Murrah, Nili-Ravi Surti have been studied extensively for production and reproduction characteristics in India. However, most of the buffaloes of the Indian sub-continent fall into the non-descript group which are designated as desi (undefined buffaloes) and cannot be categorised in any of well defined above breeds. The large population of desi buffalos in India is primarily because of the lack of organised breeding activities. (Acharya and Bhat, 1988) in the farmers buffaloes such as breed improvement societies. As process of development programmes, migration of stock from within and between breeding improvement societies. As process of development programmes, migration of stock from within and between breeding tracts and grading up of non-descript population in various states, large distinct breeds are available even in their respective breeding tracts.

Buffaloes found in the north-eastern states and in the eastern coastal region of India and in China and South-east Asian countries e.g. Philiippines, Thailand, Malaysia, Vietnam, Sri Lanka, Burma, Laos, Kampuchea, Bangladesh etc. have been classified as swamp buffaloes on the basis of their genetic constitution (2n=48) and natural habitat. The breeds included in this group in India and Manda and Parlakhemundi (Patro and Kornel, 1987).

PRODUCTION PERFORMANCE

GROWTH :

The average birth weight in Indian buffaloes have been reported to be as low as 21 kg in Surti (Thamothanan, 1980) reported from Sri Lanka as high as 41 kg in Indian Murrah (Bhat and Taneja, 1986) and higher in male calves than in female calves born. Significant effect of season, year sex, sire and sequence of calving have also been reported. Information on body weight at birth, 6 months, 12 months, 24 months and at maturity in various breeds is presented in table 1.

Growth curve from birth to 36 months of age in Indian buffaloes follows a linear trend with average daily gain of 548 g between 3-6 months and 404 g between birth to 36 months of age (Nautiyal and Bhat, 1977). Body weight as first calving in different breeds (Table 1) range from 367 kg in Dharwari to 531 kg in Nili-Ravi buffaloes (Sharma and Basu, 1984). Buffalo calves at Central Institute for Research on Buffaloes, Hisar has shown growth rate of more than 500 g per day from birth to one year of age. Some calves have body weight as high as 290 kg at one year of age/Under free choice feeding system calves weaned at birth showed higher body weights than unweaned calves (Sethi and Chopra, 1994).

The comparative growth rate in riverine and swamp breeds of different origin reported by Moran (1986) indicate higher growth rate in riverine breeds than in swamp buffaloes. Buffaloes of the European and Australian origin had higher growth rate than buffaloes of Asian origin primarily due to the fact that buffaloes in Australia and Europe have been reared for meat while in India they have primarily been reared for milk production. For milch type of animals growth rate ranging from 400 to 500 g per day upto the age of 18 months and 300 to 400 g per day from 18 months to first calving is highly remunerative.

MILK PRODUCTION :

Average lactation milk production and range of lactation milk yield reported in different breeds is presented in Table 2. Milk production as reported from different sources indicate averge lactation milk production in Murrah (1850 kg) and Nili-Ravi (1765 kg) buffaloes. However, the average from elite herds have been reported as high as 2850 kg in Murrah and 2808 kg in Nili-Ravi buffaloes from NDRI Karnal and PAU Ludhiana respectively.

In India the average first lactation milk yield in Murrah buffaloes varies from 1540 to 1868 kg (Bhalaru and Dhillon, 1978; Patro and Bhat, 1979;Reddy, 1980). First lactation yield in Nili-Ravi (1707) is almost equal to that of Murrah, however, the averages for first lactation milk yield for Bhadwari (1165 kg), Nagpuri (1026 kg) and Surti (1364 kg) are lower than Murrah and Nili-Ravi breeds. The average lactation milk yield in elite herds has been reported to be as high as 2808 kg in an average lactation length of 305 days (Tiwana, 1990) and some buffaloes yielding as high as 4000 kg of milk in a lactation with recorded peak yield as high as 20-25 kg per day.

Heritability estimates for first lactation milk yield in Murrah buffaloes range from 0.08+ 0.04 to 0.19+0.08 (Bhalaru and Dhillon, 1978; Pandey, 1983) which are slightly lower than the 0.28+0.20 for Nili-Ravi buffaloes. The heritability of second and subsequent lactation milk yield (0.22) is higher than that of first lactation milk yield (0.16) with unadjusted data (Acharya, 1988).

Studies on genetic aspects of monthly and cumulative monthly milk yield and components of lactation curve has revealed that heritability estimated for part lactation records is higher than those of total records.

LACTATION LENGTH :

Average lactation length and the range of average reported by different sources for various breeds are presented in Table 2. The first lactation length in Murrah buffaloes is around 300 days (Basu and Ghai, 1978; Reddy 1980) and in Nili-Ravi it is slightly higher (323 days). In Bhadawari, Nagpuri and Surti it ranges between 276 and 295 days for the first lactation as well as for the overall lactations (Singh and Desai, 1962; Siddappa and Gani, 1976; Deb and Kudu, 1977).

MILK CONSTITUENTS :

The average fat and solid not fat percentage at different stage of lactation in Murrah buffaloes at CIRB Hisar is presented in Table 3. The fat percentage in Murrah and Nili-Ravi is comparable however, the SNF constituents in Murrah buffaloes reported from NDRI Karnal (Singh et al, 1979) are slightly higher than Nili-Ravi breed reported from Pakistan (Asghar, 1987). Though the fat contents increase significantly with the advancement of lactation but the SNF percent remain almost constant throughout the lactation. Fat and total solids percent has been found statistically different among pregnant and non-pregnant buffaloes at the same stage of lactation (Sethi et al, 1994). All the three constituents have been reported to have low repeatability estimate of 0.167+0.014, 0.087+0.016 and 0.10+0.017 respectively.

AGE AT FIRST CALVING:

The average age at first calving in different breeds is presented in Table 2. The average age at first calving in Murrah buffaloes range from 39.9 months to 54.6 months (Bhadula and Desai, 1972; Reddy and Mishra, 1980; Chhikara et al, 1978; Jain and Taneja, 1982) which is higher than 37.6 months of age reported in Bulgarian Murrah (Defranciscis, 1988). In Bhadawari and Nagpuri buffaloes the age at first calving is slightly higher (44.3 - 54.2 months) than Surti (41.4 months) and Nili-Ravi buffaloes (41.4 months). However, Nili-Ravi buffaloes in Pakistan are reported to have higher (47.3 months) age at first calving (Ashfeg and Mason, 1954; Ahmed et al, 1983) than Indian Nili-Ravi. Swamp buffaloes have been reported to have the highest age at first calving (51 months) and the average from different sources range from 37.0 to 74.0 months.

DRY PERIOD:

The approximate average and the rage of dry periods reported for various breeds is presented in Table 3 which range from 95 days to as high as 288 days. In India the average dry period in Murrah, Nili-Ravi, Dharwari and Bhadawari breeds range from 148 days to 198 days (Basu and Ghai, 1978; Gurnani et al, 1976; Singh and Desai, 1962; Siddappa and Gani, 1976; Chaudhary and Ahmed 1078). Dry period in Nagpuri buffaloes over different lactation ranged from 95-155 (Belorkar et al, 1977; Deb and Kadu, 1977).

REPRODUCTION PERFORMANCE

Most of the buffaloes are considered to be seasonal breeders with maximum calvings taking place from July to November in almost all breeds (Nagarcankar and Rao, 1987; Chaudhary and Waheed, 1978). Rierine breeds exported to various other countries also show the similar trend of seasonal calvings from October to January in Egypt (Ragab et al, 1954) from July to October in Italy (Proto and Gargano, 1966). The above findings suggest that the buffaloes in general come in oestrus during the cold months and are subfertile during the hot months. The cause of sub-fertility has been reported as poor thermoregulation in buffaloes (Nagarcenkar and Sethi, 1988) and also poor nutrition during summer months when green fodder is almost negligible and only lingo-cellulosic material e.g. straw/dry roughages are mainly available for feeding and poor heat symptoms resulting in low heat detection rate. Investigations on management practices to overcome the problem of sub-fertility in summer months have revealed that in summer months wallowing or water sprinkling during the hot hours of the day helps in maintaining the reproduction efficiency in breedable buffaloes (Sastry et al, 1981).

SERVICE PERIOD:

The average service period in different riverine breeds reported in India varies from 90 days in Nagpuri to 211 days in Nili-Ravi from Pakistan (Table 3). The overall service period in Nagpuri and Dharwari breeds has been reported to be lower than the other riverine breeds, however, in swamp buffaloes this trait is reported to be higher than in riverine bred. Service period in all the breeds needs further investigation since this is the key reproduction trait which needs to be improved, through appropriate reproductive management.

CALVING INTERVAL:

The average first calving interval for Murrah, Nili-Ravi, Surti and Bhadawari breeds is slightly higher (Bhat and Taneja, 1986) than the overall calving interval for almost all the breeds (Lall, 1975; Singh and Desai, 1962; Chaudhary and Ahmed, 1978). The swamp buffaloes show much higher calving interval than riverine breeds (Table 3).

MEAT PRODUCTION PERFORMANCE

Meat production potentialities of riverine buffaloes of Indian origin has been undertaken more extensively in some of the european countries and in Brazil as compared to India mainly due to the meat production emphasis in those countries. Mediterranean and Egyptian buffaloes which are also of riverine type have been bred for beef production due to their excellent muscle confirmation. Swamp type of buffaloes mainly found in South-east Asian countries and in China which are extensively used for work in agricultural fields, are also usd for meat production as well.

Experimental evidence for raising buffalo calves for meat production shown body weight gain as high as 635 g per day in Murrah buffalo calves between the age from 8 to 11 months (Sharma and Talapatra, 1963; Agarwal, 1974). In non-descript Indian buffaloes growth rate of 469 to 607 g per day has also been reported (Ranjhan, 1983). Under group and individual feeding systems of management body weight gain of 541 and 534 g respectively was achieved in Murrah buffalo male calves. Average DM intake per 100 kg body weight was also higher in individually (3.17 + 0.06) than in group fed calves (3.11 + 0.04) at CIRB, Hisar (Bharadwaj and Sethi, 1994).

In Trinidad and Brazil, Indian breeds like Murrah, Surti, Jaffarabadi, Nili-Ravi and Bhadawari have been crossed with local buffaloes to raise crossbred progeny for beef production (Rastogietal, 1978). An average finished weight of 476 kg at 2 years of age was attained in these crosses giving a daily weight gain of 512 g. Higher rates of gain between 900 and 1150 g per day was achieved in China and USSR and the dressing percentage between 52 and 62% (Dzafraov, 1968; Wang pei-chien, 1978).

Dressing percentage in buffaloes range from 55 to 64 per cent depdending upon the level of protein and energy intake. (Sengar et al, 1987). In Egyptian buffaloes percentage in well fed buffalo steers weighing 435 kg was reported to be 59 per cent.

Buffalo meat is richer in protein and amino acids than the meat of other species. Water buffalo carcass is lean with low percentage of fat deposition, has rounded ribs, a higher proportion of muscle and less fat. Flavour is comparable to that of beef in steaks as well as in processed meat products. Buffalo meat is superior to beef in palatability and tenderness (Borghese et al, 1978).

Of the total buffalo population in India about 30 per cent are young calves of which half the number are male calves. These calves with appropriate feeding can raised upto 18 months to achieve at least 300-350 kg weight. This can result into quality meat production from buffaloes. With future trends of biotechnology and genetic selection, Indian buffaloes have great potential as red meat producers.

The potentialities of river buffaloes as meat support the present and future requirements of rapidly growing population deserve special attention, because of its capacity to convert coarse roughages and other cereal by-products into meat economically. There is an urgent need for the development of feed lot and feltering by upgrading the non-descript buffaloes with males of elite breeds available in the country for developing the stock for quality meat production.

GENETIC IMPROVEMENT PROGRAMMES

For genetic improvement in buffaloes systematically selective breeding in milch breeds and use of high pedigreed bulls in non-descript buffaloes has been undertaken. Progeny testing have shown some genetic improvement over number of generations in a few institutional and organised herds.

PROGENY TESTING:

Progeny testing in India has been undertaken at Military Dairy Farms, State Govt., farms and various institutional and research herds. These herds are now the elite germplasm resource for Murrah, Nili-Ravi and Surti breeds of buffaloes and will continue to make genetic progress for wider dissemination of genetic material developed at these institutions.

Results of progeny testing at various military dairy farms have revealed that 13% of the bulls had a breeding value of more than+100 kg and only 4 bulls out of 98 tested bulls had breeding value above 10% of the population mean (Basavaiah, 1978). With the average generation interval of 7 years, the genetic improvement per years was upto 0.37 per cent over the population mean as against theoretically expected improvement of 1.0 to 2.0 per cent per annum (Dev, 1978; Nagarcenkar and Sethi, 1988) at heritability estimate of 0.25 and average phenotypic standard deviation of 400 litres. The slow rate of improvement indicates that the programme needed systematic approach for implementation. Other non-additive factors which cause the genetic drift also contributed to relatively low progress.

The All India Co-ordinated Research Project on Buffaloes was as started by ICAR in the year 1970 at 4 different centres. The results revealed some significant observations at Karnal and Ludhiana for Murrah (Heavy) bred but at the other two centres namely Vallabhnagar and Dharwad the asprogramme showed a very slow pace. The results of progeny testing at Karnal in the first 6 sets of bulls showed superiority of the top ranking bulls selected over the contemporaries in each set between 7.53% (4th set) to 19.99% (3rd set) showing annual genetic gain in milk production from 0.28 to 0.67% (Nagarcenkat and Sethi, 1988). Results of 7 sets of 8 bulls each at Ludhiana revealed sire index of proven bulls as high as 2224 (2nd set) on daughters performance (Tiwana, 1990) resulting in annual genetic gain of 4.5 kg milk yield averaging 0.27% of the herd average (Tiwana et al, 1985).

Buffalo Improvement Projects were taken up at several state and Central Government farms, e.g. Alamadi farm, Chennai; govt. Livestock Farm, Banawasi, Government Cattle Breeding Farm, Anjora; Government Livestock Farm, Dhamrod, for Surti breed. Most of these farms have not shown any impact of the progeny testing programme.

Progeny testing programme at Central Institute for Research on Buffaloes, Hisar was intially sponsored by the Government of India with an object to evaluate Murrah bulls on the basis of the performance of their daughters and distribution of progeny tested bulls to various breeding and farms. The number of bulls in each set ranged from 7 to 9 and the average duration of use from 26 to 36 months. The sire index based daughters contemporary comparison method ranged from 1803 in the first set t 1434 in the 3rd set with declining trend upto the 8th set.

The possible causes of slow rate of genetic improvement were the small herd size at the all centres, slow intensity of selection and non-availability of good quality bulls since at all the centres a sort of close system of breeding was followed.

CROSS BREEDING:

During the past two decades attempts have been made in several countries e.g. Malayasia, Thailand, Philippines. China, Vietnam and other countries to cross swamp buffaloes with riverine breeds e.g. Murrah, Nili-Ravi and Surti besides crossing among the riverine buffaloes in India to produce crossbreds with higher potential for milk, meat and draft power.

The origin of Mehsana and Godavari is said to have been evolved from crossing of Surti and local buffalo cows with Murrah bulls respectively. In an experiment at NDRI, Karnal significant increase in milk yield and improvement in reproduction traits was observed in Murrah X Surti crossbred buffaloes (Sharma and Basu, 1984). In terms of efficiency of milk production (milk yield per day of calving interval), the crossbred (3.4 kg) were even reported to be better than the Murrah (3.2 kg).

In Bulgaria, Murrah buffaloes were reported to the superior than Bulgarian buffaloes both for body weights and milk yield while the Murrah & Bulgarian crosses were close to Murrah for body weights at different age groups. The milk yield and total fat in the crossbred were close to the mid parent value (Nagarcenkar, 1976).

There is genetic diversity among river and swamp type buffaloes. Inspite of the genetic diversity among the two types of buffaloes, crossbreeding between the two has resulted in fertile hybrids (FI) with diploid number of chromosomes equal to 49 as a result of 4/9 tandom fusion of long metacentric chromosomes. The experimental evidences in back cross and F2 progenies indicate buffaloes with diploid number 48, 49 and 50 (Basrur, 1988) however, Ranjhan, 1987 reported only two populations with 2n=49 and 2n=50 speculating the possibility of early phasing out the population of 2n-48 from the normal theoretical expectation of 1:2:1. However, these results are based on very small population and hence needs further confirmation. Since hybrids have been found to be fertile and there is manifold increase in the production characteristics of crossbreds therefore crossbreeding of swamp buffaloes with various breeds of river buffalo has been undertaken in Philippines, Vietnam, China, Indonesia, Malaysia, Brazil and several other countries.

GENETIC AND PHENOTYPIC TRENDS:

Phenotypic performance of the daughters of the bulls under progeny testing at the erst while Progeny Testing Farm, Hisar (CIRB) and the herd averages from 1970 to 1986 indicate declining phenotypic trend of about 15 per cent in daughters performance and 22 per cent in the overall herd performance (Sethi, 1992). Data on 209 records of first lactation traits in Murrah buffaloes at National Dairy Research Institute, Karnal (El-Arun and Tripathi, 1987) indicated significant change in phenotypic trend in first lactation milk yield and 305 days milk yield. However, genetic as well as environmental trends were non-significant for all the traits. At military dairy farms the estimated genetic gain was reported as 15.88 kg (0.9%) per annum of the population mean. The esimates of annual genetic in lactation yield reported from Egypt were 0.04 to 0.80%.

These estimates are lower than the estimates of % reported in temperate breeds of dairy cattle. In most of the herds selection was effected for sires based on their pedigree performance either on single trait basis or multi trait selection.

Based on the date from Mathura, Madhuri-Kund, Babugarh and Chak-Ganjaria in Uttar Pradesh from 1967-1983 (Sharma and Singh, 1988) it was found that selection index incorporating age of first calving, first lactation.

STRATEGIES FOR ENHANCING GENETIC IMPROVEMENT ASSOCIATED PROGENY TESTING:

To overcome the problem of small herds in progeny testing the concept of Associated Herds Progeny Testing has been introduced in India where several herds with common technical programme will work together to achieve the objective. This programme has been undertaken under Network programme for the improvement of Murrah and Surti breeds of buffaloes at Central Institute for Research on Buffaloes. Hisar under the coordinating unit of Network. The model of network project on Murrah buffaloes has been prepared which elucidates the concept of Associated Progeny Testing while came in operation from July, 1993.

1. Participating Institutions and population size

	Test Herd	Elite Herd
CIRB, Hisar	316	18
PAU, Ludhiana	193	26
IVRI, Izatnagar	5	99
CIRB, Sub Campus, Nabha	3	72
CCS HAU, Hisar	18	92
CBBF, Alamadi	3	125
NDRI, Karnal	75	125
	147	1022

(i) Population size has increased from mere 150-200 animals in each herd to 1022 buffaloes for test matings and 147 elite buffaloes for nominated matings.

(ii) Selection of proven sires: From the progeny tested bulls available at various institutions 5 top proven, bulls with sire index ranging from 2224 to 1826 kg were selected for nominated matings with the 147 elite buffaloes. At the end of each cycle 4-5 proven bulls need to be selected from among the tested bulls which shall be used for elite matings.

(iii) Selection of elite dams and nominated matings: From the total population of all the centres 147 buffaloes were selected using either of the following criteria -

a) Best lactation yield >= 2500 kg
b) First lactation yield >= 2300 kg
c) Breeding value >= 1950 kg

List of elite dams needs to be updated every quarter on the basis of information on their milk production and after every calving fresh allotment for nominated mating shall be made.

(iv) Selection of test bulls: 15 bulls were selected for the 1st set on the basis of following criteria -

a) Sons of elite dams
b) Semen freezability
c) Murrah characteristics
d) Sons of proven/recognised sires.

This criteria will be used in future for selection of 15 test bulls in each set.

(v) Semen freezing from test bulls and storage of semen: Selected bulls are maintained at the respective institutions from where it is selected. About 6000 doses of semen are frozen from each bull, 1000 doses for testing mating and 5000 doses for future use till the bull is evaluated.

(vi) Selection and rearing of young males: All the male calves born out of elite matings stand primarily selected as future test bull. These male calves are reared at the respective centres and final selection is made on the criteria as laid above for selection of test bulls. Besides growth pattern at periodic interval is also imposed for selection of bulls.

(vii) Test matings: All breedable females identified in the test herd at the respective centres are inseminated with the frozen semen of test bulls in such a manner that mating system is randomised for all the bulls. Test mating for each bull in the set is performed simultaneously for a cycle of 18 months in order to obtain at least 60 to 70 pregnancies from each bull. About 16-20 recorded daughters per bull are expected to be obtained from all the centres.

(viii) Data Recording: Information on various parameters concerning inseminations, pregnancies, daughter born to each bull, monitoring the growth of each calf till maturity and subsequently milk yield is to be collected for evaluation of the sires.

(ix) Sire Evaluation: Daughers 305 day 1st lactation milk yield will be used for estimation of sire indices. Bulls will be ranked on the basis of sire index and top 20 to 25% bulls will be selected for elite mating.

TABLE-1

RANGE OF AVERAGES FOR BODY WEIGHT AT DIFFERENT AGE IN DIFFERENT BREEDS OF BUFFALOES.

	Birth weight	Age (Months)			
		6	12	24	Maturity
Murrah India	29 - 32	112 - 127	185 - 213	376	447 - 500
Murrah Italy	29.6	166	294		-
546					
Nili-Ravi India	31.0	134 - 145	219 - 243	-	510 - 531
Nili-Ravi Pakistan	29.4 - 37.8	94.4	132.4	-	436
Surti India	-	70 - 80	109 - 135	205 - 318	-
Surti Sri Lanka	21	-	-	-	-
Dharwai	-	-	-	-	367

TABLE-2

PRODUCTION PERFORMANCE OF DIFFERENT BREEDS OF BUFFALOES

	Age at Ist calving (months)		Lact. Yield (kg)		Lactation length (days)	
	Av.	Range	Av.	Range	Av.	Range
Murrah	43.0	39.9 - 54.5	1850	1476 - 2515	315	267 - 365
Nili-Ravi	42.0	41.4 - 47.3	1765	1596 - 2808	309	-
Surti	39.0	26.5 - 45.0	1364	1304 - 1693	313	300 - 373
Bhadawari	46.0	44.3 - 54.2	1181	-	276	-
Nagpuri	48.0	44.3 - 55.6	1103	926 - 1175	270	-

3

CO-OPERATIVE ROLE IN DAIRY DEVELOPMENT

Milk production assumes second priority after rice cultivation in Indian agriculture. The village economy is incomplete for even marginal farmers if they lack one or two bovine animals. The fact that about 75% population of India is engaged in agricultural activities has put the organised milk production on the prime priorities of Government and other organizations. In this context operation flood and consequent thresh-hold of white revolution has come through the cooperative pattern of milk production management. Consequently more than 5 million farmers are today organised into about 0.5 lac of village milk cooperatives and the total turnover of Dairy sector has reached to Rs. 30,000 crore per annum (Shah et al., 1995). The milk production in Indian set up is largely a source of supplementary income to the farmers who produce milk basically for self consumption and may spare the surplus for the market. The problems of Dairy Industry in the Indian context are unique in the sense that through India accounts for probably the largest bovine population in the world yet it contributes only five percent of the total world milk and milk products. The main impediment in the Indian Dairy has been the low intensity dairying based on poor yielding cattle fed on crop residues and labour intensive management.

However, with the efforts of different agencies in various states, the development of cooperative systems in the sector which has tried to integrate both technology of milk production and its subsequent marketing had led to steady growth of five percent per annum. Since the cost of production per litre of milk has been found to have inverse relationship with the productivity, the aim of cooperative movement in India has been to upgrade the productivity alongwith the efficient marketing management so that a fruitful source and sink relationship is maintained to the benefit of even marginal farmers.

The cooperative and organised milk production gained momentum only after the independence. Earlier Dairy activity was limited to household activity only except for a few trading cooperatives of milk and ghee in some isolated cities. These cooperatives and trading societies represented and interest of trading merchants only till late fifties. In the post independence era the orientation of cooperatives started changing towards the utilization of surplus to market orientation, integration of producers into cooperative systems with upgradation of Dairy production from subsistence to commercial production. Thus during the las two decades one can see that the marketable surplus of milk in rural areas has increased manifolds both in absolute and relative terms. The immediate effect of this enhancement in marketable surplus has been the direct supply of milk and milk products to the consumers both in the urban and rural areas. However, one can see declining trend in processing of surplus milk to ghee, khoa, etc. in rural areas, which does not commensurate with the increase in milk production. Cooperatives with a thrust on direct marketing of milk, played a major role in this respect.

The Dairy processing in India can be divided into private, cooperative and Govt. agencies besides, the traditional unorganised sector. At present all the aforesaid components of organised sector use modern methods technologies and management systems. The cooperative sector is examplified by the Anand Pattern of dairy cooperatives. The cooperatives being welfare oriented; production systems of the society have multifaceted activities and attention is given to all the finer aspects from maintenance of cattle to the utilization of end product i.e. milk. Broadly speaking, nine different activities are involved in dairy economy (Table 1). Most of these activities are now being looked after by the cooperatives as compared to private, government or the unorganised sector.

TABLE 1

	Traditional/ Unorganised		Modern/ Organised		
	Private	Coop.	Private	Coop.	Govt.
1. Trade in cattle buffaloes and bullocks	*****				
2. Procurement and marketing of liquid milk	****	*	*	****	**
3. Marketing of ghee, khoa & other indigenous products	****	*	**	***	
4. Marketing of butter baby food				****	
5. Production and marketing of pelleted cattle feed		*	***	****	
6. Supply of veterinary cover	**		****	*****	
7. Supply of A land other breeding Services				****	
8. Supply of indigenous feeds	****				
9. Lease markets/costracts for bullocks	****				

Adopted from shah et al., 1995

* Degree of significance

At present milk cooperatives represent the major share of organised milk production. These are functionally multipurpose societies organised on principle of federalism. Besides, there are various levels of control at village, district and state level. The whole structure is based on "Milk Producers Cooperative Society" at village level. The milk producers cooperative society is managed by elected representatives amonst the milk producers and look after the interest of milk producers; through providing marketing facilities and the key inputs like fodder seeds, loans upgradation of cattle veterinary facilities etc. so that the milk production is enhanced. At district level, about one thousand village cooperatives are clubbed into a "District Cooperative Milk Union". The main objective of District cooperative union is to process the pooled milk in a dairy plant and its subsequent marketing. The District level cooperative is managed by a Board of Directors elected from amongst and chairman of Dairy cooperative socities. A modern distinct cooperative milk union employs professionals like Dairy Technologies and Managers. This becomes more pertinent in view of the multifareous activities like manufacture of milk powders, butter, cheese, milk beverages etc. for effective marketing purpose. The district level union also undertakes transfer of improved technologies in Animal Husbandry practices, promotion and arrangement of quality feed and fodder to primary societies. The different district milk cooperative unions ultimately culminate into milk federation of respective state. It regulates the marketing of milk and milk products at inter and intra state levels through National Milk Grid.

The cooperative dairy movements has gone a long way in utilization of dairy surplus and make it accessible to public both at rural level during the past decades. At the rural level the cooperative system has brought awareness amongst the villagers towards an aggressive dairy farming instead of traditional sustenance based milk production. This attitude has further geared the villagers towards community development through organizational set ups in other sphere also. The interaction brought by cooperatives for production and collection of milk amongst the villagers and different communities in a village on a common plateform has also helped in mitigating the cost barrier in may areas. The cooperative movement at village level envisaged facilities in terms of inputs like improved feeds, veterinary services, dairy plants etc, and above all inculcation of general and collective responsibilities for successful and viable running of the cooperatives. Therefore, dairy cooperative movement has proved to be an instrument of social and economic change at village level. The cooperative movement has thus exposed the villagers to processes of development, modern scientific ideas and creation of infrastructure.

The cooperatives, in initial stages have played a significant role in livestock trading and its productivity enhancement. Nevertheless, the role of Govt. agencies is of equal importance. An impetus was provided for the improvement of livestock through improved breeding, feeding and management. No doubt, this vaccuum was catered to by Govt. and now by other commercial sectors.

The success of cooperatives can be judged by the amount and scale of patronage and allegiance they command from the basic milk producer members in the villages, on one hand and the consumers particularly in the urban areas on the other hand. This development of source and sink relationship by the cooperative movement has resulted in the circulation of money to the tune of several crores with economic benefits at various levels besides, creating employment opportunities. The dairy cooperatives system over a period of time has succeeded in offering to their members or the milk producers remunerative prices and a dependable market for their surplus; However, since the cooperatives has been sluggish in providing efficient technical inputs and in many cases due to poor management practices, the economic impact is not going to very significant in the context of present day competitive market economy.

There has been a change due to cooperative movement for subsistence dairy enterprise to market oriented one by providing a perpetual regenerating, and a remunerative market for milk round the year. This has resulted in enhancement of the memberships of cooperatives on one hand and also a desire on the part of members to increase their productivity of livestock by proper scientific breeding, quality feeding and management practices. The overall impact at various levels is indicated in the Table 2.

As a result of successful Operation Flood programmes under the cooperative movement the house hold economics of producers increased over the past years resulting in enhancement in their house-hold income and expenditure and thereby increasing their living standards particularly in respect of their nutrition. Owing to the success of cooperatives, there has been an unprecedented incresae of milk production in the country. The near self sufficiency and self reliance in milk production is also reflected by the fact that India refused commodity aid in this sector for the first time. The success of "Anand Pattern" milk cooperative movement was appreciated worldwide and a ministerial level meeting of six Asian Countries comprising Vietnam, Indonesia, Philippines, China, Pakistan and India resolved to replicate the same pattern in their respective countries and establish an international Centre at anand for sharing the experiences of operation flood (Patel, 1992).

One of the main contributions of operation flood at the national level has been the development of infrastructure in milk processing and marketing. The National Milk Grid alongwith well organised milk supply schemes working in different parts of the country has made it possible to swiftly collect process and transport the available surplus milk and despatch it under hygenic conditions to the consumers in milk scarce area. As a result the milk market has expanded manifolds catering to about 300 million consumers at present in different parts of the country.

The network of cooperative institutions created through the operation flood programme now comprised about 70,000 dairy cooperatives in 170 milk sheds, encompassing 8.4 million milk producer families. Average milk procurement by these cooperatives has now reached some 12.3 million kg per day, of which 8.2 million litres are marketed as liquid milk, while the remainder is converted into products such as milk powder, butter, cheese, ghee and a wide range of traditional milk products. Milk processing capacity of approximately 15.6 million litres per day, chilling capacity of 6.5 million litres per day and milk powder production capacity of 726 tonnes per day have been established through the programme. One of the challenging aspects of dairy development in a tropical or subtropical country is the movement of milk over long distances. In operation flood, this has been made possible through the operation of about 140 insulated rail milk tankers, each with a capacity of 40,000 liters, supplemented by another 25 rail tankers of 21,000.

TABLE - 2

	Pre Cooperative Stage	A young but effective cooperative	The Cooperative matures: So does the dairying in the village.	A modern coopertative with infrastru-ture to sustain cross breeding on major scale
	Main Characters	*Main Characters*	*Main Characters*	*Main Characters*
a)	High draft power orientation	Increase in the feeding of cattle feed, grain and green fodder.	Increase in ratio of animals in milk to bovine holdidngs.	Intensive campaign is launched to introduce A.I.
b)	Low yield/animal low ratio of animals in milk to livestock holdings.	Increase in yield/ animal.	Culling of un productive animals begins.	Largest possible number of local animals to be covered by A.I. with semen of properly chosen exotic species.
c)	Bulk of milk output used for self consumption.	Increase in pro-portion of milk output sold.	Longer lactation lengths shorter calving patterns increase in breed ing efficiency.	Elaborate support structure enable farmers to raise cross-breds.
d)	Low real cost of milk production	Buffalo emerges as main dairy animal.	Emergency of lease markets for bullocks.	Economics of dairying under-goes major cha-nge. Use of land to support live-stock increases.
e)		Economics of dairying and opportunity costs of feeds became important	Constraints impo-sed by traditional milk production technologies begin to be felt by producers.	Real cost of milk production falls.
f)				Milk procurement by coop. rises rapidly with salutary effects on its economics.

Adopted from Shah et al., 1995

liters capacity, Approximately 1,000 other insulated road milk tankers operate throuoghout the country as well. This has enabled the operation of a national milk grid, balancing regional fluctuations in milk procurement and bridging demand and supply gaps resulting from concentrated production of liquid milk in selected milk sheds. To balance, seasonal variations in milk supply and demand caused by low milk production during the summer months, a large milk powder storage capacity has been created for buffer stocking (Banerjee, 1994).

The cooperative movement has also encouraged the development and establishment of milk producing units on small scale level providing regular source of income to the farmers. The expansion of cooperative movement has resulted in increased demand of dairy equipments, feed industry and indirectly the milk product industry also. India is now exporting the dairy equipment machinery. The milk production in the country has increased from 20 million MT to 60.8 million tonnes (Paroda, 1995), milk powder production has risen from 22,000 MT in 1969-70 to 1,60,000 MT in 1992-93 (Sahni, 1993) per capita availability of milk which had declined consistently during the two decades between 1951 and 1970, drooping to 107g at the start of operation flood, is now 187 g per day; despite a substantial increase in population as a result of the awareness generated among producers by the cooperative movement in all facts of dairying.

Although till recently cooperative dairying has proved a bone for small producers particularly small farmers and landless labourers by providing livelihood and security to such segments of society but now with the advancement of technology and its incorporation in the cooperative and other organised sectors, there is a tendency of more benefits to large units only. Unless proper remedial measures are taken, the present day capital intensive dairying involving high technology may ultimately ease out the small producers from advanced cooperative systems. In this aspect exposure of the rural small producers to scientific improvement of livestock and management at village level is of utmost importance. The need of the hour for the cooperative is to come face to face in the aforesaid challenges so that the cooperative movement is rejuvenated for rural human resource development and upliftment of marginal farmers.

4

INCREASING IN MILK PROTEIN BY FEEDING

Milk composition affects the price received. Although the pricing basis used initially rewarded fat content more than protein, in the last few years the balance has swung in favour of a higher milk protein analysis.

Therefore, the cow feeding strategies applied by the producers today seek to keep milk volume-or 'yield' - and fat within quotas limits, while maximising the protein. A BSAS report from nutritionists at the University of Reading and Trident Feeds noted that these goals are not easily reconciled. It is relatively straightforward to control the milk fat content by nutritional means, but feeding for more protein is more difficult and certainly less predictable.

SODA GRAIN FOR PROTEIN BOOST

However, some quite significant improvements have been obtained from giving the cows a supplement which is rich in energy. Several studies have shown a valuable protein increase results from processing feedstuff starch sources to change the nature as well as the amount of carbohydrate in the diet.

One example of how that has been put into practice in the UK concerns an ingredient known locally as soda grain. Proving increasingly popular in feeds on British dairy farms, this ingredient takes the form of whole wheat treated with caustic soda (sodium hydroxide or NaOH) to reduce the rate of degradation in the rumen.

A typical soda grain treatment described to the BSAS meeting involved adding 30 kg of sodium hydroxide per ton of wheat, plus water to bring the total drymatter to 700 g/kg and storing for 5 days before feeding. The use of soda grain was said to be associated with consistent improvements in milk protein content observed on a number of farms.

In one recent test the caustic treated material was compared with wheat that had been milled through a 3 mm screen, both being employed to provide increasing amounts of wheat starch to Holstein cows which were also allowed grass silage to appetite. The study, by the ADAS farm advisory service, confirmed that a higher intake of dietary starch from either source was able to raise milk protein. But it also shows an essential difference between the wheat ingredients, in that only in the case of the ground wheat was the greater starch intake per day also accompanied by a lift in the milk yield.

Positive benefits on milk protein content from feeding NaOH-treated or rolled wheat have been established by a Reading University experiment. Soda grain was compared with 50:50 mixture of rolled wheat and sugarbeet feed, for Friesian dairy cows in their early or middle lactation. The cows received there as supplements to their ad libitum access to grass silage, including wheat in their diet significantly enhanced the protein level of their milk. However, although both supplements gave the same response for milk protein, the rolled wheat-sugarbeet feed mixture differed from soda grain in also leading to an increase in milk yield and milk fat.

ALTERNATIVES FOR EXTRA RUMEN BYPASS ENERGY

An alternatively grain treatment for reducing rumen degradability was discussed by animal production specialists from Finland's agricultural research centre in Jokionen. They outlined promising results from cooking the barley, before mixing it with sugarbeet pulp and rapeseed meal into a concentrate to accompany grass silage.

In their studies the basal concentrate was a 2.8 mixture of sugarbeet pulp and either untreated or cooked barley, which for some cows supplemented using untreated or treated rapeseed meal. This protein addition did increase both total yield and protein yield, but the treatment of the rapeseed meal obtained no extra response.

By contrast, cooked barley proved better than the raw cereal despite apparently depressing the cows' daily intake of silage and of total drymatter. Both milk yield and protein yield were maintained; the milk contained less fat besides having slightly more protein.

Combinations of barley or unmolassed beet pulp with rapeseed meal were reported by IGER grassland research institute scientists in Wales to give an acceptable concentrate for feeding at low levels to dairy cows given high-digestibility grass silage. But replacing the rapeseed in the concentrate with a 1:3 blend of whitefish and soyabean meals had the effect of elevating protein and fat in the milk white reducing yield.

Energy-rich supplements can be produced using root starches as well as cereal sources, University of Newcastle investigators pointed out. They fed Friesia-Holstein cows during lactation with concentrates of the same 180 g/kg crude protein value, in which manioc (cassava or tapioca) replaced all or part of the barley-wheat cereal present. Interestingly, neither the all-cereal nor the all-root starch option resulted in the best cow performance. For yields of protein, lactose and milk fat this came from a 0.25:0.75 cereal-root mix. At the other end of the scale was the blend of 75% cereals with 25% manioc.

Across all combinations, however, there was no significant effect of dietary treatment on the proportion of protein in the milk. It required the extra daily milk production on the 25%-75% concentrate to obtain the appreciable rise observed in milk protein yield.

What degree of milk protein manipulation is possible by these feeding techniques?

The result from Findland, for Finish Ayrshire cows, pointed to protein content of 31.4 g/kg when the cows received simply grass silage and uncooked barley. Adding the rapeseed meal and cooking the barley raised this to 32.2 g/kg. The Holsteins in the British ADAS test provided 32.9 g protein per kilogram of milk where soda grain was giving them a daily starch intake of 1.9 kg, rising to 34.5 g protein on a 4.6 kg/day intake. For the Friesians at Reading University in the UK, the 30.1 g/kg protein results of unsupplemented controls rose to a peak 33.2 g/kg after feeding soda grain. Completely replacing barley and wheat with tapioca in the concentrates given Friesian-Holsteins at Newcastle University reduced their milk protein proportion from 30.8 g/kg to 30.1 g/kg.

5

ASEPTIC PACKAGING OF FOOD AND BEVERAGE

Aseptic packaging is neither a major breakthrough technology that will revolutionise all food business nor a mature or declining technology whose future has been shattered by regulatory disapprovals. Further, concepts of aseptic processing and packaging which are somewhat removed from the core of the original technologies are gradually being adopted to both said and pumpable foods for extended shelf life refrigerated distribution.

The classical technology encompasses independent sterilisation of product and package and assembly under sterile conditions to deliver food capable of being distributed under ambient temperature conditions. In this manner, much lower thermal inputs may be imparted to reasonably homogeneous pumpable food, usually beverage, and its packaging. Thus, heat sensitive foods such as milk may be effectively stabilised. Further, because of the ability to sterilise the package by one of several methods not necessarily involving high heat means that virtually any size, shape, or composition package may be the container.

Today, the most widely used systems are those of Sweden's Tetra Pak using chemical sterilization and paperboard/plastic/aluminium foil composite brick-shaped packages. But more than forty different supply companies offer aseptic packaging systems of various types ranging from fractional mililitre bottles to 2000 litres or larger size bulk flexible bags.

DOLE ASEPTIC CANNING

Dole canning lines employ superheated steam as the sterilant for metal cans ranging in size from 100cc to 400cc, with reliable results. Dole systems seem to have fallen into a category of beginner's aseptic packaging, with food companies starting with these very high speed units and eventually converting to plastic cup and tub packaging whose variable costs tend to be lower than for metal cans. Oddly, the capital costs for Dole lines are lower than for systems using chemical sterilants.

Just to demonstrate their continuing viability, a number of new Dole aseptic canning line have been recently installed for packging dietary type milk-based liquid meals which were introduced in the American market with modest success. The packages are 340cc two-piece steel cans. The products are distributed in the traditional manner of aseptic packages, i.e., under ambient conditions.

PLASTIC CUP LINES

A pharmaceutical company is aseptically packaging some of its nutritional liquid diet using the FMC

Freshfil performed cup deposit/fill/seal system. Developed by the United Kingdom's Carnauld Metal box, the system employs multilayer high oxygen barrier cups and heat sealed flexible lamination closure materials with hydrogen peroxide spray as the sterilant. Also using the Freshfil system is a major breakfast cereal company for its portion size precooked and ready-to-microwave-heat oatmeal cereal. Again, the packages are performed coextruded sthylene vinyl alcohol/polypropylene closed with aluminum foil flexible laminations. Earlier, these systems were used to aseptically package cheese sauce/dips in barrier plastic cups.

All of these products are or were low acid homogeneous or nearly homogeneous fluids. They may be readily heat sterilised in continuous heat exchangers and transferred into the packages by reliable fillers without finite risk microbiological recontamination.

THERMOFORM/FILL/SEAL: LOW ACID FLUID FOODS

Milk puddings and analogous dairy foods are aseptically packaed on French ERCA or German Bosch thermoform/fill/seal systems beginning with roll stock multilayer barrier sheet. Both systems use a traditional polystyrene/

polyvinylidene chloride (PVDC) sheet material for ease of in-line thermoforming. Sterilisation on the Bosch system is with hydrogen peroxide immersion. The ERCA system employs a complex process of relying on the heat of plastic extrusion to effect the sterility of the material followed by protecting the clean surface with an added film that is removed immediately prior to filling. The ERCA system avoids any hint of residual chemicals.

Both systems are relatively expensive to acquire and install, but offer the benefit of low material costs, and so far packagers with high output requirements, total systems costs can be the lowest of any aseptic cup system. Output speeds can be in the range of hundreds of 50cc to 250cc cups a minute.

German Hassia thermoform/fill/seal equipment is unique in that it uses high pressure temperature steam to both sterilise the package materials and to thermoform the base plastic sheet into cups.

Both Hassia and Bosch thermoform/fill/seal equipment are being used for aseptic packaging of unit portion size liquid coffee lighteners. This trend is away from the use of irradiation sterilised preformed polystyrene cups on Purity and Portion Packaging deposit/fill/seal equipment, due largely to the higher output and lower total system cost for larger packagers.

THERMOFORM/FILL/SEAL: HIGH ACID PRODUCTS

The application of thermoform/fill/seal aseptic packaging systems for low acid foods does not in any way preclude their employment for high acid foods which are much less concern from a microbiological safety perspective. Thus, ERCA systems have been successfully used for aseptic packaging of juices and other fruit beverages, apple sauce and, with modification, fruit pieces. In both Australia and the United States, ERCA thermoform/fill/seal equipment has integrated hot filling under aseptic conditions coupled with post filling cooling to deliver ambient temperature shelf stable fruit pieces in unit portion size plastic cups.

Aseptic thermoform/fill/seal systems are being applied for tomato type sauces and pastes in Australia.

DEPOSIT/FILL/SEAL SYSTEMS

Refrigerated milk puddings and fruit flavoured gels in unit portion size multilayer barrier plastics have expanded significantly, increasing the primary market for convenient-to-eat desserts. Packages are usually performed high barrier multilayer plastic cups with heat sealed flexible aluminium foil structure closures. Packaging is on machines such as German Hamba or Gasti which are engineered and operated in aseptic modes, but whose mechinsms are not regarded as truly aseptic by some regulatory agencies. In those territories, the product output is classified as ultra clean but not sterile. The product is distributed under refrigeration, a factor that helps to retain its flavour attributes as well as ensure its microbiological safety.

An increasing number of products are being processed and packaged under aseptic conditions to significantly prolong their refrigerated shelf lives. Apple, cranberry and blended fruit sauces for desserts and garnishes are, of course, high acid products. Such products are stabilised by thermal processes and aseptically packaged for ambient temperature distribution in high barrier plastic cups and trays. High oxygen barrier is important for fruit products because of their oxygen sensitivity. Packaging is in preformed coextruded polypropylene/ethylene vinyl alcohol cups, in the case of those packaged on to Crosscheck system. This system is unique among all aseptic packaging systems because it was engineered specifically for acid fluid foods. It uses a non-invasive sterilisation system and eliminates oxygen from the package before filling. Sterilisation on the Crosscheck system is with hot water.

Fruit sauce products are also aseptically packaged on thermoform/fill/seal on ERCA or Bosch systems. Juices are aseptically packaged in unit portion sizes on Hassia thermoform/fill/seal equipment using superheated steam as both the sterilant and the thermoforming pressure source.

ASEPTIC PACKAGING IN BOTTLES

In both North America and Europe during 1993 and 1994, aseptically packaged fruit beverages have appeared in polyster bottles in sizes are large as 1800cc and as small as 454cc. The aseptic technologies employed are the French Serac in which the premade bottles are washed with mixtures of aqueous chlorine and oxonia and rinsed with distilled water prior to aseptic filling. An analogous system from France's Remy is used to aseptically package flavoured water in polyester bottles.

For perspective, however, most ambient temperature shelf stable polyester bottles of fruit beverages are hot filled rather than aseptically filled. Hot filling requires the employment of special bottle structures that permit the walls to collapse inwardly damaging the bottle as a result of the vacuums developed from steam condensation upon cooling. Shelf life in polyester bottles is not as long as it is with coextruded multilayer barrier bottles, but is evidently acceptable in several territories.

At least two American packagers are delivering fruit flavoured high acid drinks in high density polyethylene bottles whose sterility is achieved by employing aseptically blow mold/fill/seal technologies from suppliers such as Germany's Rommelag or the United States Automatic Liquid Packaging. The primary bottles are fabricated from high density polyethylene which is a low barrier material, and so the gas barrier is built into a coextruded ethylene vinyl alcohol-based shrink film package. A similar type of packaging is offered by Japan's Kogyo which preforms the containers under sterile conditions and transfers them under clean conditions for aseptic packaging.

FLAVOUR SCALPING FROM ASEPTIC PACKAGES

Increasingly, juice and fruit beverages companies are employing technologies to significantly prolong the refrigerated shelf lives of their products packages in gable top barrier papaerboard cartons and plastic bottles. More than seven weeks of chilled quality retention is now commercially achieved for pasteurised fruit beverages and four weeks for unpasteurised, all employing aseptic packaging. Accompanying the long shelf life, however, has been scalping or removal of desirable flavour components from the contained product by the interior polyolefin layer. This problem has been largely overcome through the incorporation of ethylene vinyl alcohol on the interior layer in gable topo cartons, an International Paper development, or nylon used by other suppliers. Nylon has also been the interior layer choice for coextruded polyethylene bottles for pasteurised and unpasteurised juices, also, of course, for chilled distribution. The relative interness of polyester with contained fruit beverages obviates any need for an extra layer on the interior of aseptically packaged polyester bottles.

ASEPTIC PACKAGING FOR CHILLED FOODS

Aseptic technologies are being integrated with product formulation, reduced water activity, high pH and chilled distribution to deliver foods with excellent initial quality for extended periods. Chilled puddings cited above fall into this category, but in Japan, precooked rice has emerged as another important class. Rice is a true particulate product, and so the aseptic packaging of this product represents a most intriguing advance from the classical technology. Control is achieved by water activity control, mechanical removal of oxygen and by insertion of oxygen scavenger sachets. Shelf life is limited not by microbiological problems but rather by biochemical degradation of the rice starch itself.

BULK ASEPTIC PACKAGING

Probably the greatest growth in aseptic packaing has been in the realm of bulk packaging of high acid fluids foods in barrier flexible pouch packages. The best known are those produced in preformed pouches incorporating valves through which the valve areas cleaned with chlorine compounds immediately prior to filling. Companies such as Scholle and Liqui Box are supplying the complete systems which are applied for high acid pumpable foods such as tomato ketchup and sauces.

For bulk packaging of low acid pumpable foods such as cheese sauces and dips, aseptic vertical form/fill/seal systems for Bosch are employed. These systems employed roll stock high barrier transparent multilayer films which are sterilised in-line by liquid hydrogen peroxide. Some of the sauces incorporate small particles which do not necessarily retain their integrity during the sterilisation process.

PAPERBOARD COMPOSITE BRICK AND BLOCK PACKAGING

It is important to note that, despite scant mention of paperboard composite systems such as those from Sweden's Tetra Pak, Germany's Combibloc and Japan's Fuji, these constitute the largest category of aseptic packaging systems by any measure of number of installations, volume packaged, number of units packed, etc. The overwhelming majority are applied for milk, with fruit beverages as an increasingly stronger second. Among the recent developments in this packaging system class have been larger sizes for the Combibloc and easy open and reclosure featuers for both Tetra Pak and Combibloc.

Recently, Tetra Pak has been testing silica coating as the primary barrier for its brick packages. By replacing aluminiuum foil in its paperboard structures, a similar barrier is effects with material that can then be more readily recycled. Combibloc is experimenting with ethylene vinyl alcohol as the primary barrier material in its paperboard structure.

ASEPTIC PROCESSING

Little commercial aseptic packaging of significant sized particulates is underway because of the continued difficulty of thermally sterilising discrete particulates in continuous flow. This paucity of commercial installations has not deterred development.

Ohmic or electrical resistance heating of foods to sterilisation temperatures is under intensive study with a prototype system capable of sterilising large particulates. The resulting sterile product can be as high quality as minimally processed foods (for example, blanched vegetables) provided the electrical conductivity of the solid food matches that of the liquid carrier fluid. Ohmic sterilisation is reportedly being used in Europe for sterilisation of pet foods, followed by aseptic packaging in brick paperboard composite packages and for aseptic packaging in fruit in Japan.

Although not Ohmic heating, Raztek high frequency electrical resistance thermal sterilisation of liquid eggs is being performed commercially. The eggs are packaged aseptically in gable top paperboard cartons, but distributed under refrigeration.

In a longer term development, Maxwell Laboratories' joint venture company Foodeo in the United States is developing pulsed electrical discharges to sterilize food in depth, another variant on the basic electrical resistance heating principle. Ohmic and pulsed electricity represent potential technologies to heat sterilise solid products without excess thermal damage.

In another technology development from the Maxwell Laboratories group, pulsed high-intensity light is being developed to sterilise surfaces such as those of package materials before aseptic packaging. If it works, non-thermal. non-chemical technology for surface sterilization will be available.

6

TECHNOLOGY/PROCESSING OF DAIRY AND DAIRY PRODCUTS

MILK SHAKE

Milk shake, a product of Western origin, is obtained by freezing mix very similar to soft serve icecream mix and speed mixing the frozen product in a mixer to make it pourable and generate foam in it. It has lower fat and sugar contents and higher milk solids-not-fat (msnf) content than icecream. In view of the increasing popularity of milk based frozen products, a study was undertaken to standardize the method of manufacture of milk shake. The study was also extended to obtain the product in a powder form which could easily be reconstituted by housewives.

COMBINATION

Of the various combinations studied, the one with fact and msnf levels of 4 and 13% respectively, was found to be the most acceptable with respect to the whipping ability of mix and foam stability and sensory evaluation of the milk shake prepared therefrom.

STEPS IN PROCESSING

The ingredients required i.e. whole milk, skim milk powder, sugar and stabilizer (sodium alginate) were weighed and mixed as follows. Sugar (at the rate of 10%) and stabiliser (at the rate of 0.4%) were dry-mixed first. The milk was warmed upto 40° C and the skim milk powder was slowly added to it with continuous stirring. The temperature of the mixture was then raised to about 70°C before adding the sugar stabilizer mixture. After thorough mixing. After thorough mixing, the liquid was filtered through muslin cloth and while at about 60°C it was homogenized in two stages first at 175 kg cm^2 and seemed at 35 Kg/cm^2 pressure. The homogenized mix was pasteurised at 70°C for 30 minutes. The mix was then cooled to about 10°C and aged for 2-3 hr at 6°-10°C. Following the aging, the milk shake mix was frozen in a soft-serve ice-cream freezer using strawberry flavour (0.1 ml/ltr). The drawing temperature varied between -2°C to -6°C. The frozen mix was blended in a mixer for 90-120 sec to produce milk shake.

DRIED MILK SHAKE MIX POWDER

The milk shake mix was also spray dried and powder contained 3.3% moisture; 15.1% fat, 17.7% protein and the rest being carbohydrate and ash. Its solubility index was 0.45 mi, and bulk density 0.44 g/ml (loose) and 0.59 g/ml (packed).

The dried milk shake mix powder could be reconstituted by mixing calculated amount of crushed ice (to adjust the solids level at 28% in the final product) and blending in a mixer for 9C-120 sec. The reconstituted product when subjected to sensory evaluation was found to be quite acceptable. However, it scored slightly less than fresh milk shake, on account of slight chalkiness and too large ice crystals. Aging of the reconstituted milk shake for 2 to 3 hours in refrigerator prior to mixing in a mixer would, however, help improve the accetability of the product.

STERILISED CREAM

Economic utilisation of seasonal and regional surpluses of milk is of great importance to the dairy industry and while the solids-not-fat content is used for the manufacture of dried milks, the surplus fat is used for the production of ghee. Prenaration of sterilised cream would be a very profitable proposition for the utilisation of surplus milk fat and can fetch a much higher return by nearly 100% per unit weight of fat as compared to ghee. The product can be made either on a small scale or on large scale depending on the demand, in any dairy equipped with the usual facilities for milk handling.

COMPOSITION

The product has the following approximate composition

i) Fat - 20-21%

ii) Milk SNF - 6%

iii) Stabiliser - 0.2 to 0.3%

iv) Water - 72.7 - 73.8% (by difference)

STEPS IN PROCESSING

i) Adjustment of the fat level of cream to 20% (minimum)

ii) Forewarning to 85° C and holding for 15 minutes.

iii) Homogenisation at 65-67°C at a pressure of 175 kg/s.cm² for the 1st stage and 35 kg/s.cm² for the 2nd stage.

iv) Addition of trisodium phosphate as a stabiliser @ 0.2% by weight of cream.

v) Canning the cream in suitable size containers and leak detection

vi) Sterilisation at 114±1°C for 14-15 min. and rapid cooling.

vii) Testing the final quality of the product.

ADDITIONAL REQUIREMENTS OF EQUIPMENT

i) Homogeniser

ii) Can filling and seaming equipment

iii) Steriliser.

The cost of the equipment depends on the proposed capacity of handling.

The product has an acceptable shelf life to about six months and can be used in beverages like coffee, tea and fruit-cream etc. The contents of the tin are to be shaken thorough before opening.

DAHI FROM SWEET CREAM BUTTERMILK

Buttermilk is the fluid portion left behind after churning of cream or 'dahi' during butter manufacture. Since buttermilk is largely defatted cream, its composition is much like that of skim milk. It is estimated that 1.5 million tonnes of milk is annually used for the production of creamery butter and therefore nearly 8,000 tonnes of buttermilk solids are available for utilization. While a small portion of the by-product thus obtained is utilized for the manufacture of infant food, skim milk powder etc., a major portion does not find economic disposal, and is merely wasted.

This investigation was undertaken with a view to evolve a suitable technique for the manufacture of dahi from sweet-cream butter milk. Dahi is used as a part of diet in this country on account of its virtues from the nutritional standpoint. It has been resorted that nearly 7.8 per cent of all milk produced in the country is used for dahi manufacture. If an acceptable quality of dahi could be made from buttermilk, not only it will open a way for its utilization but may also release part of milk currently used for dahi for other uses.

COMPOSITION

Dahi was made with cow and buffalo buttermilk using cultures such as *Str.lactis, Sir.diacetilactis.* **L.F-40** and *Str. Thermophilus* and *L. bulgaricus* (1:1) with or without increasing total solids content by the addition of skim milk powder. The dahi thus made was analysed for total solids, fact, total nitrogen, non-protein nitrogen, per cent lactic acid, curd tension and diacetyl content, and sensory evaluation by a panel of judges, and compared with skim and whole milk dahi.

It was observed that dahi of acceptable quality from sweet cream buttermilk could be prepared by subjecting the buttermilk to cream separation (if desired) at 55°C, (optionally adding 1 to 2 per cent skim milk solids) and heating it to 90°C for 30 min. before cooling to 30°C, inoculating with one per cent of a culture of *Sir. Lactis* (for cow butter milk) and 0.5 per cent of culture of *Str. Diacetilactis* (for buffaloe buttermilk) and finally incubating in for 16 and 12 hours respectively.

ACIDOPHILUS MILK

Acidophilus milk is a sour milk product that have been allowed to ferment under conditions that favour the growth and development of a large number of lactobacillus, acidophilus organisms. Acidophilus milk differs from Indian dahi in that the milk used in the preparation and the type of micro-organisms involved are different. The final product differs from dahi in body, texture, consistency, flavour, chemical composition and in antibacterial activities.

Uses

Products of mixed fermentation such as acidophilus yeast milk being rich in alcohol and carbon dioxide excite the respiratory and central nervous systems. This improves the process of oxidation and reduction in the organisms and hence there is an increase in the oxygen flow to the lungs. In the Soviet Union, acidophilus yeast milk is widely used in treating tuberculosis.

The recent emphasis on feeding lactobacilli is attributed to the side effects of antibiotics. Antibiotics damage the intestinal microflora and intentinal discomforts caused by flatulence and diarrhoea. Induction of *Lacidophilus* into the intestine accelerates return to normalcy in the intestinal microflora. A Rumanian strain of *L. acidophilus* is claimed to have been produced for treatment of gastrointestinal disorders but also produces a feeling of general vigour and health. It has been reported that acidophilus milk products combind with chemo-therapeutic preparation can also be used effectively for several disesaes, such as typhoid, para-typhoidpsoriosis, osteomyelitis, pneumonia, migraine and urological infection. Experiments have revealed that the body weight of a hild, or an animal increases when fed with acidophilus milk preparations.

Preparation

L. acidophilus-based fermented products differ in the type of starter culture and milk used for their preparation. Acidophilus sour milk, as the name indicates, is a sour milk beverage made out of standardized milk, acidifying it by means of pure culture of acidophilus rods (*L. acidophilus*). Milk culture of *L. acidophilus* has the therapeutic value described earlier but does not possess the buttery acetaldehyde flavour of the regular fermented milk products such as dahi and yoghurt.

The procedure for the preparation of acidophilus sour milk has been standardized. The milk used for the preparation of acidophilus sour milk is standardised to 3.5% fat and 8.5% SNF content. For this preparation standardized milk is sterilized and is cooled to 40°C. The milk is inoculated with 24 hours old pure starter culture of *L. acidophilus* at the rate of 2 to 3% and filled into 200 ml glass or plastic container and incubated at about 39°C for 8-12 hrs. the product is then cooled and stored at 5-8°C till it is consumed.

The product so obtained is sout with 1 to 1.2% lactic acid (pH 3.7-4.0). The product should contain more than 2000-3000 million viable *L. acidophilus* organisms/ml which possess satisfactory antibiotic effect against I; coli as well as other pathogenic and non-pathogenic undesirable bacteria of the intestinal tract.

The viability of the organisms is of primary importance in the use of acidophilus milk. The acidophilus sour milk can be preserved upto a week below 5°C.

FLAVOURED TYPE OF MILK BEVERAGE FROM CHEESE WHEY

In most of the cheese producing countries utilization of cheese whey has become a problem, on the other hand it is an excellent source of protein "ranks high in nutritive value only next to egg protein", lactose minerals and water soluble vitamins. Utilization of cheese whey for the manufacture of flavoured type milk beverage is a most logical use of return to the human food chain in a palatable form, in the light of growing global food shortage.

To standardise the method of manufacture of flavoured type milk beverage, a base material (prepared by taking whey 4.5% skim-milk acidified with HCL heated to 90° C followed by filtration through muslin cloth) was obtained in the form of curd. This curd was mixed with part of separated whey in a proportion so as to obtain 3.0% protein level followed by neutralizing with 10% sodium hydroxide solution, preheating to 65°C, homogenization at 2.000 and 500 psi. pasteurizing at 75°C and finally cooling it immediately. The product with 6% pineapple or rose flavour had a good acceptability. It has shelf life of about 7 days under refrigerated conditions.

YOGHURT FROM BUFFALO MILK

It is an undisputable fact that the enormously increasing popularity of yoghurt, now becoming available throughout the world, is primarily based on the cultural and biochemical performance of lactic cultures namely *Streptococcus thermophulus* and *lactobacillus bulgaricus*. These are the corner stones upon which the success or failure of yoghurt processing hinges.

Although our knowledge regarding the growth and biochemical performance of yoghurt lactic cultures in cow milk has been well established there is paucity of information on this aspect in milk of other species like buffalo. Attempts have been made to obtain information on the ability of lactic cultures in the preparation of three types of yoghurt namely, plain yoghurt, fruit yoghurt and sweetened yoghurt by the procedure indicated in the flow sheet.

Processing

Cow and buffalo milk samples are individually steamed for 30 min. cooled to a temperature of 43°C and then inoculated at 3% level with *Sir thermophulus* and *l.b. bulgarous* an equal proportions (1:1). The contents are mixed thoroughly and filled in glass bottles covered with lids or aluminium foil caps, transferred to water bath maintained at 42°C±0.5°C. After incubation for 3.0-3.5 hrs when the coagulum is formed, the bottles are removed from water bath, cooled at 30°C for 1/2 hr and transferred to refrigerator for overnight storage.

Fruit/Sweetened Yoghurt	Plain Yoghurt	
	Milk (cow buffalo) (Perform compositional test)	
	Standardisation (A-C)	(A) Adjust fat (2-3%) (B) Add NFDMS (2%) (C) Add Gelatin (0.5%)
	Stir	
	Homogenisation	
	Heat Treatment	(Steaming for 30 minutes)
	Stir	
Add Sugar (5-6%)- Inoculation with	Yoghurt starter (3%)	S.thermophilus+L.. bulgaricus (1:1)
	Stir	
Add Fruit Pulp (15-20%)		
	Stir	
	Incubation	(45°C for 3.5 hrs.)
	Cooling (20°C) & quality evaluation (1-2)	1. Subjective Tests (Sensory Evaluation) A. Body B. Texture C. Flavour 2. Objective Tests (Laboratory Analysis) A. Chemical B. Physical C. Microbiological
	Storage at 5°C	

PROCEDURE FOR THE MANUFACTURE AND QUALITY EVALUATION OF PLAIN/SWEETENED/FRUIT YOGHURT

CHEDDAR CHEESE FROM COW MILK

Cheese is one of the most important dairy products in the world market. The growth rate in production of cheese is increasing steadily the world over. It provides one of the best methods of conserving and preserving milk solids. The standard method for its production is as follows:

Manufacturing Method

1. Selection of milk : Fresh, good quality milk, free from antibiotics and preservatives.

2. Selection of starter : A good, active and uniform starter is essential.

3. Clarification and Standardization of milk: Casein/fat ratio (CF)-0.7.

4. Psteurization : 63°C 30 min or 72°C 15 sec.

5. Cooling to 30°C.

6. Adding starter (LF-40) at 30 C: 1% by wt....0.

7. Adding rennet when titratable acidity of milk incresaed by 0.01 to 0.02% : 2.5g/100 lit. — 45-60 min.

8. Cutting the coagulum whey acidity 0.1% — 30 min.

9. Cooking : start at 30°C — 15 min.

10. Cooking/stirring : finish at 38° C 90 min.

11. Draining, when whey acidity is 0.13-0.16% or about 0.02% than cutting acidity — 10 min.

12. Packing the curd, after piling, acidity of whey should be 0.17 to 0.20% — 10 min.

13. Cheddaring periodical turning of blocks and piling and repiling till whey acidity reaches 0.45 to 0.5% 2 hrs.

14. Milling........................... — 10 min.

15. Salting : 2% by wt. of curd, in three applications. — 30 min.

16. Hooping : After the salt has dissolved completely. — 10 min.

17. Pressing : Max. pressure of 2 kg/cm² to be applied slowly. — 30 min.

18. Dressing the cheese : The hoops are removed from the press, cheese cloth is pulled to remove all the wrinkles and pressed again overnight. — 10 min.

19. Removing cheese from press, when the rind becomes free from openings. — 12-24 hrs.

20. Drying the cheese : Dry at 10-15°C till dry, clean and bright surface is obtained. — 2-5 days.

21. Paraffining : Dip the cheese in paraffin heated to 105° C.

22. Ripening at 8-10°C 4-8 months

CHEDDAR CHEESE FROM BUFFALO MILK

In the manufacture of cheddar cheese from buffalo milk, the basic steps remain the same as applied to cow milk, however, certain modifications have to be introduced to get desirabe product. Out of the three methods recommended (Czulak, Burde and Presalting) the last one results in superior product. The salient features of Presalting method are described as below:

1. The standardized (C/F, 0.7) and pasteurized (63° C/30 min) Buffalo milk is cooled to 28°C followed by addition of common salt @ 1% with thorough mixing.

2. After 15 min. an active starter culture (LF-40) is added @ 2.5%. Supplementation of regular culture with 0.5% *Lcasei* enhances flavour development. After about 10 min. Hansen's calf rennet powder (2.5 g/100 lit) is dissolved in tap water (20 times) and added to milk with thorough mixing. Substitution of calf rennet with microbial rennet, viz. Modilase, Noury and Marzyzme have stimulatory effect on flavour development.

3. After setting (50-55 min.) the curd is cut with 1.4 cm knife. Precaution should be taken to judge the exact cutting time. Delay in cutting results in a tough coagulum which hampers uniformity of the cubes and higher losses in whey due to breaking up into small particles.

4. The stirring is started after 10-15 min. of cutting and the curd is cooked to 35-36°C in 40-45 min. After proper cooking the curd is left in whey undisturbed for 5-10 min. and then whey is drained. The curd expels moisture at a very fast rate and even a delay of 10 min. in drainage of whey was found to result in excessive drying and hardening of cubes, which ultimately led to tough body and mechanical openness in the pressed cheese. Hence, draining has to be quick and cooking time of 1 hr to be critically observed.

5. Higher piling during cheddaring helps obtaining good texture at the end. It is essential to develop a good texture resembling chicken breast type during cheddaring to ensure proper milling, salting, pressing and rind formation.

6. After pressing, green cheese blocks are transferred to cold storage for drying. The temperature of cold storage should be maintained preferably between 10-15°C. After proper drying generally in 2-3 days, the cheese blocks are paraffined. It is recommended to ripen the cheese for about 3 weeks followed by completion of curing at 8-10°C.

MOZZARELLA CHEESE

Mozzarella cheese originated from buffalo milk in Italy. It is a soft, white, unripened, plastic curd cheese with bland but mildly acidic flavour. It has special melting and stretching characteristics. It is mainly used in preparation of bakery products like pizza. Recently, the production of mozzarella cheese is increasing in our country. Its manufacturing method is shown as below :

1. *Selection of Milk* : Fresh, good quality milk, free from antibiotics and preservatives. Buffalo, Cow or mixed milk can be used. Originally made from whole raw milk, it can now be made from pasteurised milk, partially skimmed milk.

2. *Selection of Culture* : A good, active, uniform culture containing, *S. lactis S. thermophilus* and *L. bulgaricu* is often used. Also *S. thermophilus* and *L. bulgaricus* in the ratio of I:I can be used.

3. Clarification and standardization of milk to any desired fat level, mostly 3.2%.

4. Pasteurization : 72°C/16 second.

5. Cooling to 31-23°C.

6. Addition to starter at the rate of 0.5-2.0%.

7. Addition of rennet @ 20 ml. or 2.5 g/100 lit. after the acidity has increased by 0.02% to give a coagulation time of 25-30 min.

8. The curd is cut and left undisturbed for 10-15 min. followed by cooking slowly upto 38-39°C for 30-45 min.

9. Whey is drained off and the curd is allowed to ripen to an acidity of 0.65 to 0.70%.

10. The curd is cut into pieces and stretched in hot water (82-85°C) for proper development of body and texture.

11. The curd is moulded by filling hot, plastic curd into hoops.

12. The moulded cheese in water at 10°C for 1/2 to 1 hr for hardening.

13. The cheese blocks is then transferred to a 16-20% brine solution at 8-10°C for sufficient time to allow 1.6% salt in cheese.

14. Dry off the cheese for about an hour and pack in PVDC film or laminated pouches (moisture and airtight) preferably under vacuum.

COTTAGE CHEESE

Cottage cheese is a soft, unripened variety made from skim-milk to which cream and salt may be added. It is pleasant, mild in flavour. It is a good sourceof quality protein and low in calories which is highly suitable to those conscious of over weight. Its manufacturing method is shown as follows :-

1. Selection of milk: Fresh, good quality milk, free from antibiotics and preservatives.

2. Selection of starter : A good, active and uniform starter is essential.

3. Standardization of milk : SNF of milk to 9.0% by fortifying with skim milk powder.

4. Pasteurization 63°C/30 min. or 72°C/16 sec.

5. Cooling : 30 ± 1°C.

6. Addition of Calcium Chloride @ 10g/100 lit.

7. Addition of starter culture @ 6% — 0

8. Addition of rennet @ 0.04g/100 lit. — 75 min.

9. Cutting of curd at whey acidity 0.5% — 240 min.

10. Cooking start — 15 min.

11. Washing of curd : First wash Temp. 27°C. — 10 min.
    Second wash Temp. 17°C — 10 min.
    Third wash Temp. 8°C — 10 min.

12. Creaming of curd with dressing containing 18% fat.

PROCESSED CHEESE

Processed cheese is made from natural ripened cheeses. Cheese of different age is blended together and processed into a final product with pleasant flavour and smooth body and texture. The basic objective of processing is to blend natural cheese, water emulsifying salts into a homogenous mixture and pasteurise to obtain an end product which has sufficient fluidity for convenient packging and which posseses long keeping quality. As per PFA process cheese should contain not more than 47% moisture, not less than 40% fat on dry matter basis and not more than 3% common salt and emulsifiers. Its manufacturing technique is as follows :

Manufacturing Method

1. **Selection of Cheese** : The selection is determined chiefly by age, acidity, flavour, body, texture and composition of lots of cheese available. It is recommended that in order to obtain best quality product, the cheeses should be at three different stages of ripening :

a) Current these 25% not over 1 month old.

b) Short held cheese 50% about 3 months old.

c) Aged cheese 25% 6 months or more.

2. **Cleaning, Shredding and Mixing** : The paraffin and other non-edible portion of natural cheese is trimmed off. The trimmed cheese is then ground.

3) **Selection of Emulsifier** : Emulsifying agents are used to prevent the separation of cheese into its three main Constiuents (fat, protein and water) during processing and also to improve the body and texture of finished product. The most common emulsifiers used are sodium citrate and disodium phosphate. Normally they are added at the rate of 2%. They may be added to the cheese during grinding or melting.

4. **Processing** : The purpose of actual processing is to blend the cheese and added substances into a homogenous mixture, to pasteurise it and to attain sufficient fluidity for convenient packaging. This is accomplished by heating and stirring and by addition of suitable emulsifying salt and water.

The cheese is pasteurised in a steam jacketed kettle fitted with double action agitator. The ground cheese remains crumbly until a temp. of abour 49°C is reached. Beyond this point the cheese becomes sticky, stringy and plastic and may effectively retain or reincorporate the fat without the addition of emulsifying agent. The heating and stirring are continued until final temp. is reached (75°C) followed by packaging in presterilized containers. The sealed tins are gradually cooled to 22°C. The packages should not be kept under refrigeration until they have attained this temperature.

SURTI CHEESE

Surti cheese is a form of cottage cheese popular in Western India. So far this delicious cheese has been made only under cottage industry using indigenous utensils and wicker baskets. The present technique is described for commercial production of Surti Cheese and make possible to utilise and surplus milk in market milk plants more economically while ensuring the quality of Cheese comparable to that made by the indigenous process. The major production steps are as follows :

Steps in processing

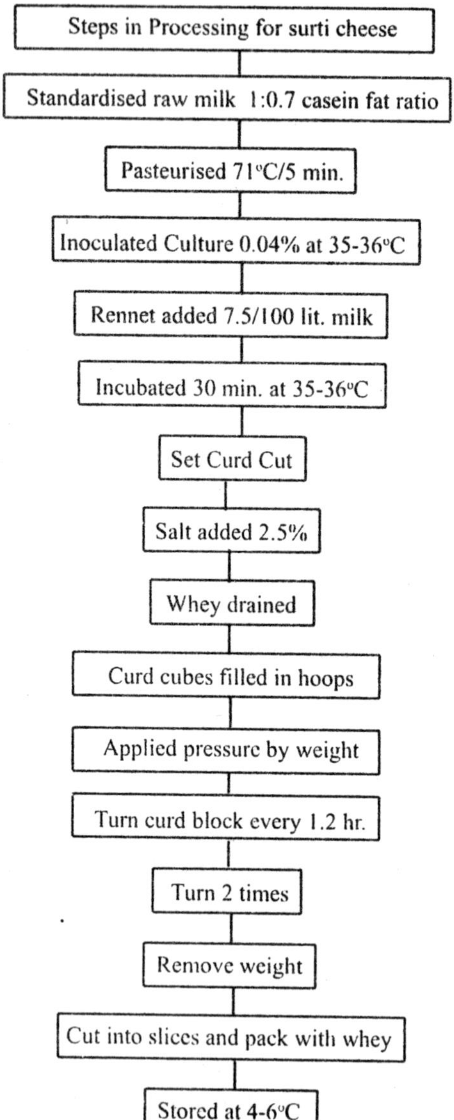

Composition

Average Composition of Surti Cheese : Fat 13% Moisture - 72% TS 28%

SOFT CHEESE

Steps in Processing

Varieties made from cow milk are quite popular in Western countries. In the context of popularising this type of highly nutritive dairy product in India NDRI has studied and standardised one soft sweet cheese variety. The major steps for the production of sweet cheese are described below:

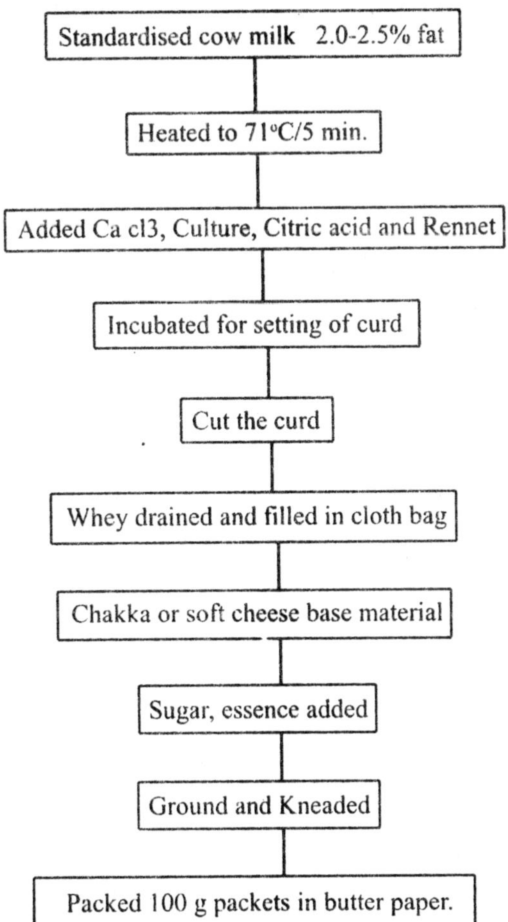

Composition

The composition of Sweet Cheese may range from fat 12-16%, TS-35-40% moisture - 60-65%. Sugar 25-30% by weight of soft cheese and essence 1 ml per kg of mix.

RICOTTA CHEESE FROM DIFFERENT WHEY SYSTEMS

Ricotta cheese originated from Italy is a soft, granular variety having a bland taste. Its physico-chemical characteristics are midway between those of Chhana and Khoa. Ricotta cheese in its fresh formis quite suitable for the partial replacement of Chhana and Khoa for the manufacture of a number of sweets (such as Sandesh, Burfi, Gulabjamun, etc) and Indian culinary dishes (such as stuffed potatoes, tomatoes, etc). No special equipment is needed for the manufacture of Ricotta. In fact, the same equipment which is used for production of case in cheese or paneer, can be employed. The process involved is relatively simple and is suitable for both small and large scale handling

Process of Manufacture

1. Adjust the pH of whey of 6.6 of 6.8 using calcium hydroxide.

2. Add 10% whole milk (cow or buffalo) to the above whey,

3. Heat with direct stream injection o 95°C and hold for 10 minutes.

4. Add sufficient citric acid (30% solution) with very slow stirring till granular curd appears and whey clears (pH 5.9-6.1). Allow the curd to settle.

5. Collect curd in a muslin cloth. Continue draining overnight.

6. Pack the product in suitable containers.

7. Yield of product is about 7%.

Composition

Moisture	75.0%
Proteins	12.4%
Fat	8.6%
Lactose	3.0%
Ash	1.0%

CHEESE SPREAD POWDER

Processed cheese prepared from blending of differently aged cheese varities is very popular. Cheese spread commonly used as a paste for sandwitches, is another cheese based product. However, certain sections of the population in India are not used to strong cheese flavour. Taking into consideration the requirement of mild flavoured and smooth textured cheese product, a method for the manufacture of cheese spread powder has been developed.

Steps in Processing

The cheese spread was prepared by blending equal proportion of young (2 months old) and fully ripened (7-8 months) lots of buffalo milk cheddar cheese. Minced cheese alongwith predetermined amounts of moisture, butterfat, salt and emulsifying agents (trisodium citrate and trisodium orthophosphate in the ratio of 5:1) at 2.0% were mixed thoroughly in a cheese processing kettle. Gelatine (0.3% in dissolved form), flavouring agents like tomato juice, onion juice etc (optional at 5.0% of the blend) were added at 60°C. The temperature was raised at 71°C with constant stirring and preservations (nisin or scorbic acid) were added at the rate of 0.02%. The hot slurry was then homogenised in a single stage homogeniser at 100 kg/cm^2 and collected in presterilised lacquered tin cans, covered with lids and seamed immediately. The seamed cans were kept in hot water at 80°C for 5 minutes and then kept at room temperature for 24 hours and transferred to cold store.

Besides the ready to use form, cheese spread was also prepared in the free flowing powder form. For this purpose, the homogenised cheese slurry without any added preservatives was adjusted to 35% total solids and then spray dried at an inlet air temperature of 160°C and outlet air temperature of 100°C. The dried product was packed in lacquered tins under nitrogen packing.

Composition

Particulars	*Cheese spread*	*Dried cheese spread*
Fat	21.50%	56.00%
T.S.	42.50%	96.50%
Moisture	57.50%	3.50%
Salt	1.00%	2.00%

The samples of cheese spread powder were acceptable upto 6 months storage at room temperture.

PANEER

Panner is primarily acid coagulated milk solid used as an ingredient in cooking of vegetables in Northern India. Mostly, buffalo milk is used for the production of paneer. The best quality product is made from milk of 6.0% fat content. Packed paneer could be stored for 3 days without any loss of freshness when refrigerated.

Steps in Processing for Paneer Manufacture

Standardised buffalo milk 6.0%

↓

Heated to 82°C/5 min.

↓

Cooled to 70°C

↓

Coagulated by 1% citric acid.

↓

Whey drained out.

↓

Milk solids filled in hoops.

↓

Pressed by weight

↓

Weight removed

↓

Cut into pieces.

↓

Dipped in chilled water for 1-2 hrs. at 4-6°C.

↓

Chilled water drained out.

↓

Packed into desired weight and stored at 4-6°C.

Composition

The average composition of paneer may be fat - 26% moisture 55% and T.S. 45%.

CHHANA MAKING

It is recognised that good quality chhana for rossogolla cannot be made from buffalo milk as the balls do not swell during cooking as those made from cow milk chhana. The rossogollas prepared from buffalo milk chhana also showed shattering during cooking and dark colouration.

The comparative study of the physico-chemical properties of chhana from cow and buffalo milk and their admixture was carried out to develop an appropriate technology for production of good quality chhana from milk and to minimize losses of milk solids in whey. The factors studied in this investigation included kind of milk-type of coagulant and temperature and pH of coagulation.

Steps in Processing

The coagulation of cow milk at pH 5.7 resulted in very soft chhana with high moisture and increased losses of milk solids in whey while at pH 5.1, channa was soft and cohesive with minimum losses of milk solids in whey. Buffalo milk followed a similar trend although the effect was less pronounced. Temperatures above 70°C caused grainy texture and increased hardness while lower temperature produced highly sticky chhana which was difficult to drain. Compared to lactic acid, citric acid produced more cohesive chhana with lower losses of milk solids in whey. Best quality chhana from cow milk was obtained by coagulating milk at 70oC at pH 5.1 using 2% citric acid solution as coagulant. This combination of factors for buffalo milk coagulation produced less cohesive chhana. Treatment of buffalo milk with 0.05% sodium citrate before boiling, dilution of milk with 25% water, and coagulation with 1% citric acid solution improved the softness and product can be comparable with cow milk chhana.

DRIED CHHANA

Chhana, also called paneer in some regions of the country, is an Indian whole milk product which constitutes an important base for sweets like Sandesh and Rossogolla. However, it is mostly prepared on small scale by the disorganised sector of dairy industry for obvious reasons of its low shelf life and difficulties in transportation. Since, it was felt that drying of chhana and consequent increase in its shelf life would help in the growth of this product a method for production of dried chhana, as detailed below, was standardised. The dried chhana is suitable for preparation of Sandesh.

Steps in Processing

Raw cow milk is standardised to 4% fat, given first boil in the coagulation vessel and then lowered to 80±5°C. The emulsifier tri-sodium citrate @ 0.02% of milk is added as an aqueous solution. The milk is kept covered and left undisturbed for 2±1 hrs. Then coagulating acid (1-2% solution of lactic or citric acid) is added to milk with gentle stirring. At the end of coagulation (pH-5.4), the contents are poured over a piece of muslin cloth stretched over another vessel. The coagulated milk solids stay on the top of the cloth while the whey passes through it.

The Chhana is transferred to milk can and calculated amount of water is added as to give 19-21% total solid in the slurry. After premixing with the held of a plunger, the mix is further passed through micro-pulveriser to give a smooth slurry. The slurry is dried in a spray-drier using an inlet air temperature of 195±5°C and an outlet temperature of 100±2°C. The dried product is promptly removed from the drying chamber, cooled, packaged and stored at room temperature.

Composition

The average percentage chemical composition of dried chhhana is: Moisture 3.5%, Fat 41.6%, Protein 46.3%, Lactose 4.2% and Ash 4.4%. The storageability of chhana powder is 2 and 4 months at 20±2°C under air tight and nitrogen gas packing respectively. The powder is dehydrated back to chhana for preparation of Sandesh.

PREPARATION OF SANDESH FROM CHHANA

The channa is first kneaded, then ground sugar added @ 30% of chhana and mixed with it. The mix is baked on a very slow fire, stirring all the time. Crushed cardamon, if desired, is added towards the end. When mixture starts forming balls, it is poured into tray and left for cooling and setting. It is then cut in desired size and decorated with pista and silver paper.

FROM DRIED CHHANA

The dried chhana is rehydrated with warm milk in the ratio of I:I of weight, left for 15 minutes, then Sandesh is made from this chhana as above.

SRIKHAND

Srikhand is a fermented and coagulated delicacy popular in the Western part of the country. The technology of Srikhand begins and the production of Dahi, from which whey is drained out and a semi-soft material is produced after mixing sugar and essence.

Steps in Processing to make Srikhand

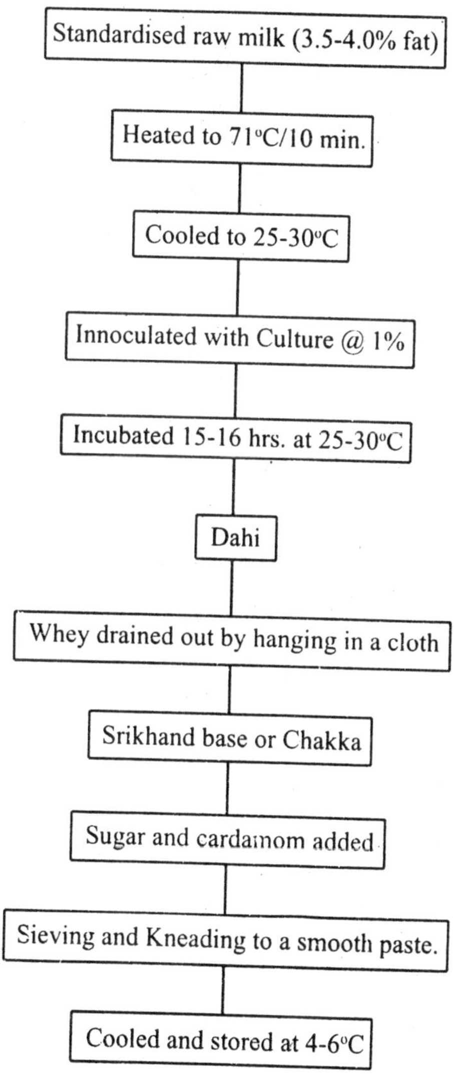

Composition

The composition of Srikhand may range from : fat 5-15%, moisture 40-45% and sugar 45-55%. The product is expected to keep at least for two weeks when refrigerated.

KHOA

The dairy plants in India usually face the problem of using surplus milk during winter. It has now been demonstrated that the organized dairies can profitably divert part of this surplus milk and some of the standard quality milk for the manufacture of Khoa. The problem concerned with limited shelf life of Khoa due to microbial spoilage and chemical deterioration was the major impediment in the adoption of this product by the organised sector. Small scale sector engaged in the manufacture of Khoa was also confronted with the limited shelf life of Khoa leading to uneconomic marketing situations. Investigations were, therefore, conducted to standardise a process for the manufacture of Khoa with long shelf life using readily available packaging materials and permitted chemical additives.

Increasing the Shelf Life

The non-availability of tin sheets and prohibitive costs of tin containers warranted us to find out a suitable substitute. The flexible packaging materials such as food grade polyethyene, parchment paper, and laminated pouches were used. Khao samples packed in sterilized four ply laminates afforded the same protection as tin containers. The product kept in good condition upto 13 days at 30°C. Khao should be lifted while hot (70°C) in these containers and sealed employing all the aseptic precautions.

The shelf life of Khoa was increasded to 75 days at cold room temperature of 7°C. Incorporation of 0.02% butylated hydroxy anisole (by weight of fat content in Khoa), addition of 0.2% potassium sorbate and mixing of nisin (100u/gm) improved the shelf life of Khoa upto 20 days at 30°C and 125 days in the cold stores. The studies showed that incorporation of potassium sorbate and nisin considerably enhanced the shelf life of Khoa without impairing its flavour and other marketable characteristics.

UTILIZATION OF BUTTTERMILK AND SOYABEAN FOR THE MANUFACTURE OF SOFTY ICE-CREAM

Buttermilk is an important by-product of butter industry. It is estimated that nearly 0.92 million tons of buttermilk is produced annually in the organised dairy sector. There is, however, little evidence of its economical utilization. The composition of buttermilk is quite similar to skim milk, except for little higher concentration of fat, mainly phospholipids. The utilization of buttermilk for popular frozen desserts such as softy ice-cream will conserve the solids of milk.

Buttermilk powder is considered to be an excellent replacement for the skim milk powder in the ice-cream mixes, Soyabean is unique, in that it produces more protein per acre than any other protein source and its protein contains, in nearly optimum proportions, all the essential amino acids except sulphur containing AA's. Two kgs of soy flour contains as much protein as 14 litres of milk. Soyabean acts as a moistrue retainer, emulsifier, stabilizer binder, as well as enhances the shelf life of products and improves product appearance. It helps food processors to produce generally high quality food at comparatively lower production cost.

The present study was, therefore, undertaken to develop a softy ice-cream using buttermilk and soyabean. It was expected that the product would not only be cheaper but also nearly equal in nutritional value.

Steps in Processing

The process, as standardized, entails in presoaking the soybean overnight in sodium bicarbonate solution, blanching and dehulling. The cotyledons thus obtained were ground in various ratio with buttermilk. Fat and sugar were then added and the mixture was pasteurised and homogenised. The mix was cooled and aged, and then frozen in a softserve ice-cream freezer.

Composition

In order to get the most acceptable product, various combinations of soybean: buttermilk solids were tested, such as 1.1:1, 1.3:1, 1.5:1, 2:1 etc. The first combination was liked most and the second was the next best. Amongst additional source of vegetable oils, three oils/fats locally available were tried, these were coconut, groundnut oil and hydrogenated vegetable fat. Of these, the last did not impart any of its own flavour to the product and, therefore, was found to be the most acceptable. Softy ice-cream was thus made using 1.3:1 of soybean and buttermilk solids, using hydrogenated vegetable fat for subsequent trails. By varying the fat, SNF and sugar concentration, the most acceptable combination was found which was respectively, 9%, 12% and 15%.

It was observed that addition 0.1, 0.2 or 0.3% sodium alginate brought about unusually large increase in the viscosity of the mix, which was not appreciated by judges. It was then felt that there was no need for addition of a stabilizer in the soybean-buttermilk softy ice-cream.

The final softy ice-cream mix was spray dried and stored in tin (packaged with/without nitrogen) and polyethylene containers and stored at 30°C±1°C and 5°±2°C to assess the shelf life of the product. From this storage study, it was observed, from physico-chemical and sensory properties (of reconstituted, softy ice-cream) that the product packaged in tins could be stored for 9 months at 30°±1°C and more than 12 months at 5°±2°C. While in polyethylene bags, the product had acceptable quality for 5 months at 30°±1°C and 9 months at 5°±2°C.

COFFEE/TEA WHITENERS

In metropolitan cities, a large amount of milk is used for the preparation of coffee/tea. Use of coffee/tea whiteners for this purpose will encourage the use of fluid milk for other purposes, such as feeding children, elderly group of people, etc.

Method has been standardised for the manufacture of two types of coffee/tea whiteners - one which is low in fat content(LFCW), is specially meant for the group users, who like to restrict calorie intake and other with high (HFCW) which is meant for the replacement of cream for whitening of coffee/tea.

Equipment Used

1. Mixing vats
2. Plate heat exchangers
3. Homogenizer
4. Spray drier
5. Packing equipment

Steps in Processing

1. Various ingredients (cream, sodium caseinate, glucose syrup, GMS, CMC, Trisodium phosphate and sodium citrate) are mixed in the desired proportion as indicated in the table. Total solids are adjusted to 35 per cent.

2. The mix is preheated to 80°C/10 min. and then homogenised (1st stage 175 kgs/cm^2 and 2nd stage 35 kgs/cm^2).

3. This mix is spray dried, employing drying air inlet temperature of 210°C and outlet temperature of 95°C. The moisture content of the dried product should be about 3 per cent.

4. The percent is packaged under nitrogen and stored preferably below 15°C.

Composition

Constituents (%)	LFCW	HFCW
Fat	12.4	48.6
Sodium caseinate	37.0	20.8
Glucose syrup	37.0	20.8
GMS	5.6	3.8
GMC	1.2	0.7
Tri-sodium phosphate	1.2	0.7
Tri-sodium citrate	2.5	1.4

GULABJAMUN MIX POWDER

The existing method for the preparation of gulabjamun is suitable at cottage scale. Khoa is generally used as a base which causes wide variations in flavour, texture and chemical composition of the sweet. Good quality khoa may not be available all the year round in different parts of the country. In order to overcome these difficulties, a ready-to-form gulabjamun mix powder formulations based on skimmed milk powder with six months shelf life has been developed.

The formulated mix consists of skim milk powder (roller) 434 g; butterfat/vanaspati 150 g; maida 260 g; suji 150 g; baking powder 15 g and powdered cardamom 0.1 g (alternatively 2 cup SMP, 3/4 cup maida, 1/3 cup butterfat, 1/2 cup suji, 1 tea spoonful baking powder and a pinch of cardamom). All these ingredients are properly blended and packed in a polyethylene bag. The mix powder stays well for about 6 months at room temperature and can be conveniently used in the preparation of gulabjamun at any time.

The production of gulabjamun starts with the preparation of sugar syrup. Equal proportions (on weight basis) of water and sugar are boiled till a syrup of about 60% concentration (one thread consistency) is obtained. The dirt and impurities gathering at the surface are removed with the help of a perforated laddle and the syrup strained through a nylon/muslin cloth.

For the preparation of dough and balls, mix instant gulabjamun mix with required quantity of water (50-55 ml for 100 g mix) and knead well until smooth body is obtained.

Normally 100 g instant mix yields 13 balls. The performed balls are covered with a wet cloth to arrest evaporation of moisture and case hardening until they are transferred to the frying pan. Deep fry the balls in refined vegetable oil or hydrogenated fat (Ghee optional) at 125-130°C for 20 minutes till the colour becomes brown. Drain the excess fat from the surface of the fried balls and finally transfer them into the sugar syrup maintained at 60°C. Soak for atleast 2 hours. Pack the sweet in presterilised polystyrene containers and serve hot.

BUTTER POWDER FROM BUFFALO MILK

Free flowing butter powder (80% fat) could be manufactured (see flow sheet) from buffalo milk solids. The product having the most desirable characteristics is made by taking buffalo milk cream and mixing in it reconstituted skim milk powder so that the final total solids content including 1% each of sodium citrate and glycerol monoste rate is 40% and contains 80% fat and 16.5% SNF (on dry basis).

The mix (optionally containing 0.015% BHA) is heated (65°C), homogenised (141 & 35 kg/cm^2), pasteurised (75°C for 1 min), ripened with LF-40-a mixed lactic starter culutre (at the rate of 1%) to obtain 0.12 to 0.16% lactic acidity and spray dried at 82°C outlet and 175°C inlet air temperatures. The butter powder should be immediately cooled (to 50°C) and coarse sieved to break any lumps culture, the butter powder could be dry blended with 0.5% fine sod.aluminium silicate to increase the flowability if desired. The finished butter powder contains 80% fact, 193.% SNF and 0.7% moisture.

In order to obtain a butter spread for the powder, 19% moisture (i.e. approx. 4 parts powder +1 part water) need be added and the powder reconstituted to a semi solid homogenous mass. If salt is desired in the spread, it should be added to the water before reconstituting the powder. To achieve the desirable colour and flavour, 0.5% annatoo butter colour and 4 drops of Butardol per 100 g spread respectively may be added.

When stored in tin cans or polyethylene bags, the butter powder keeps well for over one year at refrigeration (5°C).

FLOW SHEET FOR THE PRODUCTION OF BUTTER POWDER FROM BUFFALO MILK

Skim milk powder — CREAM

|

Dispersed in water — Blending — Emulsifier, anti-oxidant, sodium cirate

|

Total solids adjusted to 40%

|

Preheating (65°C)

|

Homogenization
(141+35 kg/cm^2)

|

Pasteurization
(75°C for i min.)

|

Starter culture — Ripening (to 0.12-0.16% LA)

|

Spray Drying (82°C outlet,
175°C inlet air temp.)

|

Cooling

|

Free flowing agent — Dry Blending

|

Sieving

|

Packaging

UTILIZATION OF SOUR BUFFALO MILK FOR THE MANUFACTURE OF EDIBLE CASEIN

Various process parameters for the manufacture of edible casein from fresh 0.2, 0.3 and 0.4% T.A. buffalo milk have been standardized. Optimised processes are : Neutralize the sour milks with $NaHCO_a$ to 0.063-0.090% T.A. Heat the fresh and neutralized sour milk to 50-60°C and separate them once through the triprocess machine. Pasteurise the skim milk from fresh milk byHTST method and that from neutralized sour milks by heating to 80°C. Precipitate the skim milks from fresh, 0.2, 0.3 and 0.4% T.A. milks at 35-36, 36-37, 38-39 and 40°C and 3.7,

4.0, 4.2 and 4.6 pH respectively. Give three washings to the precipitates, each 15 min. contact time with wash water at 35-37°C. Maintain the pH of wash water for first two washings at 4.0 and of last one at neutral. Press the washed precipitates overnight and shred them uniformly in trays. Dry the product in cabinet tray dryer with hot air circulation at 60-65°C. All the edible casein samples met ISI standards. Yield on skim milk basis from fresh 0.2, 0.3 and 0.4% T.A. milk was 2.83, 2.59, 2.53 and 2.40% respectively. All the samples graded good to excellent on flavour evaluation. PER of fresh milk edible casein was 2.49 and that of sour milk products, 2.02-2.15. All the casein samples showed 12 months of storageability at 30°C in polyethene bags. Sodium and calcium caseinates were also prepared from different edible casein samples. Edible caseins from different acidity milks did not significantly affect pH, solubility index, sinkability and wettability significantly of sodium and calcium caseinates. Calcium caseinates had significantly greater solubility index, sinkability, flowability and bulk density compared to sodium caseinates. Emulsifying and whipping properties of sodium and calcium caseinates were observed to be unaffected with the different acidity milk edible caseins. Sodium caseinate was observed to possess better emulsifying properties and whipping ability than calcium caseinate.

FROZEN YOGHURT FROM SOYABEAN AND BUTTER MILK

The fermented milk products like acid philus milk, Bulgarian buttermilk, Mazum, Kefir, Kusiss, Yoghurt and other related products occupy important place and are consumed regularly all over the world. Popularizing frozen yoghurt that too from soyabean and buttermilk in India will not only help to improve the nutritional status of the Indian population but also would be a possible substitute for ice-cream which is luxury item due to its high cost.

The balanced soyabean cotyledons were ground with buttermilk to get slurry havying soy-colids to buttermilk solids ratio 1:1. The slurry (11% T.S.) was homogenised at 175 and 35 kg/cm^2 at 65°C, pasteurised at 85° C and inoculated with L. Bulgarians+S. Ther. @ 3% after addition of gelatin as stabilizer. It was then incubated at 40°C for about 5 hours. The curd so obtained was added with 12% sugar in the form of syrup and synthetic pineapple flavour then mixed well and frozen. The product was hardened and stored. The product had protein 4.45% fat 2.4% ash 0.48% carbohydrate 18.26% and T.S. 25.6% and a good acceptability.

ICE CREAM POWDER

Ice cream is a delicious, wholesome, nutritious, frozen dairy food. It has occupied a unique place in the diet of the people in the West and is gaining steady in popularity all over India.

In India near16 60 per cent of milk production is from buffaloes. In the lean season, raw milk is in short supply and most of the surplus milk available in the flush season is used for preparing butter, ghee and skim milk powder. There is considerable demand for ice cream in the summer season (incidentally it is also the lean season of milk production) which can be coveniently met by driversifying a part of the milk during the flush season for the manufacture of ice cream powder.

Use of gelatin as stabilizer in the manufacture of dried ice cream mix yields ice cream having coarse body and texture characteristics and foam melt-down. Moreover, use of gelatin hurts the sentiments of a majority of the people who are vegetarians. Ice cream powder prepared using polysaccharide stabiliser of vegetable origin, and which on reconstitution with water yields ice cream of smooth body and texture characteristics has been developed recently at NDRI, Karnal.

Steps in Processing

The ingredients used are fresh milk/skim milk, skim milk powder, pregelatinized potato starch as stabilizer and Tween 80 as emulsifier. The composition of the ice cream mix is adjusted so that is contains only 25 per cent of the total sugar before spray drying. All the ingredients are weighed so that the mix contains 17.1 per cent fact, 14.2% SNF, 5.3% sugar, 0.7% pregelatinized potato starch and .07% Tween-80. Pregelatinized potato starch is mixed with little amount of sugar and added to milk/skim milk and heated, agitation. The required amount of cream is adjusted to 50°C. Skim milk powder mixed with the remaining sugar (to facilitate dissolution of powder particles) is added to the mixture with vigorous stirring. The contents are filtered through a muslin cloth and Tween-80 added to the mixture. The temperature of the contents is raised to 70°C and the mix homogenized at 176 kg/cm^2 and 35 kg/cm^2 on the first and second stage respectively. The mix is then pasteruized at 68°C/30 min, cooled to 5-10°C, aged for 16 hours and spray dried using an inlet air temperature of 73°C and an atomizer speed of 16500 r/min. The powder obtained is dry blended with refined sugar in the ratio 100 parts : 41 parts (by weight). The finished product contains 1.75% to 1.96% moisture, 24.84% to 25.13% SNF, 31.04%, 31.43% fat, 40.60% to 41.2% sugar, 1.3% pregelatinized potato starch and 0.13% Tween-80.
The powder has a shelf life of 9 months when packed in laminated polyester/ polyethylene packages and stored at 30°C.

For preparation of ice cream ; one part of powder should be mixed with 1.6 parts of potable water at 45°C cooled and frozen in a batch freezer to about

100% over run. 1 kg of powder then reconstituted in 1.6 kg of water yields 36 cups (125 ml) of ice cream.

The powder can be advantageously used by the industry and small scale manufacturer to cater to the demand for ice cream in the summer season. Small scale manufacturers who need to invest in a homogenizer and pasteurizer can prepare ice cream having the desired body and characteristics at a reasonably low cost.

AN IMPROVED INFANT FOOD FORMULA

An industrial process has been developed that permits manufacture of an infant formula which resembles human milk in the ratio of protein : fat : carbohydrates. The protein content in formula is adequate to fulfill the entire nutritional requirements of infant during the first year of the life, but without overloading the renal functions (which the presently available infant formulae do). This also permits extension of available bovine milk for the manufacture of higher quantities of infant foods, as well as reduce costs. Further modification also permits adjustment of whey protein to casein ratio, thus stimulating human milk more closely. The fat content has been modified so as to incorporate nutritionally superior middle chain glycerides from vegetable sources. Significantly, this aspect has both nutritional and cost advantages. Process has been also standardised for the manufacture of malto dextrins through starch hydrolysis suitable for incorporation into the formula in order to adjust the ratio of calorie contributing nutrients.

Another outstanding feature of the formula developed relates to the bifidus stimulating property. Animal bioassay as well as clinical studies carried out under medical supervision have demonstrated *Bifidobacterium bifidum* can be implanted in the intestinal tract through feeding of formula developed. In this manner, the improved formulation is expected to favour superior utilization of minerals, synthesise "B-Complex" vitamins in intestine, play a detoxification role in chronic liver diseases and provide protection against interopathogenic infection.

INCREASING THE SHELF LIFE OF GHEE

Ghee (Clarified butter oil) is the most important indigenous dairy product of India. About 33% of the total milk produced in India is converted into ghee. This product undergoes oxidative deterioration at ambien temperature. The oxidation of unsaturated fatty acids producers hydroperoxiders and their subsequent breakdown products viz. aldehydes, ketones, low molecular weight acids and oxyacids, cause the development of off-flavours in ghee. To prevent oxidation, the Food Adulteration Rules as amended in 1976, allow the addition of 0.02% by weight of butylated hydroxy anisole (BHA) and butylated hydroxytoluene (BHT) either singly or in combination in ghee. The continuous use of chemical antioxidants has been reported to cause taratogenic and carcinogenic effects in small animals and primates. In ancient times, edible vegetable sources such as betel and curry leaves were added to butter during clarification into ghee for unknown reasons. It is likely that they would improve the shelf life and flavour of ghee besides being safe to the health of the ghee consumers. An attempt was made to study the effects of betel and curry leaves with butter during clarifications at different concentration on flavour and antioxidative properties of ghee. Ghee samples treated Bha+BHT at 0.02% concentration curry leaves at 0.5, 0.8 and 1% and betel leaves at 0.2, 0.5 and 1% were stored at 30 Degree C and the samples were examined for peroxide value, iodene value, free fatty acidity Butyrorefractometer reading and flavour.

Changes during Storage

The initial peroxide value of ghee (0.00) did not increase up to 30 days of storage at 30°C. The control samples without antioxidants showed a steep rise in peroxide value after 60 days of storage. Ghee samples prepared with 1% curry leaves were most resistant to oxidation upto 135 days of storage and betel leaves at 1% level were second most potent as natural antioxidant. However, ghee samples treated with betel leaves at 1% concentration proved to be most acceptable and stable even after 147 days of storage at 30°C.

The extent of hydrolysis of ghee during storage was measured by titration for free fatty acidity. After 30 days of storage, there was a progressive increase in the free fatty acid contents of all the ghee samples. The control sample of ghee after 147 days of storage of 30°C showed an increase in FFA by more than 100%. Betel leaves at 1.0% conc. provided maximum protection against the hydrolysis of ghee. Sunderajan obseved that plant leaves contain phenolic compounds like hydroxychavicol, eugenol and some amino acids like, Aspargine, glycine, serine, aspartic acid, glotamic acid, threonine, alanine, proline and tryptophan. It is quite likely that these compounds might have served as potent antioxidants.

Although all the samples of ghee during storage showed varving degree of peroxide formation and increase in free-fatty acidity, only slight reduction in iodine value of treated ghee samples was observed. The initial iodine value of 35.9 in control sample of ghee got reduced to 35.6 after 147 days storage. The changes were non-significant in samples treated with higher doses of betel and curry leaves. Ghee samples treated BHA and BHT also offered similar benefits.

Ghee samples prepared with betel and curry leaves inhibited lower B.r. value. It is possible that the natural compounds which get dissolved in ghee during clarification might have lowered the B.R. values. Ghee samples were also evaluated for appearance, texture and flavour. All the samples of ghee were rated excellent at the beginning of the experiment. The judges preferred ghee samples treated with betel and curry leaves. These samples were awarded highest scores for flavour and colour. The samples treated with BHA and BHT were rated as ordinary.

It can be concluded that betel leaves and curry leaves at 1% concentration can easily act as replacers for BHA and BHT for extending the shelf life of ghee.

PROJECTED PER CAPITA MILK AVAILABILITY (1991-92 TO 2000-2001)

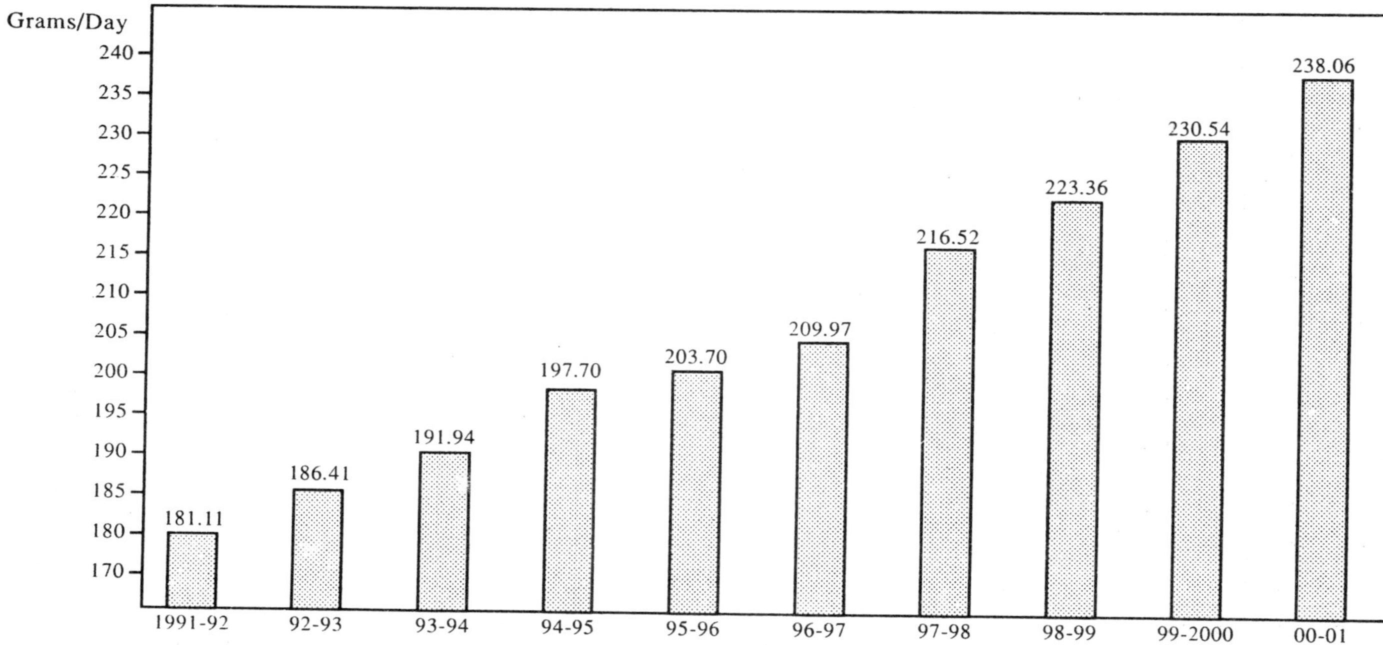

PROJECTED MILK PRODUCTION YEAR (1991-92 TO 2000-2001)

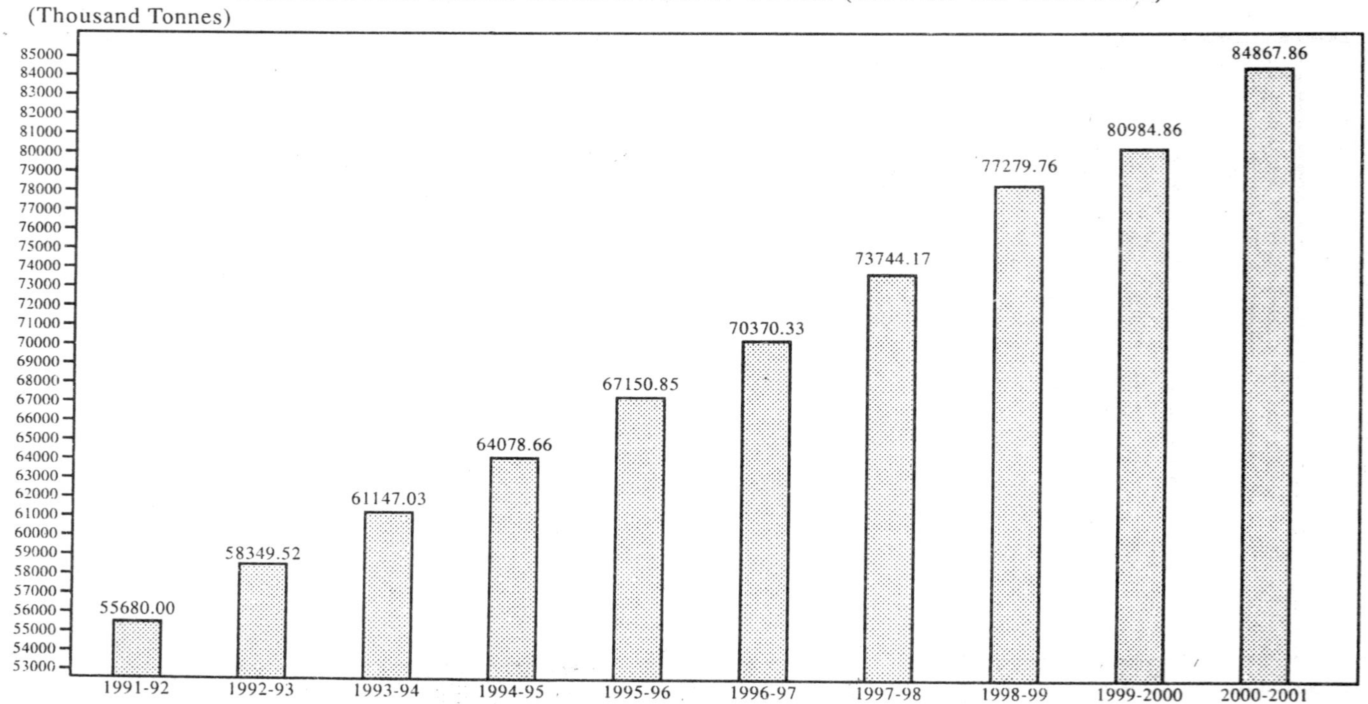

THE CHEMICAL COMPOSITION OF MILK HUMAN, COW, BUFFALO, GOAT AND SHEEP

	Human	Cow	Buffalow	Goat	Sheep
Fat	3.75	4.9	6.6	4.5	6.0
Total solid	12.57	13.7	15.8	13.5	16.3
Solids-not-fat	8.82	8.8	9.2	9.0	10.3
Lactose	6.98	4.1	5.2	4.7	4.9
Total Protein	1.63	3.4	3.9	3.5	4.8
Ash	0.21	0.7	0.7	0.8	0.8
VitaminC mg/100ml	40.00	2.5	2.8	3.5	5.5
Vitamin A(I.U.)/100ml	189.90	148.9	175.6	137.4	189.7

STATUS OF MAJOR MINERALS IN BUFFALO MILK AND COMPARISON WITH COW MILK*

Sr. No.	Minerals	Concentration (mg/100g)		Soluble % (Through rennet coagulation	
		Buffalo Milk	Cow Milk	Buffalo Milk	Cow Milk
1.	Calcium	175.50± 1.15	123.3	20.93± 0.939	35.0
2.	Magnesium	19.25± 0.381	11.1	50.64± 0.843	70.9
3.	Sodium	44.63± 0.402	58.0	95.10± 0.439	94.0
4.	Potassium	103.00± 0.913	140.0	95.15± 0.322	96.2
5.	Phosphate	97.60±1.28	95.1	32.98±0.657	44.10
6.	Citrate	163.60±2.60	176.0	85.72±1.52	91.5
7.	Chloride	62.84±0.933	104.5	99.51±0.454	100.0

* Results on cow milk from Davies & White (1958, 60)

STANDARDS FOR DIFFERENT CLASSES AND DESIGNATIONS OF MILK AS PER P.F.A.

Class of Milk	Designation	Locality	Minimum Milk fat	Percent Solid not fat
Buffalo Milk	Raw, Pasteurised, Boiled, Flavoured & Sterilised	Haryana	6.0	9.0
Cow Milk	Raw, Pasteurised, Boiled Flavoured & Sterilised	Haryana	4.0	8.5
Goat or Sheep milk	Raw, Pasteurised, Boiled Flavoured & Sterilised	Haryana	3.5	9.0
Standardised Milk	-do-	All India	4.5	8.5
Recombined Milk	-do-	All India	3.0	8.5
Toned Milk	-do-	All India	3.0	8.5
Double Toned Milk	-do-	All India	1.5	9.0
Skimmed Milk	Raw, Pasteurised, Boiled Flavoured & Sterilised	All India	not more than 0.5%	8.7

STANDARDS OF VARIOUS MILK PRODUCTS AS PER P.F.A.

1.	Cream	Milk fat 25.0% (Minimum)
2.	Dahi or Curd	Dahi shall have the same minimum percentage of milk fat and milk solids-not-fat as the milk from which it is prepared.
3.	Paneer/Channa	Moisture 70.0% (maximum) Fat - 50.0% of the dry matter (Minimum)
4.	Skim Milk Paneer/Channa	Moisture - 70.0% (Max.) Fat - 13% of the dry matter (max.)

5.	Cheese (Hard)	Moisture 43.0% (Max.) Fat - 42.0% of the dry matter (Min.) Stabiliser/emulsifier/NISIN - 0.1%.
6.	Processed Cheese	Moisture - 47.0% (Max.) Fat - 40.0% of the dry matter (min.) Salt - 3.0% (Max.) Stabiliser/Emulsifier - 4.0% (max.) or Sorbic Acid - 0.1 or NISIN - 0.1%
7.	Ice Cream	Fat - 10% (min.) 8.0% (min.) if containing fruits or nuts Protein - 3.5% (min) T.S. - 36.0% (min) Emulsifier/Stabiliser - 0.5% (max.)
8.	Milk ices/Lollies	Fat-2.0% (max.) Protein - 3.5% (min.) T.S. - 20% (min.) Stabiliser/emulsifier - 0.5% (max)
9.	Condensed Milk Unsweetened Evaporated Milk	Fat - 8.0% (min) Total Milk Solids - 26.0% (min)
10.	Condensed Milk Sweetened	Fat - 9.0% (min) Total milk solids - 31.0% (min) Cane sugar - 40.0% (min)
11.	Condensed Skimmed Milk Unsweetened (Evaporated Skimmed Milk)	Total Milk Solids - 20.0% (min) Milk Fat - Not more than 0.5% by weight
12.	Condesned Skimmed Milk Sweetned	Total milk solids 26.0% (min) Cane Sugar 40.0% (min) Milk fat - Not more than 0.5% by weight
13.	Whole Milk Powder	Fat - 26.0% Acidity - 1.2% (L.A.) Max. Solubility 98.5% (Spray) 85% (Roller), S.Index 2.0(ml) spray & 15.0 ml (Roller), Moisture - 5.0% (Max.), BHA - 0.01% Coliform 90/g. S.P.C. 50,000 (g) Sod. Citrate 0.3.

14. Skimmed Milk Powder — Milk Fat - 1.5% (max.)
Moisture - 5.0% (max.), Max/S.P.C. - 50,000/g.,
Acidity-1.5% (max) E.Col. =90/g., Sod. Citrate-0.3%
S.P.C. =50,000/g. Coliform - 90/g.

The minimum Solubility Index of the Product

	Roller Dried	Spray Dried
Solubility percent	85.0	98.0
Solubility Index	15.0 ml	2.0 ml.

15. Partially Skimmed Milk Powder

Moisture	-	5.0% (max.)
Fat	-	It should be between 1.6 to 24.0%
Acidity	-	1.5% (I.A.) (max.)
Sod. Citrate	-	0.3%
BHA	-	0.01%

The Minimum Solubility Index of the Product

	Roller Dried	Spray Dried
Solubility percent	85.0	98.5
Solubility Index	15.0 ml	2.0 ml.

16. Khoa — Moisture - 28.0% (max.); Fat - 20.0% (min.)

17. Table Butter — Fat-80.0% (min); Salt - 3.0% (max);
Curd - 1.5% (min); Diacetyl - 4.0% ppm (max)

18. Deshi Butter (Cooking): Fat - 76.0% (min)

19. Ghee — Butyro-refractomer - 40.0 to 43.0 reading at 40°C
Minimum Reichert value-28.0% of free fatty acids as 3.0
Oleic acid (max. limit) % of moisture (max. limit) 0.5.

20. Infant Milk Food — Moisture - 5.0% (max); Fat - 18.0% (min.); 28.0% max.
total carbohydrates - 35.0% (min); Milk proteins - 20%
(min.) Ash - 8.5% (max); S.P.C. - 50,000/gm.;
S.I.-2.0 ml (Spray)

21. Soy-Whey Food — Fat - 12%; Protein - 23%; Carbohydrate - 50.5%;
Ash - 5.0%; Moisture - 1.5%; (Fortification with
Vitamins & iron).

22. Coffee Complete — Instant coffee - 7.2%, S.N.F. - 20.0%; Sugar - 39.0%; Water - 25.0%; Total solids - 75.0% Milk Fat - 8.5%

23. Tea Complete — Fat-13.0%; S.N.F. - 31.5%; Sugar - 39.5% Tea solids - 14.0%; Moisture - 2.0%

BACTERIOLOGICAL STANDARDS FOR GRADING MILK

Grade	Standard plate count per ml/g	Methylene blue reduction time (Hr. Min.)	One hour Resazurin Disc No.	Presumptive coliform test
		Raw Milk		
Very good	Not exceeding 200,000	5 and above	4 or higher	Absent in 0.01 ml
Good	200,001 to 10,00,000	3 and 4	- do -	- do -
Fair	1 to 5 million	1 and 2	3.5 and 1	- do -
Poor	Over 5 million	1/2	0.5 to 0	Present in 0.01 ml
		Pasteurised Milk		
Satisfactory	Not exceeding 30,000			Absent in 0.01 ml

(Acceptance Standards for raw milk for pasteurization based on MBR time). This is a suggestion to be followed

Summer	over 1 hr
Winter	over 2 hr

Recommended standards for payment of bonus for high quality raw milk based on MBR time.

	Summer	Winter
Payment of bonus	Over 2.5 hr	Over 4.5 hr
Penalty or reduction in price	Less than 1/2 hr	Less than 1 hr

Bacteriology Standards of Milk Products

Product	Standard for satisfactory quality		Other tests	
	SPC per ml/g (maximum)	Coliform count per ml/g (maximum)		
1	2	3	4	5
1. Sterilized milk	-	-	Spore count Change in Titratable acidity	Max. 5 per ml Max after incubation for 7 days 0.02% at 37°C
2. Flavoured milk				
a) Pasteurized	50,000	10	Phosphate test	negative
b) Sterilized	-	-	Spore count;	Max: 5 per ml
3. Cream				
a) Raw	2,000,000	100	-	
b) Pasteurized	60,000	-	Phosphate test	negative
c) Sterilized	-	-	Incubation at 30°C for 14 days	No change in flavour or appearance
4. Ice Cream	250,000	90	Phosphate test	negative
5. Butter	-	10	Yeast and mould count	Max 50/g
6. Condensed milk (sweetened)	500	-	Yeast and mould	Max 10/g
7. Evaporated milk	-	-	Incubation of tins for 14 days at 30°C	No bulging due to gas production
8. Processed cheese	-	-	-do-	-do-
9. Milk Powders	50,000	90	-	-

10.	Infant milk foods	50,000	10	-	-
11.	Malted milk foods	50,000	10	-	-
12.	Processed cereals weaning foods	50,000	10	-	-
13.	Casein (Edible quality	50,000	10	Yeast and mould	Max. 50/g
14.	Vegetable protein infant food with milk, flavoured milk, malted skim milk food.	50,000	10	-	-
15.	Dried ice creaim mix sweet cream butter milk powder, partly skim sour milk powder	50,000	90	-	-
16.	Burfi	30,000	-	Yeast and mould	Max.10/g

Equipment Standards for satisfactory sterility

	Max. standard plate count/litre of capacity (Rinse method)	Max. standard plate count/900 sq. cm. of surface (Swab method)	Frequency of checking
1	2	3	4
1. Milk can/pail	1,000	-	One in every batch of 50
2. Milk bottle	1,000	-	Four bottles just before the addition of fresh lot of detergent
3. Milk receiving tank/vats	-	5,000	Once every day immediately after the preparation of equipment for operation.
4. Weighing bowl/pan	-	5,000	Once every day immediately after the preparation of equipment for operation.
5. Storage/holding transport tanks	-	5,000	-do-
6. Batch Pasteurizer	-	5,000	-do-
7. Plate heat exchanger	-	5,000	-do-
8. Surface cooler	-	5,000	-do-
9. Cotton filtercloth	-	5,000	Once every week

10. Evaporator		5,000	Every time the equipment is cleaned for operation.
11. Roller drier		5,000	-do-
12. Bottle filler	(Circulation method SPC of first litre of rinse coming out) 25,000		Coliform count not more 10 per litre.
13. HTST Plate pasteurizer	-do-		-do-
14. Homogenizer	25,000	-	Every time the equipment is cleaned for operation. Coliform: Max. 10/lit.
15. Cream separator clarifier	-do-	-	-do-
16. Spray drier	-do-	-	-do-
17. Ice cream freezer	-do-	-	-do-
18. Walls, floor etc.	-	-	Free from visible dirt and mould growth.
19. Milk crates		-	-do-

Recommended Programme of Bacteriological Quality Control at the Dairy Plant

	Name of test	Frequency of testing	Remarks
	A. Raw milk supplies at the receiving platform		
	(i) Unchilled milk		
1.	Organoleptic quality (Smell)	Each can or lot of milk daily	Unsatisfactory lots to be rejected or segreated
2.	Titratable acidity	Unsatisfactory and doubtful samples	For confirming the results of (1) above.
3.	Sediment test	Each individual milk supply to be tested once a week	Provides information about hygienic quality of milk for encouraging better quality by payment of bonus.
4.	Methylene blue reduction test.		
5.	Standard plate count	Each individual milk supply to be tested at least once a fortnight.	Information regarding source of contamination for advisory work.
	(ii) Chilled milk		
	(Test 1 to 6 as above)	-do-	-do-
7.	Temperature	Each supply of milk daily	Information regarding conditions of storage.
8.	Psychrophilic count	Each supply of milk once a fortnight	-do-

B. Pasteurized milk

(i) Pasteurised milk before despatch

(At least 3 samples of bottled and 2 samples of can milk selected at random)

1.	Temperature	Daily	Information regarding condition of storage.
2.	Phosphate test	Daily	To test efficiency of Pastcurisation.
3.	Coliform test	Daily	To test post pasteurization contamination.
4.	Standard plate count	Daily	To check general quality of pasteurized milk.
5.	Keeping quality at room temperature.	Daily	-do-

(ii) Returned milk (one or two bottles taken at random)

1.	Temperature	Daily	As above
2.	Standard plate count.	Daily	As above

C. Line testing (once a fortnight)

Test samples of milk drawn at the following stages for standard plate count.

1. Raw milk (Dump tank)
2. Freshly pasteurized milk
3. Storage tank
4. Bottle filler
5. Bottle of milk) Before despatch
6. Cane of milk) -do-

D. Other tests

1. Testing detergents for alkalinity
2. Testing chlorine solution for available chlorine
3. Checking temperature of pasteurization (Thermograph).

7

PACKAGING OF DAIRY AND MILK PRODUCTS

With substantial increase in India's milk production, which is likely to be around 60 million tonnes in 1995-96, the availability of milk and dairy products is rapidly increasing. Most of this increased milk production has been in the rural pockets of the country, while the major markets markets for dairy products are in the cities. So, the need for its transportation over long distances has become a necessity. Milk, being a highly perishable product, utmost care is needed on its preservation during storage, handling and transportation. This is also true of dairy products like butter butter, ghee, yoghurt, dairy sweets, etc..

Milk spoils fast at high ambient temperature in the presence of oxygen and other contaminating agents present in the atmosphere. Similarly, other dairy products also have a relatively short shelf-life, and major factors responsible for their spoilage are temperature, oxygen and bacteriological activity. Hence primary requirements of preservation of most the dairy products are to store it under as cool a temperature as possible, hygienically handle it and protect it from oxygen and bacterial contamination.

Organized milk marketing in India made its beginning in 1950 with bottling of milk in Mumbai, followed by Calcutta and other cities. Glass bottle is a multi-trip package for milk, and on an average each bottle performs as many as 91 trips to the consumer before it goes out of circulation. Bottles are filled on automatic filling machines at a speed of 90 bottles per minute approximately and sealed with aluminium foil. Use of multi-trip glass bottles makes prior cleaning of bottles filling necessary. Weight of empty glass bottle is also high, resulting in higher frieght cost. It is estimated that cost of bottling milk in glass bottles is around 35 paise per litre.

Today, though bottling of milk is still prevalent in many dairies, it is fast being replaced by plastic pouches. This was a new concept in that unlike multi-trip reusable bottles, plastic bags were single trip containers. Economics worked in favour of these pouches as it saved need for returning the empty containers to the dairies and its subsequent washing and cleaning before refilling for the next trip. In Mumbai, the Aarey Dairy was the first in the country to experiment with plastic pouches more than two decades ago. Today, even in smaller cities, milk pouches have become due to the convenience it offers. A good consumer response to milk pouches paved the way for the technological changes needed in the industry. Initially, the form-fill-and-seal (FFS) machines used for packaging of milk in pouches were imported but these machines are now manufactured indigenously by a number of units in the country. Availability of plastic films needed for the pouches also increased during this period, with a large number of entrepreneurs taking up the production of multi-layer films for milk packaging.

Form Fill and Seal (FFS) System

In this technique, raw materials i.e. milk and plastic film (commonly LDPE) are fed into the form-fil-and-seal (FFS) machine. First, the plastic film is formed into a tube, sealed along its length and then at bottom, thus forming a pouch. It is filled with the milk and then sealed at the top. All these steps constitute a single continuous operation in the same machine and thus, milk is handled more hygienically. The use of ultraviolet light inside the filling cabinet of the machine minimises bacterial contamination. The machine runs at a speed of about 40-60 pouches a minute. The cost of a one litre pouch ranges between 40-50 paise.

For sweetened milk, multilayer LD/LD film is also used with outer film being opaque and inner one in black colour, which helps in reducing transmission of light inside the pouch. Co-extruded multilayer LDPE/LDPE film is becoming more popular, as it helps in material saving due to its better barrier properties. Generally, 65 micron thick film is used, as against 75 micron of monolayer film. The cost of FFS machines ranges from Rs. 1,00,000/- to Rs. 8,50,000/-.

It is estimated that for a new dairy which needs to distribute 1.5 lakh litre/ day of liquid milk, it is more economical (70 per cent in capital investment) to set up LDPE pouch filling system than glass bottle filling equipment. Also, in terms of operational cost, LDPE pouches are economical. A one litre pouch costs approximately 30-40 paise. In 1994-95, about 45,000 tonnes of film was used for packaging 15 million tonnes of liquid milk.

Aseptic System :

This system has converted a highly perishable product like milk into a grocery item. The Tetra Paks are now available even with a grocery store. In this package, milk remains good for more than ten days without a need to store it in a refrigerator. This has become possible because of ultra high temperature (UHT) treatment at 140°C for 2-3 seconds of milk prior to packaging and then aseptically packing it in a carton. The packaging material (carton) is also sterilized with hydrogen peroxide. The sterile material is first formed into a tube shape, filled with milk and sealed in tetrahedron/brick shape, all done in aseptic conditions.

The machinery needed for this system is more capital intensive. The package used is LDPE-coated paperboard made locally. The tetra pack uses 170 gms paperboard laminated with 10 micron LDPE from outside and 70-75 micron LDPE from inside. The cost of 1000 ml. Tetra Pak is around 200 paise. Though this is higher than the bottle and plastic pouch system, consumers particularly in cities find it more convenient since they can buy their milk requirement once in a week or use it as an emergency stock due to its extended shelf-life.

Bulk Vending Booth

Some dairies are trying a system where milk is store in FRP (Fibre Reinforced Plastic) tanks with automatic dispensing device. This system is catching up as it reduces milk distribution cost.

To facilitate wide distribution cost, wide distribution and to reach different economic groups, milk is sold through bulk vending FRP tanks, bottles/sachets, tetra pack, etc. In 1985-86, the Delhi dairies alone distributed on an average close to 9 lakh litres of milk per day through 300 bulk-vending booths, 340 insulated containers, 245 polypack milk retail outlets and two unrefrigerated mini booths. Data on latest status is not available till date of the time of writing of this book.

Packing of Shrikhand :

With the increased availability of milk, need for marketing milk related products have also grown. Though many of these products have been traditionally made in most of the Indian homes, their commercial availability became a reality one due to the emergence of better packaging techniques. The Baroda Dairy has installed a machine in which High Impact Polystyrene (HIPS) sheets are heated and formed into cups or trays and then filled with shrinkhand which is heat-treated in order to extend its shelf life prior to filling. Sealing of the cup or tray with polystyrene film or aluminium foil coated with paper and wax follows immediately to give a continuous flow of nicely packed and sealed cups of shrikhand. The entire process of forming, filling and sealing is done as a single continuous operation, thus minimising the risk of contamination.

Plastic cups are moisture-proof, leak-proof and convenient to use. Weight of the HIPS varies from 5 gms to 35 gms and thickness between 0.3mm and 0.65 mm. These cups have capacities between 100 ml to one litre and cost in the rage of 35 paise to Rs. 2.50 with two colour printing.

Butter :

It consists primarily of about 80 per cent milk fat, 15 per cent moisture and in table butter upto 3 per cent common salt. Because of high moisture content, butter is susceptible it mould growth. Mould growth is inhibited by exclusion of air while packaging by tight wrapping or by avoiding head space in teh container. Packaging must protect the product for preservation of its flavour, body, texture, appearance, moisture and colour. Packing of butter therefore should have resistance to fat, oxygen, moisture, foreign odour and light. In India, butter is packed in bulk as well as retail packages. For bulk packaging there is no standard method, and stainless steel and in plate containers are used. For retail packaging, there is some degree of standardization.

There is an Indian Standard (IS: 2034-1961) which gives specifications for tin cans of 200 gms and 400 gms capacity. It specifies tinplate thickness of 0.24 mm and 0.17 mm respectively, and minimum tin coating of 17 g/m^2, besides many other requirements. Tinplate containers are the best for product protection, but owing to their increasing cost, very little quantity of butter is packed in the tin containers.

Flexible packaging materials like vegetable parchment paper or grease proof (GP) paper, aluminium foil, and folding board cartons which together give similar protection to the product are more commonly used. There is an Indian Standard: 7161-1973 which gives specifications for vegetable parchment paper has a good wet strength which is in contact with butter. Generally, paper of 45 gsm and above and aluminium foil above 0.009 mm thickness are used.

Butter being highly susceptible to foreign odour, one has to be very careful while choosing adhesive and printing inks used in the manufacture of the laminates. There is also another IS: 8113 - 1976 for primary cartons for packaging of 100 gms, 200 gms and 250 gms butter slabs.

Cartons protect butter while handling, after packaging in primary wrapper, in the distribution system. Since butter is stored in the refrigerator, cartons may be waxed with about 10 gsm wax on each side or laminated with a plastic film, though it is not mandatory. As most plastics have poor fat resistance, plastic films are not recommended for long term storage. However, for short term storage and packaging, many vendors of butter use LDPE or HDPE film, along with a paper overwrap.

Ghee

It is usually 100 per cent fat, obtained by boiling butter at 110°C till all water is evaporated. For long term storage, stainless steel containers or tinplate cans are desirable. Multilayer co-extruded films of LDPE/HDPE are being increasingly used for short term storage. Nylon/Surlyn based laminates are also being experimented. Generally, pastic pouches are filled on automatic FFS machines. However, if the sealing surface is contaminated with the product, sealing of the pouch becomes difficult. Packaging material should have good fat resistance and barrier properties against oxygen and moisture. IS: 11352-1985, specifications for flexible packs for the packing of edible oils and vanaspati could be a useful reference.

Cheese

Is essentially a product with high fat and moisture content. Therefore, package used for cheese should prevent moisture loss and ingress of oxygen to prevent oxidation and mould growth. It should also have fat and grease resistance and be able to prevent growth of micro-ogranisms. Oxygen is eliminated by packing cheese in hermetically sealed containers in vacuum or in inert gas atmosphere. Processed cheese is usually paked in aluminium foil in cubes with different shapes. Tinplate cans are used for 200 gms and above quantity. PVDC coated plastic films are suitable for cheese packaging as the provide good oxygen and moisture barrier properties.

Dried Milk Powders :

Since whole milk and infant milk powders are rich in fat (20-30 per cent), packaging material should provide protection against oxygen and moisture. Generally, tinplate cans are used, and packaging is done under nitrogen cover to replace air by nitrogen in the headspace of the tin cans. Skim milk powders have very low fat content and as such a good moisture barrier material is adequate for short term storage. Multiwall papers sacks with one polyethylene liner (IS: 1165-1975) is used for bulk packaging. Lined cartons are used for retail packaging. The multiwall bags can be tested for their transport worthiness according to IS: 7028. Recently, some skim milk powder has also been sold in polyethylene bags of 1 kg. Even plastic bottles of HDPE are being tried for 200 gms and 400 gms of powder.

Ice Cream

Is made by mixing milk cream, sugar, stabilisers and flavours. Since ice-cream is stored at very low temperatures, packaging material used for ice-cream should have low temperature stability. It should also provide protection against contamination, ease of opening, case of disposal, and it should also be amenable to attractive printing. Wax coated paper board is commonly used in the form of cups and cartons. IS: 7162-1973 gives specifications for waxed cartons for packaging of 300,500 and 1000 ml of ice-cream. The standard also covers packing of 100 ml chocobars. Generally, paperboard made from virgin chemical wood pulp, coated with wax, is used. Bars are generally wrapped in vegetable parchment paper. High impact polystyrene (HIPS) cups are also becoming popular.

The empty plastic cup does not support the growth of bacteria like paper packaging. Further, their comparative strength and rigidity lend themselves to its use in automatic filling equipment which is especially true of small packs of 50 and 100 ml, required in large numbers.

From the marketing point of view, possibility to get white, translucent or even transparent cups with lids or sealable closures makes it more attractive. It terms of cost effectiveness, small sizes of plastic cups are approximately 20 per cent costlier than paper cups. However, taking into account, the obvious advantages of thermoformed containers, with hygiene, extended shelf life and attractive package, the plastic packaging will get increasingly popular.

Packaging of Indigenous Products:

Pedas are first wrapped in grease proof paper and then placed in cartons lined with GP paper. Products like lassi (sweetened butter milk) in 200 ml plastic pouches packed on FFS machine is a recent introduction in the Indian market. Sweet curd is packed in HIPS cups, while local vendors used LDPE bags for loose sale of fresh curd. There is not much of organized packaging of Khoya, and materials used vary from banana leaves to grease-proof paper and polyethylene films.

8

BABY CEREAL FOOD & MILK POWDERS

INTRODUCTION

Food is composed of three main groups of constituents *i.e.*, carbohydrates, fat & protein. In addition to this there must be some inorganic minerals & organic substances *e.g.* Vitamins, Iron, Mg, etc.

There may be some foods which contain less or higher of these essential nutritional components depending upon the nutritional value. They are enriched or fortified by other components to attain the required level of nutrition.

The baby-cereal-foods is that enriched food which has a requisite level of nutrition. This requisite level is prescribed by various dietricians & physicians for children. Various experts fixed a definite calorific value for infant food & based on this the various mixtures or formulae of foods are developed. These formulae of infant food contains essential amino-acids, fats, proteins, vitamins & other essential minerals etc. which are necessary for the normal growth of child.

USES AND APPLICATIONS

By far the largest portion of the baby food products are purchased for feeding babies. One of the purposes of adding solid food to the baby's diet is to acquaint him with foods of a different consistency, texture and taste than those of liquids. Cereal is usually the first solid food offered and due to its convenience has many advantages to the mother. They can be fed with out waste in any amount desired and since they are pre-cooked are easily prepared for feeding.

Addition of cereal to the infants diet occurs at about the third month, only small amounts are used at the start, gradually increasing as the infant grow older. Mothers usually follow the pediatrician's advice as to when cereal feeding starts and often times begin with a single grain cereal rather than mixtures. This is particularly true if there is a history of allergies in the family and the pediatrician wished to avoid mixtures at the start.

In many cases, these special cereals are used by older and children, since they make an excellent hot cereal and are so easily prepared.

Pre-cooked infant cereal also have other uses, particularly in special diets, some of which are :

i) Soft diets following disease or surgery

ii) Diet following dental extraction

iii) Diet for gastro intestinal diseases

iv) Ulcer diet

v) Low sodium diet (some varieties only)

vi) Special allergy diets (single grain variety)

FORMULATIONS

Infant Food Formula

1. **Malted Food**

a)	Powdered Malt	- 28 gms.
b)	Oatmeal (Finest Ground)	- 56 gms.
c)	Lactose Sugar	- 112 gms.
d)	Baked Flour	- 454 gms.

All are mixed thoroughly.

2. Egg Containing Formula

Egg Albumen	- 5.5 %
Fat	- 0.08 %
Water	- 4.22 %
Carbohydrates	- 86.58 %
	(Of which 54 % is water soluble)
Ash	- 2.81 %
a) Calcium	- 10.11 %
b) Potassium	- 2.64 %
c) Sodium	- 25.27 %
d) Chlorine	- 36.65 %
e) H_2SO_4	- 3.13 %
f) Phosphoric acid	- 18.51 %

3. Milk Based

Sometimes referred to as humanized milk, these milk-based products are formulated to resemble the composition of human milk, but contain a lower account of carbohydrate than cow's milk. They are sold in three forms; liquid ready to use; liquid concentrates; & dry powders.

Contents of 'Cerelac' type. Infant food

Wheat flour
Partially skimmed milk
Sucrose
Corn oil
Iron salt
Vitamins

PROCESS OF MANUFACTURE OF BABY CEREAL FOOD

Once a raw materials have been approved for use, production of the cereal food can begin. In the cereal ingredients room, those materials used in small amounts per batch are carefully weighed, placed in a small container and identified by product name and batch number. It will contain the minerals, vitamins, salt and other minor ingredients.

Approximately 150 gallons of water is drawn into a mixing tank. With the agitator in motion, the amount of grain and flour per batch is shifted into the tank along with the contents of the container referred to above making a slurry of

300 lts. of dry material to 150 gallons of water. At this point, the batch may be pumped to a pressure kettle where it is completely cooked (for example, 10 to 20 minutes at atmosphere or under pressure) or it may remain in the original kettle where a similar or larger cooking process takes place.

After cooking is completed, the batch of cereal's pumped to atmospheric drum drier. The length of time necessary to pump out a complete batch of cereal varies according to the drying capacity of rate of cereal. This ranges (according to the variety of cereal) from 20 to 40 minutes. The cereal is pumped between the two drums which dry the product in a thin sheet as they rotate. The sheets are removed from the rolls by knife blades and conveyed to a flaking machine. Here the sheets are broken into small flakes which vary in size, depending on cereal variety and manufacture. At this point the flaked cereal may be conveyed directly to the packaging line or placed clean storage drums for inter packaging.

Modern packaging lines can be equipped to accomplish a multiple operation. They may assemble the package and seal the bottom, insert a pouring device, till the box with product, seal the top and in some cases, wrap the package.

MANUFACTURING PROCESS OF MILK POWDER

There are mainly two process:

i) Roller drying

ii) Spray drying

Spray Drying:

This method consists essentially in directing a spray of hot, pre-condensed milk into a current of hot air. There are three main types:-

i) Simple spray

ii) Revolving sprinklers

iii) Revolving disc.

Spray drying plant much bulkier than roller drying for given output, and spray powder costs more to produce. The product is, however, so much better, that it can only be a matter of time before nearly all milk powder is produced by the spray process. The confectionery and other industries will doubtless continue to accept roller powder.

The stages in spray drying are essentially the following :

i) Reception

ii) Clarification or filtration

iii) Cooling

iv) Storage

v) Preheating (160° to 190°F)

vi) Precondensing at about 110°F to about 42 percent total sides.

vii) Atomizing in chamber, hot air entering at about 330° and leaning at about 200°F.

viii) Separation of powder

ix) Packing

RAW MATERIAL SUPPLIERS

MILK MANUFACTURERS/SUPPLIERS

Gujarat Co-operative Milk Marketing Federation Limited
Amul Dairy Road,
Post Box. No. 10
Anand - 388 001 (Gujarat)
Ph.: 23221/23272/23319
Fax: 02692-24950

Karnal Dist. Co-operative Milk Producers Union Limited
G.T. Road Byepass
Post Box. No. 84
Karnal - 132 001
Haryana

Tamilnadu Cooperative Milk Producers' Federation Ltd.,
29 & 30 Industrial Estate
Ambattur, Chennai - 600 098.
Ph.: 044-6258520

MALT & MALT EXTRACT

Barmalt India Limited
Jharsa Road, Gurgaon
Haryana
Tel./Fax: 0124-322101/322361/321286
Agro India Malts Limited
10-A, South Side G.T. Road
Bulandshahar Road,
Ghaziabad (U.P)
Tel./Fax: 0575-757743/722387

TIN CONTAINERS

Choudhary Metal Printers
7/12, Upper Anand Parbat Ind. Area
New Delhi - 110 005.
Tel./Fax: 5729535/5726318

Arora Tin Ind.
617, Bisrekh Road
Chhaprola, Ghaziabad (U.P.)
Tel./Fax: 724173

SUPPLIERS OF PLANT AND MACHINERY

Bansal Technocrats
1/1431/18, Sharda Nagar,
Saharanpur - 247 001 (U.P).
Ph.: 0132-27914

Products: Milk Reception, Storage and Transportaion Tanks, Ghee Making Equipments (Butter Melting Vats, Prestatification Tank, Ghee Boiler, Ghee Settling Tank, Ghee Storage Tank etc.), Paneer and Khova Making Equipments, Cream Storage and Repining Tanks, CIP Unit (Manual and Automatic), Milk Pumps, SS Pneumatically operated valves, SS pipe fittings and control panels etc.

Dairy Udyog
229-A/230-A
Ghatkopar Ind. Estate
Block-C, L.B.S. Marg
Ghatkopar, Mumbai - 400 086.
Ph.: 5171636/5170938

Sangli Dairy Farms
459/3, Maruti Road,
Sangli - 416 416 (M.S)
Ph.: 75101

Hind Protective Coatings Limited
9/4, Sarvpriya Vihar,
New Delhi - 110 016.

Factory:
55,61,62, Rozka Meo Industrial Area
Sohna, Dist. Gurgaon, Haryana
Pin - 122 103.
Ph.: 6868850

HMT Ltd.,
Sree Nidhi Chambers
Senapati Bapat Marg
Pune - 4111016
Ph.: 350040
Fax: (0212) 358565
Telex: 0145-7262

Factory:
H-2, MIDC, Chikalthana
Aurangabad - 10

Products: Pasteuriser, Centrifugal Pump, Butter Making Machine, Butterfly Valves, Plate Heat Exchangers, Oil Purification & Clarification System, Ice Cream Machinery & Turnkey Projects of small & big capacity Dairy.

BOILER

Indcon Boilers Limited
D-170, Okhla Ind. Area,
Phase-1, New Delhi - 110 020
Ph.: 6811441/442

PACKAGING MACHINERIES

Nichrome International
46, Dr. B.R. Ambedkar Road
Near Sangam Bridge
Pune - 411 001 (M.S)
Ph.: 0212-622137/622259

Rado Packaging Machines Pvt. Ltd.
C-377, Sector-10
Noida - 201 301 (U.P)
Ph.: 8-555190, 8-533341
Fax: 8-525699
Products: Form Fill and Seal Machines

COMPLETE PLANT SUPPLIER

Mojj Engineering Systems Pvt. Ltd.
81-B/15, M.I.D.C., Bhosari
Pune - 411 026
Ph.: 91-212-790360
Fax: 91-212-792836

Delhi Office:
G-4, South Extension Part II,
New Delhi - 110 049.
Ph.: 011-6426632
Fax: 011-6451870

DETAILS OF PLANT AND MACHINERY

Cereal Food Section

1. Mixing and Blending equipment with agitator.
2. Sieves.
3. Cooking kettles or pressure kettles.
4. Atmospheric drum driers with internal heating provision and knife blade attachment.
5. Flaking machine.
6. Packing and sealing machine.
7. Weighing platform.
8. Boiler.
9. Chilling Plant and storage.

Milk Powder Section

1. Storage tank for milk. Capacity 350 kilos.
2. Vacuum drier

3. Pasteuriser.
4. Butteer churn.
5. Vacuum evaporator.
6. Lab equipment.
7. Generator.
8. Pumps, Vales and fittings.
9. Miscellaneous.

PLANT ECONOMICS

Rated Plant capacity = 500.00 KG/day MILK POWDER

LAND & BUILDING Rs. 11,75,000.00
(Land Area Required 500 sq.mt.)

LIST OF PLANT & MACHINERY

1. Storage tanks
2. Feed pump
3. Preheater, jacketed type
4. Precondenser
5. Spray drier with atomizer
6. Condenser
7. Baby Boiler
8. Chilling plant
9. Packing unit
10. Laboratory testing equipments
11. Miscellaneous equipments *i.e.* sieves valves etc.

FIXED CAPITAL

1.	LAND & BUILDING	Rs.	11,75,000.00
2.	PLANT & MACHINERY	Rs.	10,85,000.00
3.	OTHER FIXED ASSETS	Rs.	2,82,000.00
	TOTAL	**Rs.**	**25,42,000.00**

LIST OF RAW MATERIALS

1. Milk
2. Citric Acid
3. Mangnesium Oxide
4. Miscellaneous Chemicals NaCl CaCO3 etc.
5. Tin Containers

TOTAL WORKING CAPITAL/MONTH

1.	RAW MATERIAL	Rs.	7,96,000.00
2.	SALARY & WAGES	Rs.	1,52,875.00
3.	UTILITIES & OVERHEADS	Rs.	76,000.00
	TOTAL	**Rs.**	**10,24,875.00**

TOTAL CAPITAL INVESTMENT

TOTAL FIXED CAPITAL	Rs.	25,42,000.00
TOTAL WORKING CAPITAL FOR 3 MONTHS	Rs.	30,74,625.00
TOTAL	**Rs.**	**56,16,625.00**

TURN OVER/ANNUM

Milk Powder 150000 kg. Rs. 1,80,00,000.00

PROFIT = RECEIPTS - COST OF PRODUCTION
= 1,80,00,000.00 - 1,38,82,282.50
= 41,17,717.50

PROFIT SALES RATIO = Profit / Sales x 100 = 22.88 %

RATE OF RETURN = Operating profit / T.C.I x 100 = 73.31 %

BREAK EVEN POINT (B.E.P) = 39.45 %

9

CASEIN FROM MILK

INTRODUCTION

Milk & Milk products are indispensable to the growth of the child & to the health of the adult. For the infant, milk is a perfect food; for the growing child, milk & milk products are essential foods, and for adults and expectant mothers milk is most important food.

European countries commanding a surplus of milk production over local consumption have devised methods to utilize the excess supply in the best possible way. They are making various milk products like casein cheese, condensed milk, malted milk etc.

Chemically milk contains all the essential of a complete food to overcome the requirements of young mammals. It in a mysterious fluid containing about 101 different substances & no one can produce artificial milk by any type of blending. Casein, which is normally in suspension, thickness & settler down, carrying with in it the undissolved substances, & leaving milk serum in which soluble salts, lactose, certain proteins, ferments, coloring matter etc. are present.

Normally the composition of milk is as given blow :

Water	86.60%
Casein	3.40%
Fat	3.25%

Milk Sugar	4.55%
Albumin	0.45%
Ash	0.75

Casein occur extensively in milk secretions. It forms nearly 20% of the solid contents & about 85% of protein content of milk. Casein in precipitated from milk by the addition of dilute aids and by certain enzymes as pepsin & rennin (chymosin). It is insoluble in water & in alcohol. In milk it is dissolved in water in the form of Calcium casseinate'; which is responsible for white colour of milk.

Casein is an important bye-product of milk, that can be manufactured very easily. After the extraction of butter, the residue is usually thrown off. This can be utilized in making casein.

Fresh milk when heated to boiling paint does not coagulate. However, a thin membranes of casein is formed on the surface, but no real coagulation occurs.

The composition of milk from various animals :

SOURCE	CARBOHYDRATE	PROTEIN	FAT
HUMAN	6.2 - 7.6%	2.0 - 6.0	2.0 - 6.2
COW	4.1 - 6.8%	2.5 - 4.0	3.0 - 6.0
BUFFALOW	4.5%	4.3	7.5
GOAT	4.5%	3.7	4.8
SHEEP	4.9%	6.5	6.9
MARE	5.7%	1.3	1.2

The manufacture of casein can be produce maximum from sheep milk and it is said that sheep milk can be maximum received from Rajasthan. So it is advised that sheep milk can be received from Ajmer and jaipur for the manufacture of Casein.

Casein made from butter separated milk "Skim Milk". In order to obtain the protein from the milk rapidly, a little quantity of acid is added. By doing so, the milk will coagulate and water will be separated.

Casein is sold in granular or powder form. it is an essential raw material by which a number of items are produced. In the past few years, the plastic was prepared from casein which was known as casein plastic. In recent years there have, however, been absolute by other durable cheap and better plastics made from synthetic material.

USES & APPLICATIONS

Casein in made exclusively for export, with little for internal consumption. Casein prepared on a large commercial scale is used as a patent food. About 25% of the ordinary 'cheddar cheese' consists of casein.

Pure casein is a white, amorphous, hygroscopic powder without taste or odour.

The casein is used in various Arts & industries. It has a good demand from pharmaceutical industries as a good nourishment. Another extensive use of it is a substitute for celluloid. Together with formaldehyde, it forms plastic transparent substances of great cohesive power, which can be dyed, polished, & produced in any shape. It is the re-called artificial horn, which comes into the market in a variety of forms, such as gallalith etc. It is also used as insulating material in electrical industry. Cylinders & plates for photography, as well as films, are made by casein. Artificial tortoise shell, Amber, ivory, combs are derived from casein. Super calendered & photographic paper, wall-paper, & colored paper are also manufactured by it; in order to obtain a high glaze & be able to stand being immersed in water.

Soaps become softer and more durable, the addition of casein. It is also combined with lime to attain favourable qualities. Glue, becomes capable of reristing dampness, and is therefore used in ship building, where ordinary glue in ineffective.

Casein is also used for manufacture of plywood. Casein colors are also extensively in demand, for their excellent covering power. In the printing of staffs & in the liner industry casein furnishes the dressing material, and artist canvas in impregnated with-it. Casein is used for clearing wine.

MANUFACTURE OF CASEIN

If we want to make better quality of casein the fat content of the skim milk, from which it is made, should be minimum. Therefore it necessary, the cream may be again separated from skim milk so that its fat content is minimum.

After separating the last trace of cream from the skim milk it is heated 350°C and filled in the wooden tank equipped with a hand agitator for mechanical agitator. For co-agulation of casein 150 ml of dilute hydrochloric acid (1 part of acid into 1 parts water) and is added by spray pump slowly and starring is continued. Milk starts coagulating as the acid is added and coagulated man settles down at bottom. When complete coagulation has taken place, the mass is allowed to settle for half an hour. Now the stop coke is opened and the whey is drained over a draining cock made of wire cloth fixed in wooden frame, so that the coagulated mas is retained over it. The coagulated mass is again dropped into the tank for washing.

Now-a-days a different types of filter is using to separate whey.

Washing is done in the tank by adding dilute acid water (8 C.C. acid is 50 list of water). The acid is added sufficient quantity so that coagulation is completely under water. After ten minutes, the water is drained out. Two such type of required more. It should be remembered that washing should be such type that there should be leaving no whey.

The coagulation is hanged is a cloth so that water tickles down. Even after this process there is sufficient water present necessity squeezing and processing. For this the cloth filled with coagulation is put under two wooden frames and pressed by putting some weight.

A screw press may be used for the same purpose as it makes the pressing very easy. The casein is now from of a cake.

Now the cake should be cut in the pieces. Then the pieces are rubbed on over a 10 mesh more cloth fixed in a wooden frame. Granules of casein are obtained below the sieve.

The next step is to dry the granules. If the production is 5-10 kg. casein per day and it is sheering run that the charging can be done in open by spreading the granules over white sheets on a coat, but it larger production is required a tray dryer will be needed.

Tray dryer is a almirah which is heated inside with electric elements. Granule is placed in trays which are put in place over the sacks provided in the almirah. the heating can also be done with coal.

The granules are next ground to powder. Different types of grinding machines are available including driven. If powder is available that it is casein to run the grinder in the keep of 1/2 H.P. motor. The powder is packed in polythene bags which are placed in card board boxes. Indian standard institution has prescribed the requirement for edible quality casein code No. IS : 1167-1965.

The process can be completed in the following steps.

1. Cream separation.
2. Coagulation of whey.
3. Washing with water acid solution.
4. Removal of water from casein.
5. Pressing.
6. Granulation or powder.
7. Drying.
8. Grinding.
9. Testing.
10. Packing.

As we have seen casein is made from skim milk casein is the another name given to the "available protein" in the milk. In order to separate the protein from the milk rapidly a little quantity of acid is added.

By doing so the milk will coagulate and water will be separated.

FLOW DIAGRAM FOR CASEIN MANUFACTURE

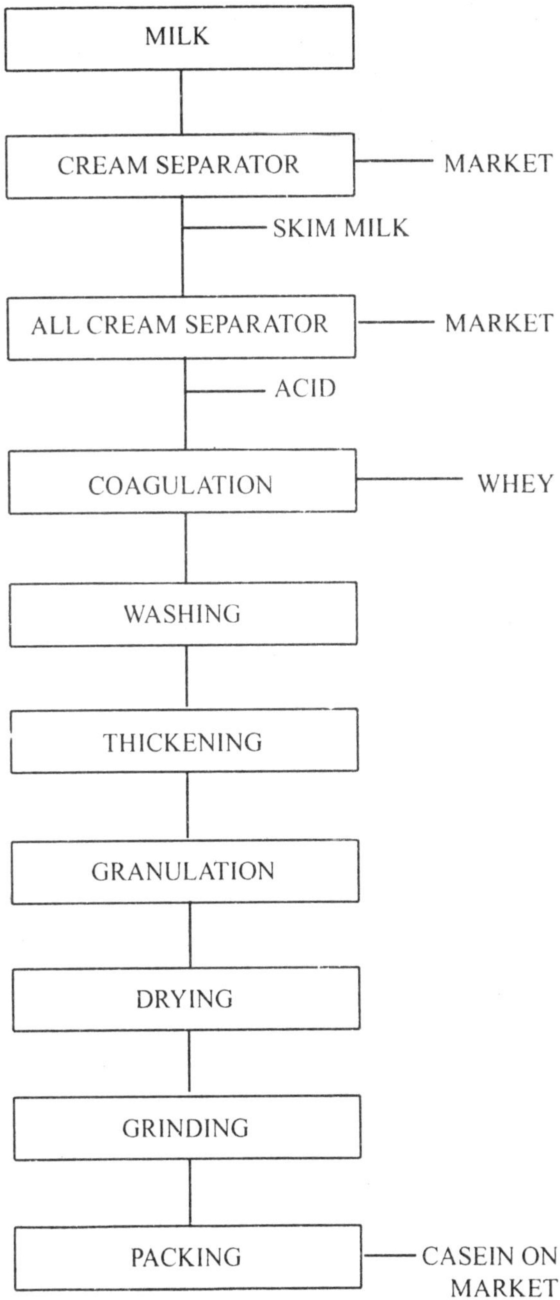

SUPPLIERS OF RAW MATERIALS

MILK MANUFACTURERS/SUPPLIERS

Andhra Pradesh Dairy Development Co-operative Federation Limited
G-28, Jangpura Extn.
New Delhi - 110 014.

Gujarat Co-operative Milk Marketing Federation Limited
Amul Dairy Road,
Post Box. No. 10
Anand - 388 001 (Gujarat)
Ph.: 23221/23272/23319
Fax: 02692-24950

Karnal Dist. Co-operative Milk Producers Union Limited
G.T. Road Byepass
Post Box. No. 84
Karnal - 132 001
Haryana

Rajasthan State Dairy Development Corporation Limited
15, Raniara Garden
Jaipur (Rajasthan).

Tamilnadu Cooperative Milk Producers' Federation Ltd.,
29 & 30 Industrial Estate
Ambattur, Chennai - 600 098.
Ph.: 044-6258520

SUPPLIERS OF COMPLETE PLANT & MACHINERY

Bansal Technocrats
1/1431/18, Sharda Nagar,
Saharanpur - 247 001 (U.P).
Ph.: 0132-27914

Products: Milk Reception, Storage and Transportaion Tanks, Ghee Making Equipments (Butter Melting Vats, Prestatification Tank, Ghee Boiler, Ghee Settling Tank, Ghee Storage Tank etc.), Paneer and Khova Making Equipments, Cream Storage and Repening Tanks, CIP Unit (Mannual and Automatic), Milk Pumps, SS Pneumatically operated valves, SS pipe fittings and control pannels etc.

Mojj Engineering Systems Pvt. Ltd.
81-B/15, M.I.D.C., Bhosari
Pune - 411 026
Ph.: 91-212-790360
Fax: 91-212-792836

Delhi Office:
G-4, South Extension Part II,
New Delhi - 110 049.
Ph.: 011-6426632
Fax: 011-6451870

CREAM SEPARATOR

M/s. Dairy Equipment Co.,
National Insurance Building, 204,
Dr. D.N. Road, Mumbai 1.

M/s. Parenco Industries.
Agarwal House,
4/14, Asaf Ali Road,
New Delhi 1.

10

CONFECTIONERY INDUSTRY - SEMI AUTOMATIC PLANT (TOFFEE AND CANDY MFG.)

INTRODUCTION

Confectionery or sweet meals are preserved edible delicacies consisting of a solid or crystalline phase and a liquid or non-crystalline phase the relative proportion of which determine the type of confectionery. The common types of confectionery are hard boiled candies, caramel and toffee, comfits or draggees, and lozenges.

Sugar is the main ingredients of confectionery. There are about 65 important confectionery factories in the country. Mainly in U.P. Bihar, Mumbai, Punjab, and Bengal. In addition , a large number of small concerns are producing sugar confectionery with indigenous equipments.

Since the product is a consumable item so this is having tremendous demand throughout the world .

PROPERTIES

Sugar confectionery is whole some and nutritious. It is a high caloric food, when eaten alone or in considerable amount, say about 100 gms. It depresses the secretion of gastric juices and delays evacuation of the stomach.

There is a resulting tendency of the stomach juices to absorb water from the lining of the stomach which in turn ease irritation.

USES AND APPLICATION

The toffee and candies are used after meal, dinners as mouth refresher. It drives away bad smell from mouth and refresh the breath. Some times it causes good sensation while chewing.

It is chewed by children, young people, young girls, young ladies etc. But mostly it is consumed by children of age group below ten.

Its main application for consumption purpose.

Formulations

1. English Toffee Nougets

Corn syrup	38 lbs
Nulomoline	10 lbs
Dairy Butter (Salted)	5 lb.
Coconut Butter (86°F mp)	10 lb.
Brown Sugar	15 lb.
Fine Granulated Sugar	20 lb.
Seat	503

Flavour with a combinations of clove oil , Almond oil and vanilla.

Place the following ingredients in a caramel cooking kettle, Nulomoline, corn syrup, butter, coconut butter & condensed milk . Give the steam valve a few turns and allow the batch to mix until the fats are melted & mixed with the other ingredients. Then add the brown and while sugar , turn the steam an full and cook the batch as rapidly as possible to a firm ball.

This toffee can be cooked quite successfully , using as much as 110 pounds of steam pressure. After the batch has been cooked to the desired consistent, turn of the heat. Add the salt & flavour and mix thoroughly . Spread the batch oil at once to cool. The gradually fold it together so as to secure an even temperature throughout the batch. It is team ready to pass through drop rolls.

After the toffee ruggets are cold, place teem in a rerolling pan. Spray then with melted land coconut butter. Then add product sugar that has been flavoured with mint oil. Allow the candies to remove until they will waled, spread them and to set. Then pack.

2. **Everton Toffee**

Sugar	4 lb
Water	3 lb
Cream of Tartar	1/2 tsp
Butter	203'

But the water , sugar , and cream of tartar into a pan and stir until they bail, but no layer. Add the butter after the other comes off the fire , but do not stir it in.

PROCESS OF MANUFACTURING

The common Confectionery are:-

1. Hard Candy or Hard Sugar Boiling, e.g. Acid drops, pear drops, bulls eyes etc.

2. Hard and pulled goods.

3. Caramel and Toffee.

4. Coated confections like pan coated confections comfits or dryers.

5. Lozenges.

6. Jelly crystal.

Manufacture of Hard Candy

A solution of cane sugar to which is versugar of glucose or a chemical reagent to bring about particle inversion is added, is cooked , is cooked in a steam jacketed kettle, and transferred under suction to a vacuum cooker and concentrated vacuum boiling gives a light coloured product. A supersaturated sugar solution with a glass-like consistency is obtained. The product is quickly cooled by spreading on an oiled, water cooled table or plate.

Flavoring and coloring material are added the product thoroughly mixed. It is cut into shapes by frame cutters.

A particular variety of hard sugar boiling is the so-called pulled or stain goods or satinettes. In their preparation, the cooled sugar boiling is kneaded. Pulled an lapped a number of times during which treatment tiny air bubbles are incorporated into the mass. The appearance of the product depends on the duration of pulling. Short pulling gives a ration, silk-like finish prolonged pulling and lapping imparts a chalky appearance.

The cooking temperature for hard boiled products is 300-310°F while 280°-290°F for pulled or sation goods. The maximum temperature employed in vacuum boiling for hard boiled products is 260-270°F.

Hard & Pulled Goods

Hard and pulled goods may be employed in the production of filled goods. Pulled candy of different colours are arranged on a table to give the required design or rolling , the batch is rolled in an automatic batch feeder by tapered rollers into a rope which is passed through sizing rolls, cut and moulded into different shapes, in automatic machines, the good are dried by and twist -wrapped.

Caramel & Toffee

Caramel and toffee contain milk and butter in addition to the usual ingredients, the former being softer. Butter is however, partly or wholly replaced by coconut or coco butter.

In the manufacturer of caramels. butter and milk are emulsified in a homogenizer to a creamy product and added along with other ingredients icing sugar, corn syrup corn flour, or cashew powder to the boiling fitted with mechanical with stirrers. The mixture is cooked (260-280) rapidly. the material is poured on oiled slabs, flavoured and moulded by castings.

Toffee is cooked to a higher temperature 290-300° that ceramelisation occurs and the resulting product is cut. The temperature employed in vacuum boilers is 230-240 °F. The product from the boiling pan is fed into an automatic bathe feeder formed into a cope by size rollers, and fed to an automatic plastic cut and wrap machines.

Plain toffee is prepared from sugar and corn syrup only while mild and fats are added to the better varieties to impart -flavour and to develop a softer and more pliable texture.

Coated Confections

These are also known as pan coated confections , confits, or dragees consists of nuts or seeds, or boiled goods or chewing gums, coated with a hard glossy sugar covering. The nuts of other center are placed in a rotating coating pan and giving and under coated of gum arabic or gelatin (10%) and sugar syrup (30°F) and a final coating of sugar.

Composition of fondants

Sugar	60 parts
Water	20"
Corn Syrup	20"
Cooking Temp.	234-240°F.

Lozenges

Lozenges are prepared by cold mixing of sugar, gum arabic, gelatin or styrene, and flavoring materials. Two types of lozenges are produced plain lozenges are made by cutting pieces from a sheet of dough and drying in air. Out lozenges, and made from mixtures of icing sugar and flavour with gum as binding materials.

Jelly Crystals

Jelly crystal is made by mixing refined sugar with gelatin solution, flavour, and colour no cooking is needed.

Confectioneries are wrapped in glassine, cellophane, or waxed paper and also packed in tin containers. Boiled good are packed in 400 gm, 800 gm . 1kg, 5 kg. containers, and toffee in 400 gm, 800 gm 1 kg. containers.

SUPPLIERS OF PLANT & MACHINERY

Dairy Den (India) Pvt. Ltd.
25, "Madhuban", Ellisbridge,
Ahmedabad - 380 006

Factory:
9-Parasbaug Society
Bh. Bational Flats
Nr. Tagore Hall
Ahmedabad, Gujarat.
Ph: Off.: (079)461205, 449538, 44816
Fact.: 77690
Fax: 91-443537
Telex: 121-7157DDPL IN

Products: Soft Ice Cream Machines, Thick Ice Cream Machines, Ice Cream Mix Plant, Homogenisors, Batch Freezers, Continuous Freezers, Fruit Feeder, Rippe Variagatore, Candy Machines, Display Cabinets of all kinds, Cream Whipping Machines, Sluch Machine, Ice Cubers, Hotel & Kitchen Equipments, Laundry Equipment, Refrigerated Juice Disperser Brand Names: DAIRY DEN (INDIA) PVT. LTD., DAIRY MAC ENGINEERING PVT. LTD., CARPGIANLISA, ZANUSSI.

3. M/s. Nagpal Brothers,
2789, Zorawar Singh Marg,
Hamilton Road,Delhi -6.

Wrapping Machine

1. M/s. R.G. K. Enterprises
Parekh Industrial Estate
Chandansar Road
Virar (E)
Distt. Thana (M.S).

Homogeniser

1. M/s. United Technologie
B 3/201, Ashokvan Borivali (E)
Mumbai - 66.

BOILER

Indcon Boilers Limited
D-170, Okhla Ind. Area,
Phase-1, New Delhi - 110 020
Ph.: 6811441/442

Folding Cartons for Butter, Cheese, Chocolate & Skimmed Milk Powder, Lined Cartons for Skimmed Milk Powder and Malted Beverages, Wunderpac Bag in Box Packing for Liquid Milk, Condensed Milk, Ice Cream Mix and Frozen Yoghurt Mix

ITC Limited (Packing and Printing Division)
90 Chamiers Road,
Chennai - 600 018 (T.N)
Ph.: 452840

Delhi Off.:
Thapar House
124, Janpath
New Delhi - 110 001
Ph.: 312727

COMPLETE PLANT SUPPLIERS

Dhiman Systems
Dhiman Group Complex,
Kapurthala Road, Nakodar - 141 310,
Dist. Jullandhar, Punjab
Ph.: 01821-20707, 20469
Fax: 21007

Branch:
53/19, Old Rajandera Nagar
New Delhi - 110 008

SUPPLIERS OF RAW MATERIALS

MILK MANUFACTURERS/SUPPLIERS

Andhra Pradesh Dairy Development
Co-operative Federation Limited
G-28, Jangpura Extn.
New Delhi - 110 014.

Gujarat Co-operative Milk Marketing Federation Limited
Amul Dairy Road,
Post Box. No. 10
Anand - 388 001 (Gujarat)
Ph.: 23221/23272/23319
Fax: 02692-24950

Karnal Dist. Co-operative Milk Producers Union Limited
G.T. Road Byepass
Post Box. No. 84
Karnal - 132 001
Haryana

Rajasthan State Dairy Development Corporation Limited
15, Raniara Garden
Jaipur (Rajasthan).

Tamilnadu Cooperative Milk Producers' Federation Ltd.,
29 & 30 Industrial Estate
Ambattur, Chennai - 600 098.
Ph.: 044-6258520

FOOD COLOURS AND FOOD FLAVOURS

Arun Chemical Industries
B-35, Mayapuri Ind. Area
Phase-I, New Delhi - 110 064
Tel./Fax: 5131625

PLANT ECONOMICS

Rated Plant capacity = 1.00 TON/day
SEMI AUTOMATIC PLANT TOFFEE & CANDY

LAND & BUILDING Rs. 12,37,500.00
(Land Area Required 500 sq.mts.)

LIST OF PLANT & MACHINERY

1. Homogeniser
2. Steam and Vacuum Pans
3. Drop cutting machines

4. Pulling machines
5. Toffee cutting machines
6. Revolving comfits pans
7. Tableting machines
8. Wrapping and packing machines
9. Kneading machines
10. Boiler 250 Kg/RH Steam
11. Pumps,Valves,fittings & other equipments
12. Laboratory testing equipment
13. Moulds, dies and other tools, jigs, fixtures

FIXED CAPITAL

1.	LAND & BUILDING	Rs.	12,37,500.00
2.	PLANT & MACHINERY	Rs.	8,30,000.00
3.	OTHER FIXED ASSETS	Rs.	1,85,000.00
	TOTAL	**Rs.**	**22,52,500.00**

LIST OF RAW MATERIALS

1. Sugar
2. Milk
3. Corn Syrup
4. Invert Sugar
5. Flavours
6. Colours
7. Butter
8. Miscellaneous Chemicals, Citric Acid Peppermint etc.
9. Wrapping Paper & Containers

TOTAL WORKING CAPITAL/MONTH

1.	RAW MATERIAL	Rs.	5,22,250.00
2.	SALARY & WAGES	Rs.	63,250.00
3.	UTILITIES & OVERHEADS	Rs.	45,000.00
	TOTAL	**Rs.**	**6,30,500.00**

TOTAL CAPITAL INVESTMENT

TOTAL FIXED CAPITAL	Rs.	22,52,500.00
TOTAL WORKING CAPITAL FOR 3 MONTHS	Rs.	18,91,500.00
TOTAL	**Rs.**	**41,44,000.00**

TURN OVER/ANNUM

1. By selling 300 tonnes of Candy & Toffee Rs. 1,05,00,000.00

PROFIT = RECEIPTS - COST OF PRODUCTION
= 1,05,00,000.00 - 86,69,797.50
= 18,30,202.50

PROFIT SALES RATIO = Profit / Sales x 100 = 17.31 %

RATE OF RETURN = Operating profit / T.C.I x 100 = 44.17 %

BREAK EVEN POINT (B.E.P) = 47.46 %

11

CONDENSED MILK (SWEETENED)

INTRODUCTION

The advent of condensed milks belongs to the nineteenth century. In 1809, nicholas Appert (1749 - 1840), a French Food Scientist, announced his discovery of a means of preserving milk (without the admixture of sugar or other preservatives) by the following method: the milk was condensed by heating it in an open vessel placed in a waterbath over fire, to about two-thirds of its original volume. The condensed milk was strained,cooled and poured into glass bottles,filling them to the brim and corking them tightly. The bottles so filled and sealed were then held in a boiling waterbath for two hours. The milk so treated was found to have very good keeping quality.

The commercially successful manufacture of condensed milk was initiated by the American, Gail Borden (1801 - 74), who is known as 'the father of the process of milk condensing'. Borden is said to have experimented for some ten years before he finally decided that a semi-fluid state, produced by evaporation in vacuo, was the best form of preservation. In 1856, he received a patent both from the U.S.A. and England. Records show that Borden manufactured sweetened condensed milk sold under the famous Eagle Brand label as early as 1856

About 1860, the Anglo-Swiss Condensed Milk Co. was organized in Switzerland by the American brothers Charles A. Page and George H.Page, with the assistance of Swiss and English capital. This company prospered and grew rapidly in Europe. About 1880, it extended its operations to the U.S.A, but in 1902 it sold its American interests to Borden. In 1904, it consolidates with Hentry Nestle of Switzerland forming the Nestle-Anglo-Swiss Condensed Milk Co.

The basic principle in the process of preserving unsweetened condensed milk by heat-sterilization was introduced by John B. Meyenberg, a Swiss, who was an operator in the original plant of the Anglo-Swiss Condensed Milk Co., Switzerland. He migrated to the U.S.A. in 1884, and in the same year was granted a basic patent on his invention of a sterilizer. Later in 1884 and in 1887, he was granted patents on his process of preserving milk. His process patents provided sterilization by steam under pressure at a temperature not exceeding 116°C (240°F), while the sealed cans were continuously agitated by the revolving reel. This innovation provided the basis for a new industry.

PROPERTIES

(a) **Specific gravity/density**

Evaporation of water in the manufacture of condensed milks raises their specific gravity/density, which is universally employed to control their composition. Baume hydrometers are widely used for this purpose. Table 8.4 gives some of the figures for specific gravity and Baume readings.

TABLE 8.4
Specific gravity and Baume readings of condensed milks

Type of condensed milk	Fat	Milk solids not-fat Percentage	Sucrose	Specific gravity 16°C (60°)	Specific gravity 49°C (120°F)	Baume Reading 16°C (60°F)	Baume Reading 49°C (120°F)
Condensed milk	9.0	22.0	43.0	1.303	1.282	33.7	31.9
Evaporated milk	9.0	22.0	---	1.083	1.072	11.2	9.7
Skim sweetened	--	26.0	45.0	1.355	1.333	38.0	36.2

(b) Freezing Point. The figures for condensed and evaporated milks are given in table 8.5.

TABLE 8.5
Freezing point of condensed and evaporated milks

Type of condensed milk	Fat	Milk solids not-fat Percentage	Sucrose	Freezing Point	
Condensed milk	9.0	22.0	43.0	-14.9	5.1
Evaporated milk	9.0	22.0	---	-1.3	29.6

ROLE OF MILK CONSTITUENTS IN CONDENSED MILKS

a. **Milk-fat.** Imparts a rich and pleasing flavour, soft body and smooth texture to both condensed and evaporated milks. Affects viscosity. Significant in flavour problems, such as rancidity,tallowiness, etc.

b. **Milk-proteins.** Technologically of great importance. Their physico-chemical reactions to processing-heat largely determine the heat-stability and viscosity of condensed milks.

c. **Milk-sugar.** Plays an important role in the control of the texture of condensed milk. The size of lactose crystals determines the relative smoothness of condensed milk. and is controlled by the procedure used for the cooling and crystallization of this product.

d. **Mineral salts.** These-particularly calcium and magnesium together with citrates and phosphates-control the salt-balance and heat-stability of milk. A disturbed salt-balance causes objectionable heat-coagulation of milk.

USES AND APPLICATIONS

Uses of Condensed and Evaporated Milks

(a) **Condensed milk**

(i) For reconstitution into sweet milk drinks;

(ii) In tea or coffee;

(iii) In ice cream preparation;

(iv) In candy and confectionery;

(v) In prepared foods.

(b) **Evaporated milk**

(i) For reconstitution into milk for feeding infants and persons with weak stomachs etc.;

(ii) In ice cream;

(iii) In tea and coffee.

Plain Condensed Milk

This is unsweetened condensed milk, made from whole milk,partly skim milk or entirely skim milk, and condensed to 2.5 to 4:1. It is used in ice cream factories and bakeries. The product is neither sterile nor preserved by sugar. Its keeping quality is similar to that of high quality, efficiently pasteurized milk.

Superheated Condensed Milk

This is plain condensed milk superheated by blowing live steam towards the end of the condensing period. The major purpose of superheating is to increase the viscosity. it is used in ice cream factories and bakeries, where it is believed to yield better results than plain condensed milk.

Frozen Condensed Milk.

This is plain condensed milk frozen to give it longer storage life. It is used largely in ice cream factories.

METHOD OF MANUFACTURING, PACKAGING AND STORAGE OF CONDENSED MILK

Details of manufacture

Basic principle. The basic principle in the production of condensed and evaporated milks is that high quality milk is filtered/clarified, standarised, forewarmed and condensed/evaporated to the desired level. The concentrated product is preserved by the addition of sugar for condensed milk and by heat-sterilization for evaporated milk.

Receiving milk. The quality of the incoming milk is one of the indispensable corner-stones upon which rest the quality and marketability of every form of concentrated milk. It is well known that the sanitary quality of the milk Cn the receiving platform depends on its background on the farm, viz.,healthy cows, clean milk production, clean utensils, freedom from colosrum,prompt cooling and refrigerated transport. However, all milk supplies must be systematically and thoroughly inspected each day by conscientious and experienced milk-graders.

When milk is received at the plant, its temperature should be at 10°C (50°F) or below. The milk should be clean sweet,free from off-flavours and odours and reasonably free from extraneous material.

Filtration/Clarification.

This is done in order to remove visible foreign matter, which is unsightly and may cause consumer complaints, from the milk.

Standardization.

This is done so as to conform to legal standards in the finished product. The standardization of raw milk is normally carried out in three stages:

(a) the first standardization, which establishes the desired ratio of Fat: SNF (usually 1 : 2.44);

(b) the second, which establishes the desired ratio of added sugar to the total milk-solids;

(c) the third, which adjusts the concentration of the finished condensed milk to the desired percentage of total solids.

Forewarming/pre-heating.

This refers to the heating of milk before it is condensed, and serves the following purpose·

(i) To ensure that the finished product is free from micro organisms and enzymes;

(ii) to ensure uninterrupted boiling in the vacuum pan;

(iii) to provide an effective means of controlling objectionable age-thickening in the finished product.

The temperature-time of forwarming/pre-heating extends over a wide range, such as 82 to 93°C (180 to 200°F) for 5 to 15 minutes; or 116 to 149°C for 0.5 to 5 minutes. The modern trend is towards high-temperature short-time heating, such as 115 to 118°C (239 to 248°F), for No.Hold/flash. the exact temperature time of heating is so controlled as to provide optimum viscosity in the manufactured product without inducing excessive thickening or thinning during storage.

Addition of sugar

(a) Purpose. Sugar is added for the purpose of preserving the condensed milk without resorting to sterilization by heat.

(b) Kind. Generally sucrose is added as it has proved most suitable. It is either highly refined cane or beet sugar. Other sweetening agents, such as corn syrup solids, glucose and dextrose, have been used to replace sugar by 5 to 25 percent. The disadvantages of these sweetening agents are their reduced sweetening capacity compared to sucrose and their adverse effects on colour and the rate of thickening in storage.

(c) Amount. This ranges from 40 to 45 percent in the finished product,which requires 18 to 20 percent sugar on milk basis.

Hunziker advocated a Sugar Ratio (sugar-in-water concentration) of 62.5 to 64.6 percent; this amount not only ensures proper protection against microbial growth, but also prevents sugar crystallization.

Condensing.

The basic principle consists in the removal of water from the standardized milk by boiling it under partial vacuum at a low temperature till the desired concentration is reached. This operation is carried out in an evaporator,

Homogenization.

Hot condensed milk is invariably homogenized before it is cooled and crystallized by standard manufactures of the product throughout the world. The object is to obtain a uniform fat emulsion and reduce fat separation to a minimum during storage. A special type of homogenizer suitable for handling a highly viscous product is used at a total pressure of 2500 psi (2000 psi in the first stage and 500 psi in the second stage).

Cooling and Crystallization.

(i) **Importance.** The cooling process occupies an important place in the manufacture of a marketable condensed milk. Prompt cooling is desirable to delay the tendency of age-thickening and discolouration,which is accelerated by prolonged exposure to heat.

Packaging.

The condensed milk is now ready for packaging. Bulk packaging may be done in barrels of various sizes, drums with polythene liners, or tin-containers. For the retail market, fillers are used to package condensed milk in cans. After filling, the cans are sealed,labeled and packed in cases for storage and distribution.

The retail cans are filled with automatic filling machines. In general, the filling machine consists of multiple-piston pumps. The cylinder charge can be adjusted to the size of the cans to be filled. It is important to fill the cans fully in order to exclude as much of the air from the container as possible.

FLOW DIAGRAM OF MANUFACTURE OF EVAPORATED MILK

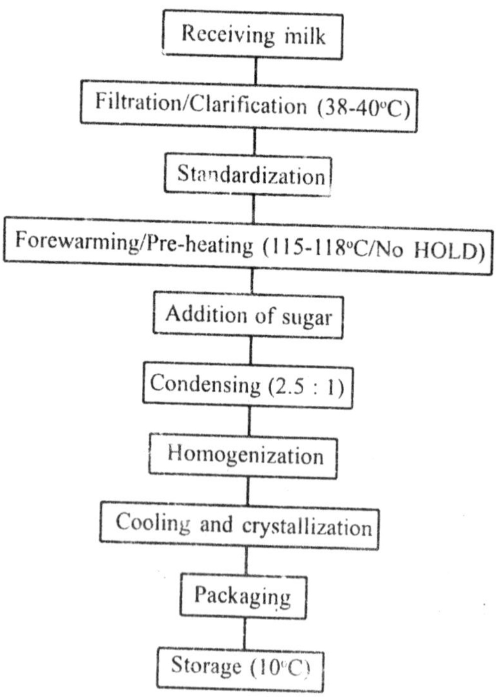

Flow Diagram of Manufacture for Condensed Milk

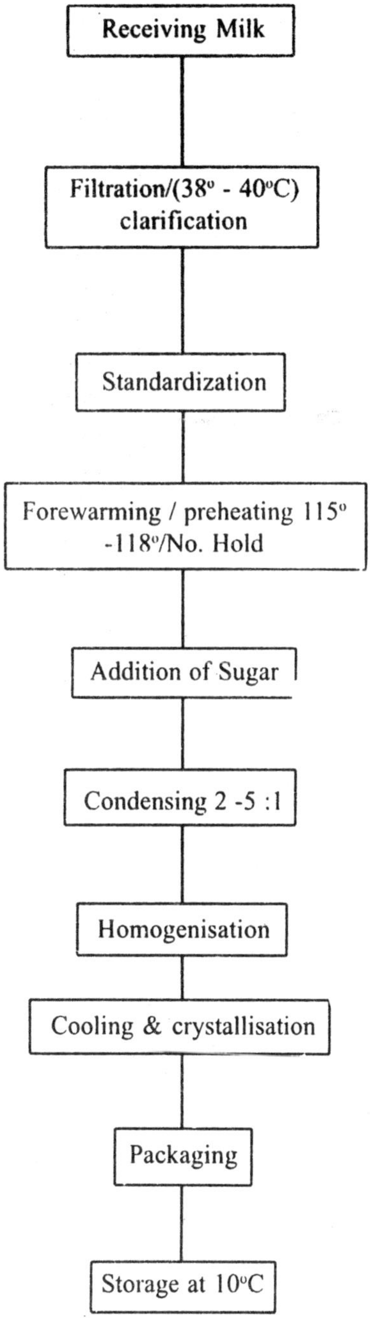

ADDRESS OF RAW MATERIAL SUPPLIERS

MILK MANUFACTURERS/SUPPLIERS

Andhra Pradesh Dairy Development
Co-operative Federation Limited
G-28, Jangpura Extn.
New Delhi - 110 014.

Gujarat Co-operative Milk Marketing Federation Limited
Amul Dairy Road,
Post Box. No. 10
Anand - 388 001 (Gujarat)
Ph.: 23221/23272/23319
Fax: 02692-24950

Karnal Dist. Co-operative Milk Producers Union Limited
G.T. Road Byepass
Post Box. No. 84
Karnal - 132 001
Haryana

Rajasthan State Dairy Development Corporation Limited
15, Raniara Garden
Jaipur (Rajasthan).

Tamilnadu Cooperative Milk Producers' Federation Ltd.,
29 & 30 Industrial Estate
Ambattur, Chennai - 600 098.
Ph.: 044-6258520

ADDRESSES OF COMPLETE PLANT AND MACHINERY SUPPLIERS

Bansal Technocrats
1/1431/18, Sharda Nagar,
Saharanpur - 247 001 (U.P).
Ph.: 0132-27914

Products: Milk Reception, Storage and Transportaion Tanks, Ghee Making Equipments (Butter Melting Vats, Prestatification Tank, Ghee Boiler, Ghee Settling Tank, Ghee Storage Tank etc.), Paneer and Khova Making Equipments, Cream Storage and Repening Tanks, CIP Unit (Mannual and Automatic), Milk Pumps, SS Pneumatically operated valves, SS pipe fittings and control pannels etc.

Dairy Den (India) Pvt. Ltd.
25, "Madhuban", Ellisbridge,
Ahmedabad - 380 006

Factory:
9-Parasbaug Society
Bh. Bational Flats
Nr. Tagore Hall
Ahmedabad, Gujarat.
Ph: Off.: (079)461205, 449538, 44816
Fact.: 77690
Fax: 91-443537
Telex: 121-7157DDPL IN

Products: Soft Ice Cream Machines, Thick Ice Cream Machines, Ice Cream Mix Plant, Homogenisors, Batch Freezers, Continuous Freezers, Fruit Feeder, Rippe Variagatore, Candy Machines, Display Cabinets of all kinds, Cream Whipping Machines, Sluch Machine, Ice Cubers, Hotel & Kitchen Equipments, Laundry Equipment, Refrigerated Juice Disperser Brand Names: DAIRY DEN (INDIA) PVT. LTD., DAIRY MAC ENGINEERING PVT. LTD., CARPGIANLISA, ZANUSSI.

HMT Ltd.,
Sree Nidhi Chambers
Senapati Bapat Marg
Pune - 4111016
Ph.: 350040
Fax: (0212) 358565
Telex: 0145-7262

Factory:
H-2, MIDC, Chikalthana
Aurangabad - 10

Products: Pasteuriser, Centrifugal Pump, Butter Making Machine, Butterfly Valves, Plate Heat Exchangers, Oil Purification & Clarification System, Ice Cream Machinery & Turnkey Projects of small & big capacity Dairy.

Industrial Refreigeration
901, Market Chambers-V
Nariman Point, Mumbai - 400 021.

Factory:
Plot No.33,
Govt. Indl. Estate
Phase-II, Pinaria,
Silvassa - 396 230
Ph.: 2041183, 2041185, 2041189
Fax: 2044944
Telex : 841130
Products: Dairy Plant and Equipments from UK and Netherlands.

BOILER

Indcon Boilers Limited
D-170, Okhla Ind. Area,
Phase-1,New Delhi - 110 020
Ph.: 6811441/442

TIN CONTAINERS

Choudhary Metal Printers
7/12, Upper Anand Parbat Ind. Area
New Delhi - 110 005.
Tel./Fax: 5729535/5726318

Arora Tin Ind.
617, Bisrekh Road
Chhaprola, Ghaziabad (U.P.)
Tel./Fax: 724173

PLANT ECONOMICS

Rated Plant capacity = 1000.00 KGS./day

CONDENSED MILK SWEETENED

LAND & BUILDING Rs. 8,00,000.00
(Area Required 500 Sq. Mts.)

LIST OF PLANT & MACHINERY

1. MILK RECEIVING SECTION:
Milk weighing machines,milk recenining tanks chain conveyers etc.

2. PASTEURIZING SECTION:
Milk tanks, milk tanks, pumps, plate pasteuriser milk fillers, water heaters- hot water pumps chilled water pumps temp recorders, etc.

3. MILK STORAGE SECTION:
Stainless steel milk tanks, milk, pumps,stainless steel pipes etc.

4. REFRIGERATION SECTION:
Refrigeration plant,compressors condensers,electric motors- Ammonia pipes etc. 10 tonnes Refrigeration

5. BABY BOILER:
Vertical multi tubular boiler,steam & water mixing batteries Rotating can washers, wash up tanks

6. CAN WASHING SECTION:

7. Laboratory equipment Gerber centrifuge dirt dusting apparatus, Lactometers centrifugal-Machines, testing apparatus etc.

8. Installation & Erection

FIXED CAPITAL

1. LAND & BUILDING	Rs.	8,00,000.00
2. PLANT & MACHINERY	Rs.	9,85,000.03
3. OTHER FIXED ASSETS	Rs.	2,20,000.00
TOTAL	**Rs.**	**20,05,000.03**

LIST OF RAW MATERIALS

1. Milk
2. Sugar
3. Cans
4. Chemicals, Preservatives etc.

TOTAL WORKING CAPITAL/MONTH

1. RAW MATERIAL	Rs.	10,06,500.00
2. SALARY & WAGES	Rs.	74,250.00
3. UTILITIES & OVERHEADS	Rs.	93,400.00
TOTAL	**Rs.**	**11,74,150.00**

TOTAL CAPITAL INVESTMENT

TOTAL FIXED CAPITAL	Rs.	20,05,000.03
TOTAL WORKING CAPITAL FOR 3 MONTHS	Rs.	35,22,450.00
TOTAL	**Rs.**	**55,27,450.03**

TURN OVER/ANNUM

1. Receipts from sale of condensed milk (200 gm pack tin)
   Quantity 1800000 tin Rs. 1,98,00,000.00

PROFIT = RECEIPTS - COST OF PRODUCTION
= 1,98,00,000.00 - 1,54,00,378.26
= 43,99,621.74

PROFIT SALES RATIO = Profit/Sales x 100 = 22.22 %

RATE OF RETURN = Operating profit/T.C.I x 100 = 79.60 %

BREAK EVEN POINT (B.E.P) = 32.47 %

12

DAIRY FARM

INTRODUCTION

More than Five percent of the world's milk comes from Buffalloes. Buffalloes milk is used in much the same way as cow's milk. It is high in fats and total solid, which gives it a rich flavour. Many people prefer it to cow's milk and are willing to pay more for it. In India, where in Mumbai area alone an estimated 10,000 new born calves starved to death each year through lack of milk. The demand for Buffallo milk in India (About 60% of the milk consumed over 80% in some states) is reflected in the prices paid for a litre of milk; about 130 paisa for cow's milk compared with about 200 paisa for buffallo milk Twelve of the Eighteen major breeds of buffallo are kept primarily for milk production (although male may be used for traction & all animals are eventually used for meat.) The main milk breeds of India & Pakistan are the murrah, Nile/Ravi.Surti, Mehsana, Nagpure, & Jafarabad.

The domesticated water buffallo is one of the gentlist of all farm animals. Despite an intimidating appearance it is more like a house hold pat-sociable, gentle, and serve. In rural Asia the care of buffalloes is after turned over to small boys & girls aged about 4 to 9.

Another belief is that the buffallo is exclusively a tropical animal. River type buffalloes, However, have been used to pul! snow plows during Bulgarian winter.

Buffallo milk has a higher content of both butter fat and non fat-solids than cows milk does. Throughout much India it is in such demand that Cow's milk is sometimes hard to sell.

Breeds: The major genetic division of the buffallo are the swamp Buffalo of the eastern half of the Asia, which has swept back horns and the river buffalo of the western half of Asia which usually has the curled horns. There is also the mediterranean buffalo, which is of the river type but has been isolated for so long that it has developed some unique characteristics.

Although there is only one breed of swamp buffalo, certain sub-groups seem to have specific inherited characteristics. Swamp buffaloes range from 250 kg for some small animals in China, 200-300 kg in Berma and 500-600 kgs in Laos. Only in India and Pakistan are there well defined breeds with standard qualities. There are eighteen (18) river buffalo breeds in south asia which are further classified as the Murrah, Gujrat, Uttar Pradesh, Central Indian & South Indian breeds. These are the five groups and main breeds :-

Groups	**Breeds**
Murrah	Murrah,Nili/Ravi, Kundi
GujratSurti, Mehsana, Jafarabadi,	
Uttar Pradesh	Bhadawari, Tarai,
Central India	Nagpuri, Manda, Pandharpuri, Sambalpur,JerangiHandi,
South Indian	Toda, south Kanara,

The best known breeds are Murrah Nili/Ravi, Surti, Jafarabadi, Mehsana, & Nagpuri.

Genetics:- The swamp buffalo has forty eight chromosomes, the river buffallo fifty similar in the two types and they cross breeds to produce fertile hybrid progeny. Cattle however, have sixty (60) chromosomes and although mating between cattle & buffaloes is common, hy-brids from the union are unlikely to occur.

Individual buffaloes show large variation in milk yield, conformation, horn shape, colour,meal production, temperament, growth rate, & other characteristics.

The large bulls that would be best for breeding purposes are often being selected as draft animals and Castrated, or sent to slaughter or shot by hunters.

YIELDS : In countries like India & Egypt, the milk yield of buffaloes is generally higher (680-800kg) than for local cattle (360-500 kg). However since selection for exceptional, large variations in yield occur between individual animals and milk production of dairy buffaloes falls short of its potential. Indian Government forms, average yields for milking buffaloes range from 4-7 kg per day in lactations averaging 285 days, Daily yields of 12 kg have been reported for some Bulgarian buffalo cows & and a daily production of over 20 kg has been reported for some remarkable animals in India. A peak milk yield of 31.5 kg/day has been recorded from a champion Murrah buffalo in the All India Milk yield competition conducted by Govt. of India.

DAIRY MANAGEMENT

The characteristics of the dairy buffalo so closely approximate those of the dairy cow that successful methods of breeding, husbandry and feeding for milk production for the cow can be applied equally to the dairy buffalo. Buffaloes however have not been breed for uniform udders and it is more difficult to milk them by machine.

USES & APPLICATIONS OF MILK

Buffalo milk can provide a wide variety of products : butter, butteroil (Clarified butter or ghee) soft and hard cheeses, condensed or evaporated milk, Ice-cream, Yogurt and buttermilk. It is of great economic importance in India in preparing tonned milk- a mixture of buffalo milk and milk made by reconstituting skim milk powder.

The richness of buffalo milk makes it highly suitable for processing. To produce 1 kg of cow's milk but only 5 kg of buffalo milk. To produce 1 kg of butter requires 14 kg of cow's milk but only 10 kg of buffaloes milk. Because of these high yields, processors appreciated the value of buffalo milk. Buffalo cheese is pure white. Cheese are becoming increasingly popular throughout the world. Demand is rising at a rate that is among the highest for any food product cheese offers particular benefit to areas where refrigeration is not widely available where transporting high protein foods to remote areas is difficult and where seasonal fluetnations affect milk supplies.

LIST OF DAIRY FARMS

M/s. HMM Ltd.,
Industrial Estate,
Dowleswaram, Rajahmundry - 533 124,
East Godawari Dist. (A.P.)

M/s. Kamadhenu Cattle Breeding & Dairy Farm,
12, Padmarao Nagar,
Secunderabad - 500 025 (A.P.)

M/s. Tisco Dairy & Poultry Farm,
P.O. Agrico, Jamshed pur - 831 009 (Bihar).

M/s. Gazipur Co-op Dairy Society Ltd.,
Vill & PO Gazipur, Delhi - 110 091.

M/s. Universal Poultry & Dairy Farm,
C/o Bhagwan Dass & Co.,
Kashmere Gate,
Delhi - 110 006.

M/s. Sterling Poultry & Dairy Farm,
Vill Ularia, Sanand Road,
PO Santhal, via Sarkhej - 382 210.
Dist. Gandhi Nagar, Gujarat.

SUPPLIERS OF CATTLES

M/s. Haryana Dairy Development Co-op Federation Ltd.,
Bhiwani,
(Haryana)

M/s. Govt. of Jammu and Kashmir,
Animal Husbandary Deptt,
Cattle Breeding Farms,
Beli Charana, Jammu Cantt.

M/s. Govt. Of Punjab,
Animal Husbandary Deptt.,
Cattle Breeding Farms - Mattewara,
Ludhiana (PB).

COMPOSITION OF CATTLE FEED

There is no definite composition to Buffalo feed compound but in general practice the following composition is followed :-

A.

Ground nut Cake	25%
Wheat bran	27%
Grain Husk	15%
Maize	30%
Mineral	1%
Salt	2%

B.

1.	Wheat or rice bran	55%
2.	Soyabean or ground nut cake	35%
3.	Molasses	8%
4.	Mineral supplement	2%

COMPOSITION OF MILK

COMPOSITION

Buffalo milk contains less water, more fat,slightly more lactose,and more protein than cow's milk. It seems thicker than cow's milk because it generally contains more than16 percent total solid compared with 12-14 percent for cow's milk. Although the butterfat content is usually 6-8 percent, it can go much higher in the milk of some well fed dairy buffaloes and in the milk of Swamp buffaloes (which are not normally used for milking). Cow's milk butterfat content is usually between 3 and 5 percent.

Because of its high butterfat content, buffalo milk has considerably higher energy value than cow's milk. Phospholipids are lower but cholesterol and saturated fatty acids are higher in buffalo milk. Studies have shown that digestibility is not adversely affected by this. Because of the high fat content, the buffalo's total fat yield per lactation compares favourably with that of improved breeds of dairy cattle, it is much higher than that of indigenous cows.

Normally the protein in buffalo milk contains more casein and slightly more albumin and globulin than cow's milk. Several researchers have claimed that the biological value of buffalo milk protein is higher than that of cow's milk, but this has not yet been proved conclusively.

COMPARATIVE GROSS COMPOSITION (IN PERCENT) OF BUFFALO AND COW'S MILK

	Total Solid	Fat	Protein	Lactose
River buffalo	17.96	7.45	4.36	4.83
Swamp buffalo	18.34	8.95	4.13	4.78
Friesian Cow	12.15	3.60	3.25	4.60
Native Cow	13.45	4.97	3.18	4.59

NOTE : In general buffalo milk is considerably higher in total solids, fat, and protein than milk from improved or native cows. Buffalo milk is slightly higher in lactose.

Source: R.E. McDowell, Department of Animal Science, Cornell University

SOME PHYSICAL CHARACTERISTICS OF MILK

Characteristics	Buffalo	Cow
Viscosity (cP)	2.04	1.86
Refractive index	1.3448	1.3338
Surface tension (dynes/cm)	55.4	55.9
pH	6.7	6.6
Freezing point depression	.560	.570
Average size of fat globules (um)	5.01	3.85
Number of fat globules (millions/mm^3)	3.20	2.96
Phosphates activity (units/100)	28	82
Fluorescence under UV light	Greenish yellow	Pale bluish

Sources: H.Laxminarayana and N.N Dastur. Buffaloes' milk and milk products. Part II. Dairy Science Abstracts 30:231-241.

MANUFACTURING PROCESS

The manufacturing process for Dairy milk is started with the milking buffaloes by hand (at small scale) & milking buffaloes by machine (at large scale).

The detailed process is given herewith :-

MILKING BUFFALOES BY HAND

The profitable operation of a dairy herd depends in a large part upon how well you milk your buffaloes. You can do everything else carefully and well, but if you do not milk your buffaloes properly, you can never be successful in dairying. Poor milking habits cause low production, mastitis, & poor quality milk. An important part of milking buffaloes is to produce the cleanest possible milk. Milk must be low in sediment.

Although machine milking is rapidly replacing hand milking, many dairymen still use the latter. In milking by hand, buffaloes must be carefully prepared to produce high quality milk.

COOLING & STORING MILK

The careless handling of milk between milking & delivering to the plant can cause high bacteria counts to develop in the milk thus a mechanical cooler is employed for the purpose. Whole of the milk should be stored at 50°F to prevent spoilage. Storage Tanks made of stainless steel are employed for storing the raw milk.

FILTRATION :

The cold raw milk is filtered, however, it can be filtered before cooling & storing in tank, but the precaution is to be taken at this stage so that no foreign matters or undesired materials may be carried on.

HOMOGENIZATION:

Filtered milk is fed into homogenizer. Homogenization is the process by which the milk is emulsified and are further divided to produce a more stable emulsion that will not separate on standing. The fat is emulsified with liquid part of milk that are water mostly. Hence, to prevent sedimentation of fat in milk. This homogenization process is done. By this way high quality homogenized milk is produced.

After feeding the milk into homogenizer, the pressure of the homogenizer is increased about 2500 psi. However, if this pressure does not produce milk that meets the standard, it may be necessary to use a pressure as high as 3000 to 3500 Lb.

CLARIFICATION:

The milk is passed through a clarified as it leaves the homogenizer. Cold milk clarification is preferred to hot milk. This clarification operation can be perform before homogenization. But the complete clarification can be achieved at this stage.

Clarifier can be replaced by cream separator but since the separator bowl is not designed to hold a large amount of sediment and consequently is not efficient for clarfifying a large volume of milk. However, This operation can be omitted to get high quality milk.

PASTEURIZATION:

In this process, the clarified milk is fed to pasteurizer and heated to the required temperature & held there during the holding period (usually at 145°F & for at least 30 minutes). Vat pasteurizer with jackets & agitators is employed for the pasteurization.

The milk is heated by hot water or steam passing into the space between the two tanks. In this process, excessive heating of any part of the milk & a consequent "cooked" flavour is prevented.

At the end of the holding period, the cold water is circulated through the jacket or coil of the pasteurizer, Temperature of the milk may be quickly lowered 10° to 15°, & at this point the heated flavour will not continue to develop. This is done to destroy all pathogenic bacteria.

REFRIGERATION OR FREEZING SYSTEM

After the complete processing of milk it is to be stored in a cold upto chilling condition so that no unwanted micro-organisms/pathogenic organism can be developed in the processed milk. It is stored until delivered for distribution i.e. for packing in Cans or pouches.

TESTING:

The testing of milk is an essential for the quality control purposes. However, testing may be done prior to storage under freezing condition. But it is better to test the final product before packing. When product is cleared from testing or quality control section then it is ready for packing & distribution & send to packing section.

PACKING:

There are two methods adopted from packing milk. Firstly packed or stored in aluminium milk cans for distribution. Secondly milk packed in plastic pouches of capacity 1/2 kg, 1 kg, & 2 kgs packs.

Milk is stored in milk cans. There will no difficulty. It is traditional. But, in pouches filling of milk is to be performed with a great care & skilled operator is to be employed for this purpose. Automatic pouch making, milk filling & pouch sealing machine is available with printing provision.

Milk filled & sealed in pouches is now ready for dispatch & distribution for marketing.

ADDRESSES OF COMPLETE PLANT & MACHINERY SUPPLIERS

Bansal Technocrats
1/1431/18, Sharda Nagar,
Saharanpur - 247 001 (U.P).
Ph.: 0132-27914

Products: Milk Reception, Storage and Transportation Tanks, Ghee Making Equipments (Butter Melting Vats, Prestatification Tank, Ghee Boiler, Ghee Settling Tank, Ghee Storage Tank etc.), Paneer and Khova Making Equipments, Cream Storage and Repening Tanks, CIP Unit (Manual and Automatic), Milk Pumps, SS Pneumatically operated valves, SS pipe fittings and control panels etc.

Dairy Den (India) Pvt. Ltd.
25, "Madhuban", Ellisbridge,
Ahmedabad - 380 006

Factory:
9-Parasbaug Society
Bh. Bational Flats
Nr. Tagore Hall
Ahmedabad, Gujarat.
Ph: Off.: (079)461205, 449538, 44816
Fact.: 77690
Fax: 91-443537
Telex: 121-7157DDPL IN

Products: Soft Ice Cream Machines, Thick Ice Cream Machines, Ice ɛam Mix Plant, Homogenizers, Batch Freezers, Continuous Freezers, Fruit ɛder, Ripe Variagatore, Candy Machines, Display Cabinets of all kinds, Cream ıipping Machines, Sluch Machine, Ice Cubes, Hotel & Kitchen Equipments, undry Equipment, Refrigerated Juice Disperser Brand Names: DAIRY DEN NDIA) PVT. LTD., DAIRY MAC ENGINEERING PVT. LTD., ARPGIANLISA, ZANUSSI.

HMT Ltd.,
Sree Nidhi Chambers
Senapati Bapat Marg
Pune - 4111016
Ph.: 350040
Fax: (0212) 358565
Telex: 0145-7262

Factory:
H-2, MIDC, Chikalthana
Aurangabad - 10

Products: Pasteuriser, Centrifugal Pump, Butter Making Machine, Butterfly Valves, Plate Heat Exchangers, Oil Purification & Clarification System, Ice Cream Machinery & Turnkey Projects of small & big capacity Dairy.

BOILER

Indcon Boilers Limited
D-170, Okhla Ind. Area,
Phase-1, New Delhi - 110 020
Ph.: 6811441/442

TIN CONTAINERS

Choudhary Metal Printers
7/12, Upper Anand Parbat Ind. Area
New Delhi - 110 005.
Tel./Fax: 5729535/5726318

Arora Tin Ind.
617, Bisrekh Road
Chhaprola, Ghaziabad (U.P.)
Tel./Fax: 724173

POUCHES (PRINTED/LAMINATED)

Flex Industries Limited
A-107/108, Sector - IV,
Noida - 201 301 (U.P)
Ph.: 85-22558

SUPPLIERS OF RAW MATERIALS

CATTLE FEED & GREEN FEED:-

LOCAL DEALERS.

The Quality Green Fodder can be grown in rest of the uncovered areas as mentioned earlier.

However, Addresses of Stockists & distributors of the cattle feed are given latter.

PLANT ECONOMICS

Rated Plant capacity =

LAND & BUILDING (Land Area Required 2000 sq.mts.)	Rs.	21,80,000.00

LIST OF PLANT & MACHINERY

1. Steam boiler
2. Homogenizer complete with accessory
3. Refrigeration system consists of air compressor, refrigerants etc.
4. Pasteurizer with cooling arrangement
5. Filter (ordinary)
6. Pouch making, filling & sealing machine complete automatic with printing arrangement
7. Milk reception tank (Stainless 20000 steel make)
8. Milk Cans (Aluminium)
9. Dies different capacity
10. Buffaloes Kundi
11. Misc. other equipments such as laboratory & testing equipments

FIXED CAPITAL

1.	LAND & BUILDING	21,80,000.00
2.	PLANT & MACHINERY	17,17,000.00
3.	OTHER FIXED ASSETS	4,20,000.00
	TOTAL	**43,17,000.00**

LIST OF RAW MATERIALS

1. Cattle feed green fodder/Cattle feed
2. Health expenses (medicines) etc.
3. Pouches
4. Misc. other items such as printing ink etc.

TOTAL WORKING CAPITAL/MONTH

1.	RAW MATERIAL	59,500.00
2.	SALARY & WAGES	38,750.00
3.	UTILITIES & OVERHEADS	15,200.00
	TOTAL	**1,13,450.00**

TOTAL CAPITAL INVESTMENT

TOTAL FIXED CAPITAL	43,17,000.00
TOTAL WORKING CAPITAL FOR 3 MONTHS	3,40,350.00
TOTAL	**46,57,350.00**

TURN OVER/ANNUM

1. By sale of 1200 x 365 litres of Milk (Dairy Farming)	Rs.	52,56,000.00
	TOTAL	**52,56,000.00**

PROFIT = RECEIPTS - COST OF PRODUCTION
= 52,56,000.00 - 28,83,617.00
= 23,72,383.00

PROFIT SALES RATIO = Profit/Sales x 100 = 45.14 %

RATE OF RETURN = Operating profit/T.C.I x 100 = 50.94 %

BREAK EVEN POINT (B.E.P) = 42.88 %

13

DAIRY EQUIPMENTS

INTRODUCTION

India new ranks forth in the world in the matter of milk production with a production level of about 24 million tonnes. Nearly 60 percent is marketed and the balance is used for home consumption of feeding calves.

The per capita consumption of milk and milk products varies from state to state. The average works out to 5.5 oz. The present per capita availability of milk is estimated at around 108 grams per head.

The total number of dairy farms/plants in India are more than 175. The average daily throughout of milk of all dairy plants is at present 2.8 million litres. There has been a spurt in milk production particularly in Maharashtra and Gujarat. The operation flood programme initiated during the forth plan with assistance from the world bank has been a major contributory factor in the regard. Co-operatives constituents a major sources of supply of milk to the dairy plants. The average daily production of milk powder and infant food is about 43 tons. Butter and ghee production amounts to 40 tonnes a day. Production of table butter, condensed milk, infant food and matted food is sufficient to meet the demand. The sizes of the dairy farms vary from 10 milch cattle to 100 animals. The animals which dry off are sold and newly calved ones are purchased to keep up the milk production.

In a few farms pasteurization equipment are installed and milk is delivered to consumers with 2 hours after milking.

DAIRY EQUIPMENTS

Items Made In India :-

The items that are made at present generally are as under.

1. Milk reception, cooling and storage receiving tanks, drip savers, centrifugal pumps, plate and surface type coolers uninsulated and cold walled storage tanks and aluminium alloy, milk cans.

Can Washing :-

Can washing, troughs, steaming blocks, rotary and straight semi automatic can washers.

Processing :-

Batch and plate pasteurisers of various sizes for milk and cream. The plates are imported.

Butter and Ghee Making :-

Manually and power operated cream separators upto 550 lph. cream ripening tanks, butter churns, butter trolleys, butter handling accessories and ghee boilers.

Cheese & Casein Making :-

Cheese and casein vats, cheese knives, curd milk hoops, presses.

Bulk Milk Handling :-

Bulk milk coolers and storage tanks.

Washing & Sterilizing :-

Milk pipe washing and sterilizing deist and cleaning in place units.

Milk Testing :-

Manually and electrically, driven centrifuges lock stoppers, lab. fitting. Recirculating and falling film type evaporator and spray dryers.

Silo Tanks :-

Other items like condensed milk coolers, certain item of ice cream making equipment etc.

The growth of urbanization in the country has opened the scope of setting up milk dairies in town and cities.

The industry is growing fast thus creating scope for the manufacture of dairy equipment.

Formerly milk men were performing preservation and processing milk food for their limited clientele in their own have storage tank and other equipment in organised dairies for improving the productivity of the operation and functions.

The following items have been reserved by the Government of India, for exclusive manufacture in the small scale sector.

1. Double cone mixer.
2. Micro Pulveriser.
3. Rotary Dryers.
4. Basket Type Centrifuges.
5. Milk cooling & Ghee settling Equipment.
6. Butter churns.
7. Curd Mills.
8. Evaporating pans.
9. Agitators.
10. Storage Tanks.

MANUFACTURING PROCESS

Metal Shearing Operations :-

Operations that cut sheet metal and even bar stock and other shapes, have various purposes. Commoin operations and the work they do are depicted in figure below.

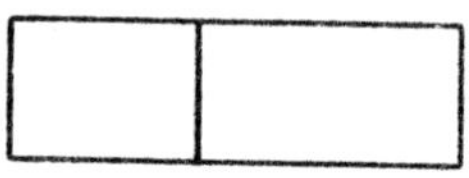

Shearing

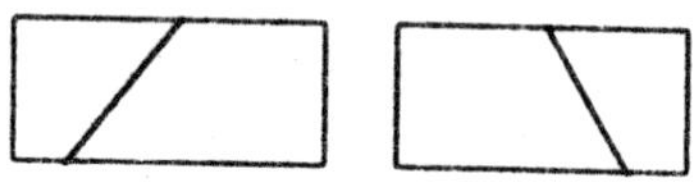

CUTTING

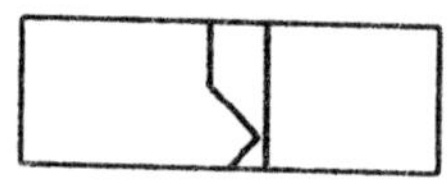

PARTING

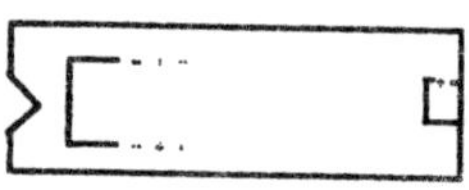

BLANKING

PUCHING OR PIERCING

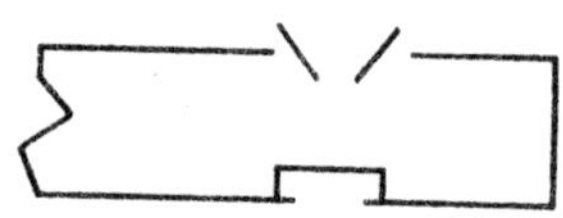

NOTCHING

SITTING

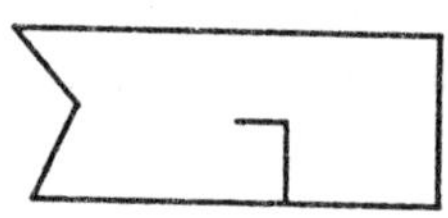

LANCING

NIBBING

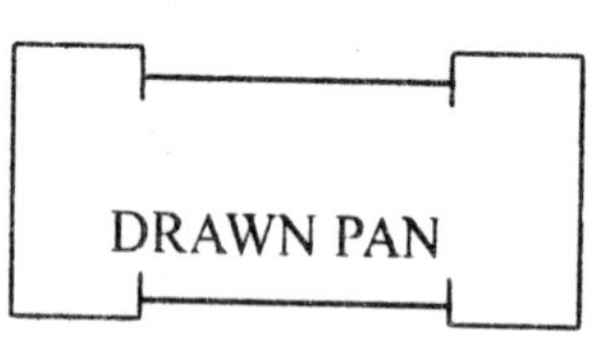

TRIMMING

Sheet metal is sheared between a punch and a dye block. The punch has the same shape all the way around as the opening in the dye block, except, it is smaller on each side by an amount called the break clearance. As the punch enters the stock, it pushes material down into the opening.

Bending :-

The bending group of operations is performed in presses (variety) dairy benches (door trim, molding etc.) forming rolls (cylinders) and roll straighteners (trips, sheets, plates).

Spring back, due to the elasticity of the metal and amount of bend may be compensated for by 1 over bending or largely prevented by striking the metal at the radius with a coining (i.e. squeezing as in the production of cones) pressure sufficient to set up compressive stresses to counter balance surface tensile stresses. A very narrow bead may be used to localize the pinch where needed and minimum danger to the press in squeezing on a large area. Under such conditions, good, sharp bends in V dyes have been obtained with two or four times the pressure required to shear the metal across the same section.

Bending Allowance :-

The thickness of the metal over a small radius or a sharp corner is 10 or 15% less than before bending because the metal moves more easily in tension than in compress iron. For the same reason, the neutral airs of the metal moves in towards the centre of the corner radius. Therefore in figuring the length of blank to be allowed for bend upto an elastic radius of two or three times the metal thickness to the length may be figured closely as along a neutral line at 0.4 ton out from the inside radius.

Gas Welding :-

The heat for gas welding is supplied by burning a mixture of oxygen and a suitable combustible gas. The gases are mixed in a torch (blow pipe) which gives control of welding flame.

Acetylene is almost universally used as the combustible gas because of its high flame temperature. This temperature, estimated to be about 6000 °F is so far, above the melting point of all commercial metals that it provides a means for the rapid localized melting essential in welding.

Oxy Acetylene Welding :-

Oxy acetylene welding of steel is performed without any flux. Fluxes are necessary for welding practically all other metals. Welding rods all other for oxy acetylene welding are covered by specifications for iron and steel gas welding rods (AWS A 5.2, ASTM A251).

Mechanised Oxy Acetylene Welding :-

Oxy acetylene welding by machine is applied in the manufacture of steel barrels, tubing, irrigation pipes and special forms fabricated of steel and many alloys. Multiple flame, water cooled machine torches make welds at rates several times that possible by the most expert hand welders. Machine welding is done with and without filler material mostly without on tubing and pipe the welds being compressed in the process to make a flush or reinforced joint.

Metal Working Equipment :-

Powder presses consists of frame of substantial construction with devices for holding the dies or tools and a moving ember or slide for actuating one portion of the dies. This slide usually receives its movement from a crank shaft furnished with a clutch for inter nutrient operation and a flywheel to supply the sudden powder requirement. Hydraulic presses have no crank shaft, clutch or flywheel but employ raw actuated by pumps.

The crank shaft is ordinarily the limiting factor in the pressure capacity of the machine and accordingly is often taken as the basis for tonnage ratings. There is no uniform basis for this rating, owing to the variations in the shaft proportions and materials and in different relative serverity of various press operations.

The speed of operation of the press depends upon the energy requirement and the crank pin velocity. The latter determine the velocity of impact on the tools in blanking the blow varies directly with the contacted speed and the thickness and hardness of the material.

Horizontal Plate Bending Machines :-

Consists of two stationery rolls and a third vertical adjustable upper roll which can be fitted obliquely for taper bending and is held in bearings with spherical seats. The diameter of the rolls can be determined approximately from the equi $r^2 = bt$ in which r is the radius of the roll, b the width of the plate or sheet and t its thickness, all in inches.

PLANT AND MACHINERY SUPPLIERS

Air Compressors

1. M/s. Bhalla Refrigeration Industries,
   Shop No.- 42, Ground Floor,
   Raghu Shree Market,
   Ajmeri Gate,
   New Delhi - 110 006.
   Phone No - 730767.

2. M/s. Renu Enterprises,
   2094 - A, Gali No - 165,
   Ganeshpura 'A',
   New Delhi - 110035.

Grinders :

1. M/s. Guru Nanak Mechanical & Engg. Works.
   B - 47, Phase - II
   Mayapuri Industrial Area
   New Delhi - 110 064.

Drilling Machine :

1. M/s. Moonlit Industries
   Railway Road
   Sirhind
   Punjab.

Lathe Machineries

1. M/s. Jay Jay Cee Engg. Corpn.,
   308/1, Shahzada Bagh,
   Old Rohtak Road,
   Delhi - 110 035.

2. M/s.Supreme Mechanical Works,
   Plot No. 612, Shastri Nagar,
   A Block, Delhi - 110 052.

Drying Oven:

1. M/s. Krishna Scientific Works
   D - 3/21, Mayapuri
   Phase - II
   New Delhi - 110064.
   Phone : 541 2360

Welding Equipments :-

1. M/s. Allied Electricals Engineering Co.,
   Bakarawadi,
   Madanzampa,
   Baroda - 1.

Welding Transformers :-

1. M/s. Contential Electronics,
   117- C- 19,
   Naroda Industrial Township,
   Ahmedabad.

Other Machines :-

1. M/s. Punjab Steel Corporation.,
   Sekhri Buildings,
   Vill Shukarpura,
   D.B. N. Road,
   Batala (Punjab)

SUPPLIERS OF RAW MATERIALS

1. M/s. A.K. Corporation Ltd.,
   Visakhapatnam,
   Andhra Pradesh.

2. M/s. Aditya Mills Ltd.,
   Stadium House,
   Block No.2,
   2nd Floor,
   Veer Nariman Road,
   Mumbai - 1.

M.S. Sheet/Rod :-

1. M/s. Hindustan Steel Traders
Plot No. N - 22
Main Road
Anand Parbat Industrial Area
New Rohtak Road
New Delhi - 110 005
Phone : 572 8474.

PLANT ECONOMICS

Rated Plant capacity	=	44 NUMBERS DAIRY EQUIPMENTS/ANNUM
LAND & BUILDING (Land Area Required 500 sq.mts.)		Rs. 7,25,000.00

LIST OF PLANT & MACHINERY

1. Cutogen 5 'Oxy Acetylene torch set complete.
2. MMC series L loyds branch plate bending machine with motor & other accessories
3. Air cooled arc welding transformer 350 amps.
4. Welding rectifier set 30 x 350 ampa
5. Argon arc welding equipment and accessories.
6. 50 P.S.I air compressor.
7. Various pneumatic tools such as chipping hammers, polishers, were brushes etc
8. Flexible shift grinder.
9. Gas welding set with accessories.
10. Universal radial drilling machine
11. S.S. & S.C lathe height of centre 1770 mm with accessories and attachments.
12. Bench drilling machine
13. Hacksaw machine
14. 5 ton chain pulley block and travelling trolley with chain
15. 5 ton hand operated gantry crave.

16. Vessel rotator stands.
17. Double ended bench grinder.
18. Work bench with vice.
19. Electrical drying oven.

FIXED CAPITAL

1. LAND & BUILDING		Rs.	7,25,000.00
2. PLANT & MACHINERY		Rs.	7,48,000.00
3. OTHER FIXED ASSETS		Rs.	1,70,000.00
	TOTAL	**Rs.**	**16,43,000.00**

LIST OF RAW MATERIALS

1. Stainless steel plates and sheets.
2. M.S. sheets rods etc.
3. Stainless steel rods and other sections
4. Purchased items (lumpsum)

TOTAL WORKING CAPITAL/MONTH

1. RAW MATERIAL		Rs.	1,28,200.00
2. SALARY & WAGES		Rs.	47,750.00
3. UTILITIES & OVERHEADS		Rs.	52,400.00
	TOTAL	**Rs.**	**2,28,350.00**

TOTAL CAPITAL INVESTMENT

TOTAL FIXED CAPITAL	Rs.	16,43,000.00
TOTAL WORKING CAPITAL FOR 3 MONTHS	Rs.	6,85,050.00
TOTAL	**Rs.**	**23,28,050.00**

TURN OVER/ANNUM

1. Storage tank (1000 litres) (Non insulated)
2. Ghee settling tank (1000 litre).
3. Ghee settling tank (3000 litre).
4. Double con mixer. (100 kg per hour
5. Micro pulverizer.
6. Evaporating pan. (Assorted sizes).
7. Butter churn 100 litres.

TOTAL Rs. 43,30,000.00

PROFIT = RECEIPTS - COST OF PRODUCTION
= 43,30,000.00 - 34,83,496.00
= 8,46,504.00

PROFIT SALES RATIO = Profit/Sales x 100 = 19.55 %

RATE OF RETURN = Operating profit/T.C.I x 100 = 36.36 %

BREAK EVEN POINT (B.E.P) = 59.12 %

14

DAIRY PRODUCTS & MILK PACKAGING IN POUCHES (GHEE, BUTTER, PANEER & CHEESE)

INTRODUCTION

Milk is an Important human food. It is palatable, easy to digest and highly nutritives. It contains proteins, fat, sugar, minerals and a liberal quantity of different kinds of vitamins.

In World milk production, India ranks next only to the United States of America and the U.S.S.R. But the milk produced in India is far from adequate for its vast population as the daily average consumption per head comes to even less than half of the optimum requirement of about 310 grams.

The importance of milk in human diet especially for children and expectant and nursing matters is vital. To meet the demand of the increasing population milk production in India has to be increased upto about 64 million tonnes by 2000 Ad. It is neither possible nor desirable to increase the cattle and buffalo population to achieve this target. This can only be achieved by stepping up milk production of our bovine population by cross breeding of cows and use of improved cows and buffaloes.

Unlike rich countries like the U.K. and the U.S. dairying in India is a subsidiary occupation of almost all the farmers. More than 60 per cent of the families involved in dairying belong to the small or marginal farmers or even agricultural labourers.

PROPERTIES

PROPERTIES OF GHEE

The colour of ghee prepared from cow milk is deep yellow , while that produced from buffalo milk is white when solid and colorless when liquid. The product from cow and buffalo has raw (bland) and slightly cooked (caramelized) flavour, depending on the quality of the raw material and of the method of production. The texture of product when no special conditions for cooling are adopted, is pasty.

PROPERTIES OF BUTTER

With reference to their effect on the body of butter, the properties of butter fat have to do briefly with its melting point. Other properties of butter fat that are of outstanding importance as related to butter are its colour, ability to absorb extranceous odours, vitamin properties to hydrolysis and oxidation leading to damaging flavour deterioration.

1. Melting point, of butter ranges from 31 to 36°C (87.8 to 96.8°F) and solidifying point from 19° to 24°C (66.2°F to 75.2°F).

2. The yellow colour of butter fat is principally due to the present of carotenes and anthophyll. These substances belong to a group of pigments. Called carotenoids which are derived from the green leaves of plants and from roots. Since green feeds are richest in carotenoids, the butter fat produced in spring and early summer is more deeply yellow than winter butter fat.

3. Butter has the property of readily absorbing odors from the atmosphere, or from other absorbing that liberate volatile substances. The pressure of foreign odors and flavors in butter depreciated its market value. It is therefore important to protect cream and butter against contact with objectionable odors from any source. This applies to the production and handling of the cream on the farm and in transit, and the transportation and the storage of butter in ware house, retail stores and the family refrigerators.

4. Prevention of the spoilage of butter fat is in an important factor in the control of the keeping quality of butter. Decomposition of butter fat many be brought about by hydrolysis or oxidation or both.

USES AND APPLICATION

GHEE, BUTTER :

1. In the production of recombined milk.
2. In ice cream manufacture.
3. As cooking fat.
4. In the confectionery industry.
5. In the manufacture of various types of fat spread.

Paneer :

It is consumed directly with or without sugar. It is used in hotel and restaurant for manufacturing Curry Pacoda, Sandwich and other things.

MANUFACTURING PROCESS

GHEE MANUFACTURING PROCESS

Direct Evaporation - This is a batch process and may be carried out either at atmospheric pressure or under vacuum . The former resembles the Indian method of ghee production. Butter is placed in a large open vat/pan which can be heated through a steam jacket or col. At first the heat is applied slowly till the butter melts. the temperature is then gradually raised, and the butter stirred, usually to 108-110°C(226-230°F). When all the moisture has evaporated, the residual butter fat is drained from the curd and filtered. the product obtained (butteroil) has somewhat darker colour when compared with other methods, it has also got a cooked flavour. Direct evaporation under vacuum does not yield much advantage either in the efficiency of production or in the quality of the finished product.

Decantation - This is also a batch process. The butter is melted and allowed to stand undisturbed for sufficient time, until it stratifies into three layers viz. top-scum, middle -fat and bottom serum. The fat layer is drawn off from the top and cooled. A clean separation cannot be obtained by this process and fat recovery is low . as such this method is uneconomic , especially when employed on a large scale.

Centrifugal separation followed by vacuum drying.- This is a more or less continuous method and yield high quality product. different varies of this process have been used in many countries for large-scale production of butter oil from butter. A typical method has been described below.

Details of manufacture - Butter (unsalted) is dumped in the butter melter, which is a vertical jacketed stainless steel cylindrical tank fitted with an agitator (provided with reduction gear to work on variable speeds) . If the butter is very cold and hard, it should be cut into small piece before heating. Then a steam inlet to the jacket is opened and the agitator run at low speed.

The tipping tank, which is jacketed at the bottom, is filled with clean water and heated to 77-79°C(170-174°F) by opening the steam inlet of the jacket. the centrifugal oil separator is then started and when it has attained full speed, the hot water from the tipping tank is run into it. When the water has completely run out, the discharge valve of the butter melter is gradually opened to allow the melt to enter into the oil separator. The rate of flow of the of the melt is so regulated as to avoid overflow. The melt is now separated into oil and serum.

The oil flows into the float-controlled balance tank and thence into the vacuum pan due to suction. Here it is dehydrated at 56-63°C (133-145°F) under a vacuum of 57-62 cm. of mercury. AT the end of the operation, the vacuum is broken and butteroil allowed to flow by gravity into he receiving kettle for subsequent cooling , packaging and storage at room temperature.

d. Directly from cream by de-emulsification and centrifugal separation - The process utilizes the principle of de-emulsification of cream used in various continuous butter-making processes. De-emulsified fat may then be melted and clarified by centrifuging and vacuum heating. However, the direct production of anhydrous milk fat from cream has yet to achieve significant commercial application.

COOLING

This is an important aspect. Butteroil should be cooled and crystallized under careful control, so as to form a large number of fine crystals. The desired result may be obtained by rapidly super-cooling (to 13-18°C) and stirring the mass during forced crystallization (by adding 5-15 percent of finely crystalline fat from a previous batch(; this yields a smooth homogeneous mass which does not separate into solid and liquid layers on standing.

PACKAGING.

Packaging. - When packaging butteroil, care should be taken to exclude oxygen. Thus, it is important to avoid re-aeration of the product as it comes out of the vacuum dehydrator in a partially or a completely de-aerated form. Care should also be taken to leave a minimum of air in the head-space of the container, or to replace the air in the head-space with an inert gas. In tropical countries, allowance must be made for expansion of the product indeciding upon the size of the container to use. While filling, the fat should run into the bottom of the container in such a way as to avoid contact with the air. Tin cans are satisfactory for both bulk and retail packaging. Wooden casks and tubs with suitable liners (butter-paper or plastic film) may be used. Cardboard containers, waxed or plastic coated,can also serve the purpose.

BUTTER MANUFACTURE PROCESS

Since butter is made primarily under the factory system, it is intended briefly to discuss the process involved in the manufacture of this product in the typical butter factory. The process involves, the following operation.

1. Separations of milk.
2. Selection of cream.
3. Neutralization of cream.
4. Pasteurization of cream.
5. Cream ripening
6. Churning.
7. Packing and printing, and
8. Marketing.

1. The ancient practice of churning milk for the production of butter of butter still is followed in limited sections. Cream rather than milk is commonly churned for reasons of economy and efficiency. A small separator(centrifugal type run by power) is used to separate cream from the skimmed milk, which is sold back to farmer or to the local market.

2. Receiving the milk or cream involves weighing sampling, testing the samples for payment. and grading. Crading is necessary to maintain quality. Were cream is received, it can be grouped occurring to the quality. so that different grands of butter can be produced. The selections of cream is usually based on flavour, odour, acidity and appearance.

The usual fat content for butter making is 32-40 % obtained by subjecting the milk to the action of powder centrifugal separators. Clarifying (the removal of leukocytes, some bacteria, and other debris) and separations the accomplished jointly large foreign bodies, are removed from cream by filtration or straining.

3. The term "neutralization" is applied to the practice of adjusting the acidity of cream. The purposes of neutralization are to

a. Improve flavour.

b. Prevent fat losses that result when pasteurized high acid cream and churned, and

c. Improve keeping quality.

Neutralization is in the reduction of acidity in cream to about 0.12-0.15% (pH 6.8-7.0) by addition of alkaline salts like calcium oxide, cal. hydroxide calcium carbonate, magnesium oxide. etc. Fresh sweet cream separated in the plant requires no neutralization where as farm separated cream usually goad.

4. Pasteurization of the cream, as with the market milk, renders the product safe fro a public health stand point. and improves it keeping quality the as standard requires not less than 165°F. for 30 minutes or 185°F for 15 sec. for proper pasteurization. A temperature of 180-185°(82.2 to 85.0°C) is most common. The simplest design of flash pasteurized for cream in a hollow drum of flash pasteurized for cream in a shallow drum with a double wall. Objectional flavours and odours can be removed from cream by using a vacuum chamber in conjunction with pasteurization.

5. The cream is cooled immediately after pasteurization. Much butter is made without the use of starter cultures. As used in the butter industry, starter is a culture of lactic acid producing bacteria used alone or in combination of with citric acid fermenting bacteria. These are added prior to churning.

6. Cream ripening refers to the fermentation of cream intended for butter manufacture. following pasteurization the cream is cooled to 68° to 72°F and added 5-10% of the starter. By holding the cream at 70°F (21.1°C) for several hours, a fermentation takes place. A characteristic flavour and aroma will be imparted to be cream to be carried into the resulting butter.

7. The natural colour of butter varies under different conditions from a yellowish white to a yellow. The market demand that butter be uniform in colour. It is therefore standard practice to added edible colours to cream before churning. usually based on flavour, odour, acidity and appearance.

The use fat content for butter making in 32-40% obtained by subjecting the milk to the action of powder centrifugal separators. Clarifying (the removal of leucocytest, some bacteria, and other debris) and separations the accomplished jointly. Large foreign bodies, are removed from cream by filtration or straining.

PANEER MANUFACTURING PROCESS :

Paneer is primarily acid coagulated milk solid used as an ingredient in cooking of vegetables in Northern India. Mostly, buffalo milk is used for the production of paneer. The best quality product is made from milk of 6.0% fat content. Packed paneer could be stored for 3 days without any loss of freshness when refrigerated.

Step in Processing:

1) Standard Buffalo milk 6.0%	2) Heated to 82PToPTC/5 min	3) Cooled to 70°C
6) Milk solids filled in hoops.	5) Whey drained out.	4) Coagulated by 1% citric acid.
7) Pressed by weight.	8) Weight removed.	9) Cut into big pieces.
12) Packed into desired weight and stored at 4-6°C.	11) Chilled water drained out.	10) Dipped in chilled water for 1-2 hrs. at 4-6°C.

Composition :

The average composition of paneer may be fat-26% moisture 55% and T.S. 45%.

FLOW SHEET FOR MANUFACTURE OF BUTTER FROM MILK

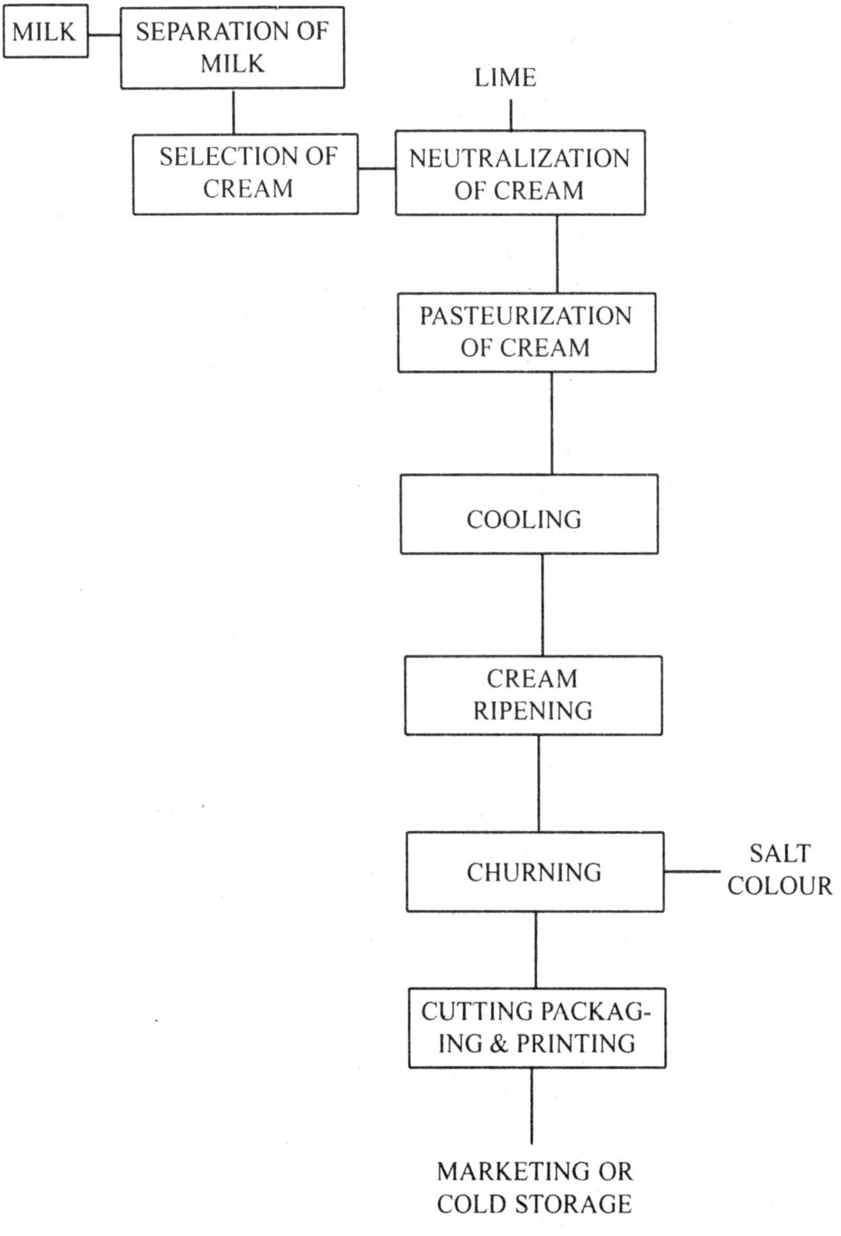

FLOW DIAGRAM FOR GHEE

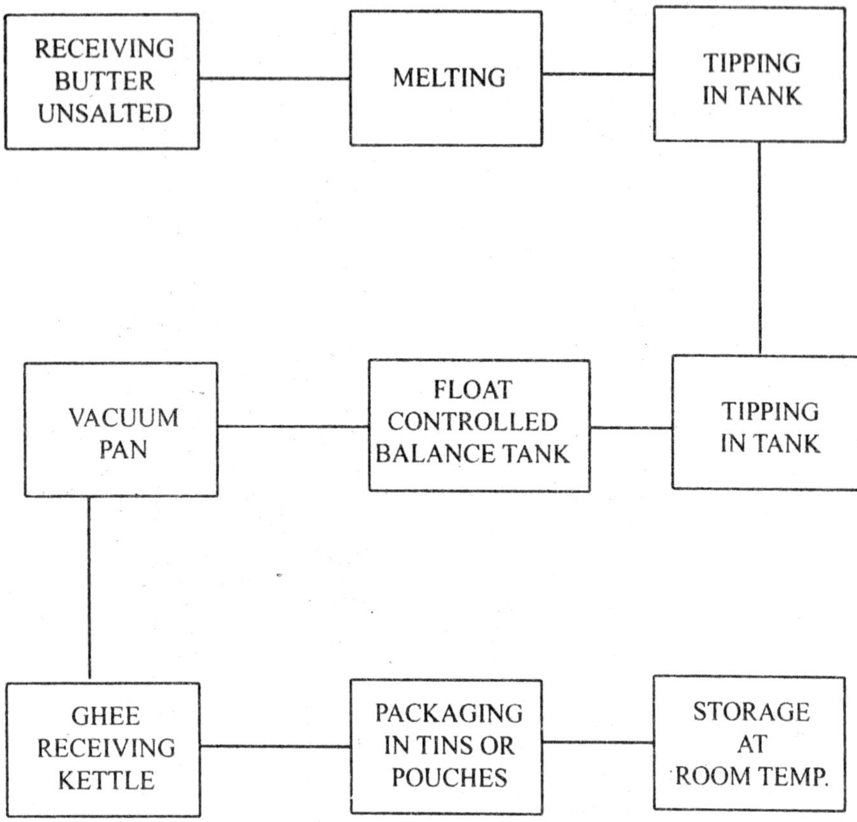

SUPPLIERS OF COMPLETE PLANT & MACHINERY

Bansal Technocrats
1/1431/18, Sharda Nagar,
Saharanpur - 247 001 (U.P).
Ph.: 0132-27914

Products: Milk Reception, Storage and Transportation Tanks, Ghee Making Equipments (Butter Melting Vats, Prestatification Tank, Ghee Boiler, Ghee Settling Tank, Ghee Storage Tank etc.), Paneer and Khova Making Equipments, Cream Storage and Ripening Tanks, CIP Unit (Manual and Automatic), Milk Pumps, SS Pneumatically operated valves, SS pipe fittings and control panels etc.

PLASTIC MILK CANS

Ashish Engineers
857, Somwar Peth,
Tale Gaon, Dabhade,
Dist. Pune - 410 506 (M.S).
Ph.: 02114-2615, 2521

MILK FAT TESTER

Electronic Milk Fat Tester
B-815, Phase-1, Badli Ind. Estate
Delhi - 110 042.

DAIRY EQUIPMENTS

Bansal Technocrats
1/1431/18, Sharda Nagar,
Saharanpur - 247 001 (U.P).
Ph.: 0132-27914

Products: Milk Reception, Storage and Transportaion Tanks, Ghee Making Equipments (Butter Melting Vats, Prestatification Tank, Ghee Boiler, Ghee Settling Tank, Ghee Storage Tank etc.), Paneer and Khova Making Equipments, Cream Storage and Repening Tanks, CIP Unit (Manual and Automatic), Milk Pumps, SS Pneumatically operated valves, SS pipe fittings and control panels etc.

Dairy Udyog
229-A/230-A
Ghatkopar Ind. Estate
Block-C, L.B.S. Marg
Ghatkopar, Mumbai - 400 086.
Ph.: 5171636/5170938

Goodwell Industries
New Colony, Opp. Railway Good Sheds
Faridabad (Haryana)
Ph.: 8123698

Malahar Industrial Associates
834, Mini Nagar, Rawal Pada
Dahisar (E) Mumbai - 400 068.
Ph.: 8114536

Sangli Dairy Farms
459/3, Maruti Road,
Sangli - 416 416 (M.S)
Ph.: 75101

Hind Protective Coatings Limited
9/4, Sarvpriya Vihar,
New Delhi - 110 016.

Factory:
55,61,62, Rozka Meo Industrial Area
Sohna, Dist. Gurgaon, Haryana
Pin - 122 103.
Ph.: 6868850

BOILER

Indcon Boilers Limited
D-170, Okhla Ind. Area,
Phase-1, New Delhi - 110 020
Ph.: 6811441/442

PACKAGING MACHINERIES

Nichrome International
46, Dr. B.R. Ambedkar Road
Near Sangam Bridge
Pune - 411 001 (M.S)
Ph.: 0212-622137/622259
Rado Packaging Machines Pvt. Ltd.
C-377, Sector-10
Noida - 201 301 (U.P)
Ph.: 8-555190, 8-533341
Fax: 8-525699

Products: Form Fill and Seal Machines

Samarpan Fabricators Limited
Plot A-182/A-183, Road 16/Z
Wagle Ind. Estate,
Thane - 400 604 (M.S)
Ph.: 5321842, 5320373, 5320029
Fax: 91-22-5320033

Products: Form Fill Seal Machine, Flexible Laminated Films, Blister Packaging Machines (Auto and Semi-auto), Thermo Forming Machines, Shrink Wrapping Machines, Strip Packing Machines etc.

POUCHES (PRINTED/LAMINATED)

Flex Industries Limited
A-107/108, Sector - IV,
Noida - 201 301 (U.P)
Ph.: 85-22558

COMPLETE PLANT SUPPLIER

Mojj Engineering Systems Pvt. Ltd.
81-B/15, M.I.D.C., Bhosari
Pune - 411 026
Ph.: 91-212-790360
Fax: 91-212-792836

Delhi Office:

G-4, South Extension Part II,
New Delhi - 110 049.
Ph.: 011-6426632
Fax: 011-6451870

SUPPLIERS OF RAW MATERIAL

CORRUGATED BOXES

A.B. Packaging
RZ-34F/2B, Main Sagarpur
Gali No. 4, Near DESU Sub Station
New Delhi - 110 046
Ph.: 5593683/5618656

Arihant Print 'O' Pack Pvt. Ltd.
G-969, Ind. Area, Phase -III,
Bhiwadi - 301 019 (Rajasthan)
Ph.: 01493-20322, 20922
Delhi Ph.: 7247362
Fax: 91-11-7427440

HYDROCHLORIC ACID

Gulati Acids and Chemicals
37/1, Old Nazafgarh Road,
Near Haryana Roadways Workshop
Gurgaon (Haryana)
Tel./Fax: 8-329729

Shahan Shah Chemicals
Delhi Rohtak Road
Ismaila, M.I.E
Bahadurgarh - 124 507, Haryana
Tel./Fax: 311840/311844

ALUMINIUM CANS

Khambete Kothari
Cans and Allied Products Pvt. Ltd.
Jalgaon - 425 003 (M.S)
Ph.: 24750

PLANT ECONOMICS

Rated Plant capacity = 1390.00 KG/day
PANEER, GHEE, BUTTER & CASEIN

LAND & BUILDING Rs. 34,75,000.00
(Land Area Required 1500 Sq.mts.)

LIST OF PLANT & MACHINERY

1. Centrifuge or Cream separator with accessories
2. Pasteuriser with cooling arrangements and accessories (plate heat exchanger)
3. Refrigeration system consists of air Compressor, refrigerator and circulating tank.
4. Filter ordinary.
5. Milk reception tank (Stainless steel) with arrangements.
6. Water Softener unit.
7. Steam boiler
8. Miscellaneous equipments as laboratory testing equipments.
9. Automatic Pouch filling & sealing machine.
10. Vacuum Pan Evaporator
11. Vertical Storage Tank with stirrer (S.S)
12. Vertical storage tanks (SS)
13. Neutralization tank (SS)
14. Pasteurization vessel (SS)
15. Fermenting tank (SS) with heating cooling arrangements.
16. Churner (SS)
17. Ghee receiving kettle
18. Pipe fitting, pumps, motor, valve and other miscellaneous machinery.
19. Screw Press.
20. Oscillating Granulator.
21. Tray Dryer.
22. Grinding Machine.

FIXED CAPITAL

1. LAND & BUILDING	Rs.	34,75,000.00
2. PLANT & MACHINERY	Rs.	24,11,000.00
3. OTHER FIXED ASSETS	Rs.	5,05,000.00
TOTAL	**Rs.**	**63,91,000.00**

LIST OF RAW MATERIALS

1. Milk
2. Chemicals for butter paneer.
3. Hydrochloric Acid
4. Cans, Polyethene, packets, Corrugated boxes etc.

TOTAL WORKING CAPITAL/MONTH

1. RAW MATERIAL	Rs.	22,70,400.00
2. SALARY & WAGES	Rs.	2,22,488.00
3. UTILITIES & OVERHEADS	Rs.	2,14,000.00
TOTAL	**Rs.**	**27,06,888.00**

TOTAL CAPITAL INVESTMENT

TOTAL FIXED CAPITAL	Rs.	63,91,000.00
TOTAL WORKING CAPITAL FOR 3 MONTHS	Rs.	81,20,664.00
TOTAL	**Rs.**	**1,45,11,664.00**

TURN OVER/ANNUM

1. Paneer 60000 Kgs.
2. Butter 150000 Kgs
3. Ghee 186000 Kgs
4. Casein 21000 Kgs.
5. Milk 600000 litres in pouches

TOTAL Rs. 4,18,50,000.00

PROFIT = RECEIPTS - COST OF PRODUCTION
= 4,18,50,000.00 - 3,61,85,297.08
= 56,64,702.92

PROFIT SALES RATIO = Profit / Sales x 100 = 13.54 %

RATE OF RETURN = Operating profit / T.C.I x 100 = 39.04 %

BREAK EVEN POINT (B.E.P) = 51.15 %

15

DAIRY FARM AND DAIRY (MILK) PRODUCTS
(PASTEURIZED MILK,BUTTER,GHEE & PANEER)

INTRODUCTION

A dairy is a place for handling milk and milk products. Technology refers to the application of scientific knowledge for practical purposes. Dairy technology has been defined as that branch of dairy science which deals with the processing of milk and the manufacture of milk products on an industrial scale. In developed dairying countries such as the U.S.A., the year 1850 is seen as the dwiding line between form and factory scale production. Various factors contributed to this change in these countries, viz concentration of population in cities where jobs were plentiful, rapid industrialization, improvement of transportation facilities, development of machines etc, whereas the rural areas were identified for milk production, the urban centers were selected for the location of milk processing plants and product manufacturing factories.

These plants and factors were rapidly expanded and modernized with improved machinery and equipment to secure the various advantages of large scale production. This heralded the advent of dairy technology in these countries.

USES AND APPLICATION

MILK

1. Milk is used as a food.
2. Used as a complete food for infants.
3. It is used to prepare curd, butter, ghee,cream and ice cream etc.
4. Milk is used in all homes.
5. It is used in hotels and restaurants as milk food preparation and in the preparation of tea or coffee.

GHEE AND BUTTER:

1. In the production of recombined milk.
2. In Ice cream manufacture.
3. As cooking fat.
4. In the confectionery industry
5. In the manufacture of various types of fat spread.

PANEER:

1. Paneer can be either directly consumed with sugar.
2. Paneer can be used for manufacturing of curry of different varieties.
3. Other sweet dishes can also be prepared from paneer.
4. Paneer is also used to prepare paneer pulao etc.

MANUFACTURING PROCESS

The manufacturing process for Dairy milk is started with the milking cows by hand (at small scale) & milking cows by machine (at large scale).

The process is given here with :-

MILKING COWS BY HAND

The profitable operation of a dairy herd depends in a large part upon how well you milk your cows. You can do everything else carefully and well, but if you do not milk your cows properly, you can never be successful in dairying. Poor milking habits cause low production, mastitis, & poor quality milk.

An important part of milking cows is to produce the cleanest possible milk. Milk must be low in sediment.

COOLING & STORING MILK

The careless handling of milk between milking & delivering to the plant can cause high bacteria counts to develop in the milk thus a mechanical cooler is employed for the purpose. Whole of the milk should be stored at 50°F to prevent spoilage. Storage Tanks made of stainless steel are employed for storing the raw milk.

FILTRATION :

The cold raw milk is filtered.

STANDARDIZATION:

Milk is Standardized according to B.I.S Specification on according to requirements by wholesaler.

HOMOGENIZATION:

Filtered milk is fed into homogenizer. Homogenization is the process by which the milk is emulsified and are further divided to produce a more stable emulsion that will not separate on standing.

CLARIFICATION:

The milk is passed through a clarifier as it leaves the homogenizer. Cold milk clarification is preferred to hot milk.

PASTEURIZATION:

In this process, the clarified milk is fed to pasteurizer and heated to the required temperature & held there during the holding period (usually at 145°F & for at least 30 minutes).

REFRIGERATION OR FREEZING SYSTEM

After the complete processing of milk, it is to be stored in a cold upto chilling condition so that no unwanted micro-organisms/pathogenic organism can be developed in the processed milk. It is stored until delivered for distribution i.e. for packing in Cans or pouches.

PACKING:

There are two methods adopted for milk packaging. Firstly packed or stored in aluminium milk cans for distribution. Secondly milk packed in plastic pouches of capacity 1/2 kg, 1 kg, & 2 kgs packs.

Milk is stored in milk cans. There will no difficulty. It is traditional. But, in pouches filling of milk is to be performed with a great care & skilled operator is to be employed for this purpose. Automatic pouch making, milk filling & pouch sealing machine is available with printing provision.

Milk filled & sealed in pouches is now ready for dispatch & distribution for marketing.

MANUFACTURE, PACKAGING AND STORAGE OF PASTEURIZED MILK PROCESS FLOW DIAGRAM

RECEIVING MILK
(GRADING, SAMPLING, WEIGHING, TESTING)

|

PRE-HEATING (35-40°C)

|

FILTRATION/CLARIFICATION

|

COOLING AND STORAGE (5°C OR BELOW)

|

STANDARDIZATION

|

PASTEURIZATION (63°C/30 MTS OR 72°C /15SEC)

|

HOMOGENIZATION (2500 PSI)

|

BOTTLING/PACKAGING

|

STORAGE (5°C OR BELOW)

MANUFACTURE OF BUTTER

DEFINITION:

Butter may be defined as a fat concentrate which is obtained by churning cream, gathering the fat into a compact mass and then working it.

According to the PFA, Rules (1976) table (creamery) butter is the product obtained from cow or buffalo milk or a combination thereof, or from cream or curd obtained from cow or buffalo milk or a combination thereof, with or without the addition of common salt and carotene as colouring matter. It should be free from other animal fats, wax and mineral oils, vegetable oils and fats. No preservative except common salt and no colouring matter except annattor or carotene may be added. It must contain not less than 80 per cent by weight of milk fat, not more than 1.5 per cent by weight of curd and not more than 3 per cent by weight of of common slat. Diacetyl may be added as a flavouring agent but, if so used, the total diacetyl common must no exceed 5 ppm. Calcium hydroxide, sodium bicarbonate, sodium carbonate, sodium polyphosphates may be added, but must not exceed the weight of butter as a whole by more than 0.2 per cent.

COMPOSITION:

According to the PFA Rules (1976), table creamery butter should contain not less than 80 per cent fat, not more than 1.5 per cent curd and not more than 3.0 per cent common salt. The typical composition of Indian butter has been given in Table 4.1

Table 4.1

COMPOSITION OF INDIAN BUTTER

Constituent	Percentage
Butter fat	80.2
Moisture	16.3
Salt	2.5
Curd	1.0

Since butter is made primarily under the factory system. It is intended briefly to discuss the process involved in the manufacture of this product in the typical butter factory. The process involves, the following operation.

1. Separations of milk.
2. Selection of cream.

3. Neutralization of cream.
4. Pasteurization of cream.
5. Cream ripening
6. Churning.
7. Packing and printing, and
8. Marketing.

GHEE MANUFACTURING PROCESS

Direct Evaporation. This is a batch process and may be carried out either at atmospheric pressure or under vacuum. The former resembles the Indian method of ghee production. Butter is placed in a large open vat/pan which can be heated through a steam jacket or col. At first the heat is applied slowly till the butter melts. The temperature is then gradually raised, and the butter stirred, usually to 108-110°C (226-230°F). When all the moisture has evaporated, the residual butter fat is drained from the curd and filtered. The product obtained 9(butteroil)) has somewhat darker colour when compared with other methods. It has also got a cooked flavour. Direct evaporation under vacuum does not yield much advantage either in the efficiency of production or in the quality of the finished product.

Decantation- This is also a batch process. The butter is melted and allowed to stand undisturbed for sufficient time, until it stratified into three layers viz. top-scum, middle-fat and bottom- scum. The fat layer is drawn off from the top and cooled. A clean separation cannot be obtained by this process and fat recovery is low. As such this method is uneconomic specially when employed on a large scale.

Centrifugal Separation followed by Vacuum Drying- This is a more or less continuous method and yield high quality product. Different varies of this process have been used in many countries for large-scale production of butter oil from butter. A typical method has been described below.

Details of manufacture- Butter (unsalted) is dumped in the butter melter, which is a vertical jacketed stainless steel cylindrical tank fitted with an agitator (provided with reduction gear to work on variable speeds). If the butter is very cold and hard, it should be cut into small pieces before heating. Then a steam inlet to the jacket is opened and the agitator run at low speed.

The tipping tank, which is jacketed at the bottom, is filled with clean water and heated to 77-79°C (170-174°F) by opening the steam inlet of the jacket. The centrifugal oil separator is then started and when it has attained full speed, the hot water from the tipping tank is run into it. When the water has completely run out, the discharge valve of the butter melter is gradually opened to allow the melt to enter into the oils separator. The rate of flow of the melt is so regulated as to avoid overflow. The melt is now separated into oil and serum.

The oil flows into the float-controlled balance tank and then into the vacuum pan due to suction. Here it is dehydrated at 56-63° (133-145°F) under a vacuum of 57-62 cm. of mercury. At the end of the operation, the vacuum is broken and butteroil allowed to flow by gravity into the receiving kettle for subsequent cooling, packaging and storage at room temperature.

PACKAGING

PACKAGING. - When packaging butteroil, care should be taken to exclude oxygen. Thus, it is important to avoid re-aeration of the product as it comes out of the vacuum dehydrator in a partially or a completely de-aerated form. Care should also be taken to leave a minimum of air in the head-space with an gas.

SUPPLIERS OF PLANTS & MACHINERIES

Bansal Technocrats
1/1431/18, Sharda Nagar,
Saharanpur - 247 001 (U.P).
Ph.: 0132-27914

Products: Milk Reception, Storage and Transportation Tanks, Ghee Making Equipments (Butter Melting Vats, Prestatification Tank, Ghee Boiler, Ghee Settling Tank, Ghee Storage Tank etc.), Paneer and Khova Making Equipments, Cream Storage and Repening Tanks, CIP Unit (Manual and Automatic), Milk Pumps, SS Pneumatically operated valves, SS pipe fittings and control panels etc.

Dairy Equipments

Bansal Technocrats
1/1431/18, Sharda Nagar,
Saharanpur - 247 001 (U.P).
Ph.: 0132-27914

Products: Milk Reception, Storage and Transportation Tanks, Ghee Making Equipments (Butter Melting Vats, Prestatification Tank, Ghee Boiler, Ghee Settling Tank, Ghee Storage Tank etc.), Paneer and Khova Making Equipments,

Cream Storage and Repening Tanks, CIP Unit (Manual and Automatic), Milk Pumps, SS Pneumatically operated valves, SS pipe fittings and control panels etc.

HMT Ltd.,
Sree Nidhi Chambers
Senapati Bapat Marg
Pune - 4111016
Ph.: 350040
Fax: (0212) 358565
Telex: 0145-7262

Factory:
H-2, MIDC, Chikalthana
Aurangabad - 10

Products: Pasteuriser, Centrifugal Pump, Butter Making Machine, Butterfly Valves, Plate Heat Exchangers, Oil Purification & Clarification System, Ice Cream Machinery & Turnkey Projects of small & big capacity Dairy.

Packaging Machineries

Nichrome International
46, Dr. B.R. Ambedkar Road
Near Sangam Bridge
Pune - 411 001 (M.S)
Ph.: 0212-622137/622259

Rado Packaging Machines Pvt. Ltd.
C-377, Sector-10
Noida - 201 301 (U.P)
Ph.: 8-555190, 8-533341
Fax: 8-525699

Products: Form Fill and Seal Machines

POUCHES (PRINTED/LAMINATED)

Flex Industries Limited
A-107/108, Sector - IV,
Noida - 201 301 (U.P)
Ph.: 85-22558

CANS AND CAN WASHING SYSTEM ALUMINIUM SEAMLESS

1. M/s. Mulakhraj & Co.,
   204 Azad Market,
   Delhi - 110 006.

2. M/s. Agricultural Supplements and Brass Utensils,
   Court Road,
   Jagadhri - 145 003.

ALUMINIUM CANS

Khambete Kothari
Cans and Allied Products Pvt. Ltd.
Jalgaon - 425 003 (M.S)
Ph.: 24750

LABORATORY EQUIPMENT:-

1. M/s. Bharat Laboratory (Regd),
   8, Amrit Kaur Market,
   Opp. New Delhi Railway Station,
   P.B. No. 180,
   New Delhi - 110 001.

MILK RECEPTION TANKS:-

M/s. Filtron India,
'Gokul' Feruguson Road,
Pune - 411 005.

SUPPLIERS OF POUCHES FILLING & SEALING MACHINES

1. M/s. Somani International corpn,
   Maker Chambers,
   V. Nariman Point,
   Mumbai-400 021.
   (For getting imported machine only)

COMPLETE PLANT SUPPLIERS

Mojj Engineering Systems Pvt. Ltd.
81-B/15, M.I.D.C., Bhosari
Pune - 411 026
Ph.: 91-212-790360
Fax: 91-212-792836

Delhi Office:
G-4, South Extension Part II,
New Delhi - 110 049.
Ph.: 011-6426632
Fax: 011-6451870

Products: Complete Turnkey Basis Plants for Dairy Industry i.e. Milk Powder Plant, Cheese Plants, Casein Plants etc.

SUPPLIERS OF RAW MATERIALS

CATTLE FEED & GREEN FEED:

LOCAL DEALERS.

The Quality Green Fodder can be grown in rest of the uncovered areas

RAW MATERIAL FOR POUCHES

M/s. Prem Plastic Industries,
9988-B/1, Sarai Rohilla,
New Rohtak Road,
New Delhi - 110 005.

M/s. Chemiplast Industries,
55, Industrial Area,
Sector-1, Parwanoo,
Distt. Solan (HP).

FOREIGN MACHINERY SUPPLIER ADDRESSES

Farm Dairy Equipment:-

1. Etscheid Anlagen GmbH.
   Industrigelande,
   5466, Neustadt/Wied (Fernthal)

PLANT ECONOMICS

Rated Plant capacity = 2000.00 LTR/day
DAIRY FARMING & DAIRY PRODUCTS

LAND & BUILDING (Land Area Required 3 acres)	Rs.	30,80,000.00

LIST OF PLANT & MACHINERY

1. Milk storage tank (S.S)
2. Centrifuge or cream separator with accessories
3. Pasteuriser with cooling arrangements and accessories (plate heat exchanger)
4. Refrigeration system consists of air compressor,refrigerator and circulating tank.
5. Filter ordinary (S. S. body)
6. Milk reception tank (Aluminium with pump arrangement inlet and outlet
7. Water softener
8. Steam boiler
9. Miscellaneous equipments as fat testing, bacteriological testing, pH testing etc.
10. Instrumentation for process control equipments pumps, valves and others
11. Homogenizer
12. Deaerator
13. Pouch Weighing, filling and sealing machine (automatic type)
14. Automatic milking machine with compressor system
15. Water storage tank (sintex type)
16. Aluminium Cans for milk

FIXED CAPITAL

1. LAND & BUILDING	Rs.	30,80,000.00
2. PLANT & MACHINERY	Rs.	17,15,000.00
3. OTHER FIXED ASSETS	Rs.	35,95,000.00
TOTAL	**Rs.**	**83,90,000.00**

LIST OF RAW MATERIALS

1. Grass, Kutti, Cattle feed, and other average
2. Other Laboratory chemicals
3. Printed Pouches (Polyethene) for ghee, milk and butter packaging - material and others
4. Medicines.

TOTAL WORKING CAPITAL/MONTH

1.	RAW MATERIAL	Rs.	3,10,000.00
2.	SALARY & WAGES	Rs.	64,750.00
3.	UTILITIES & OVERHEADS	Rs.	43,400.00
	TOTAL	**Rs.**	**4,18,150.00**

TOTAL CAPITAL INVESTMENT

TOTAL FIXED CAPITAL	Rs.	83,90,000.00
TOTAL WORKING CAPITAL FOR 1 MONTH	Rs.	4,18,150.00
TOTAL	**Rs.**	**88,08,150.00**

TURN OVER/ANNUM

1. By sale of 10,800 Kgs. of Ghee
2. By sale of 54,000 Kgs. of Butter
3. By sale of 28,800 Kgs. Paneer
4. By sale of 5,40,000 Lits. Milk in

TOTAL Rs. 1,00,80,000.00

PROFIT = RECEIPTS - COST OF PRODUCTION
= 1,00,80,000.00 - 72,28,567.00
= 28,51,433.00

PROFIT SALES RATIO = Profit/Sales x 100 = 28.29 %

RATE OF RETURN = Operating profit/T.C.I x 100 = 32.37 %

BREAK EVEN POINT (B.E.P) = 48.91 %

16

FLAVOURED MILK (PASTEURIZATION OF MILK)

INTRODUCTION

The freezing of fluid milk and concentrated milk is not being practical on any large commercial scale, but since there is a growing demand for this product, the industry should develop into a sizable one. At the present time, frozen milk is of value only in those places where fresh milk is scarce, expensive or not available. There has long been a demand for milk that would retain its natural flavour on shipboard during long voyages; like wise in the tropical countries where cows are few and good milk is very scarce.

Web and Hall in 1935 concluded that fresh milk could be pasteurized, condensed to one third its weight, canned and frozen without any detrimental effect to the body and flavour of the product. A good quality milk resulted when the product was held frozen and then reconstituted within a four week period. Miller in 1938 reported that resident of the canal zone had been using frozen milk supplied to them from washington by the Government. This product was concentrated prof to freezing and storage. When thawed, the same amount of water as originally removed was added to the product and a natural flavoured whole milk was obtained. Corley and Doan in 1940 studied various treatments of concentrated milk by Roadhouse and Henderson in 1940 dealt with the quick freezing of whole milk. All investigators reported success and advocated the freezing of milk as a treatment that has possibilities in the preservation of milk for future use after a period of low temperature storage.

Resident of the temperature and northern zones are familiar with the changed appearance of milk that has been foreign while on the back door stop during periods of below-freezing atmosphere temperatures. During this slow freezing, the solid constituents become concentrated in the unfrozen portion while the frozen portion contains most of the water and there is considerable separation of the fat emulsion. In studying these physical changes, Doan and feather man in 1937 showed that the concentration of milk solids in milk before freezing aided in stabilizing the fat emulsion and that a concentration of three to one gave satisfactory results. They also showed be homogenized prior to freezing. If the milk is properly homogenized, either before or after the evaporation, fat separation should not occur. Homogenization not only reduced the oiling off tendencies but also appeared to aid in preventing tallowy flavour.

Pasteurization not only retards the rate of thickening of concentrated frozen milk during storage, but also retards the development of tallowy, flavours. However, if the milk is contaminated with copper, it is impossible to avoid a tallowy flavour regardless of any treatment to regard, its development. Stainless steel or glass lined equipment is necessary for both the pasteurizing and concentrating operations in order to pressure the natural flavour of the milk. Enamel lined tin cans should be used for the finished product.

Essentially, the treatment of milk for freezing, is the same as that for canned evaporated milk, except for the last step in the process, in that the milk to be frozen is not sterilized by heat. The canned product may be frozen by almost any method, the simplest and commonest being to stack the cans in a cold storage room at 0°F or below.

Coal field (anon 1955) reports having a frozen milk concentrate which when diluted with two parts of water and stirred tastes exactly like regular bottled milk. He pasteurized milk at 180°F fr. 16 seconds, homogenized at 2000 lbs. pressure and then condone sed, using a partial vacuum, until two thirds of the water had been removed. He then pasteurized and homogenized the concentrated milk (using the same temperature, time and pressure), poured it into cans, sealed, the froze. Coal field reported that this second heating solved the problem of destablization of the protein. Other investigation such high temperature, although they used a longer time.

For instance Doan (1948) recommended a heat treatment at not over 170°F. For 15 min in order to obtain maximum protein stability web (1951) reported that lower stability would result at pasteurization greater than 155°F. For 30 min or 170°F, for one minute.

The acceptance of frozen concentrated milk by consumers will probably depend on three things, all three important. First, the quality must be substantially equivalent to the fluid milk now available. This point can doubt less be met but the frozen product can never the better than the fluid and, if inadvertently held too long, might be inferior.

The dating of packages, giving the time limit for holding would seem to be necessary. Secondary, a product must be relatively convent to use. In this respect, frozen milk would never equal fluid milk which requires no preparation. However, it might enjoy some popularity because of its space saving characteristics, its longer keeping period and the fact that it can be reconstituent to various degree for different purposes.

USES

The purposes of pasteurization of milk are two fold.

1. To make milk safe for human consumption by destroying all bacteria that may be harmful to health (public health aspect).

2. To improve the keeping quality of milk and milk products (product aspects).

Pasteurization of milk may then be defined, in a lay language, as the process of heating milk and other fluid milk products to pre-determined temperature for a period of time sufficient to render the product free of undesirable enzymes and disease-producing micro-organisms.

Further, flavours are added to the milk to give it better tests, so that its sales increase.

FLAVOURING ESSENCE

Strawberry Essence:-

Straw berries, fresh	-	16 ounces,
Angelica (california)	-	6 fluid ounces
Brandy (california)	-	6 ounces
Alcohol	-	8 ounces
Water	-	Q.S.

Mash the berries to a pulp in a mortar or bowl, and transfer to a flask, along with the Angelica, brandy, alcohol and about 8 ounces of water, let macerate over night then distill off until 32 ounces have passed over. Color strawberry red. The addition of a little essence of vanilla and a pint of lemon improves this essence.

Vanilla Essence

Vanilla beans chopped fine	-	30 ports
Potassium Carbonate	-	1 ports
Boiling water	-	1,450 ports
Alcohol	-	450 ports
Essence of musk	-	1 port

Dissolve the potassium carbonate in the boiling water, add the vanilla, cover the vessel, and let stand in a moderately warn place until cold. Transfer to a wide mouthed Jar, add the Alcohol, Cork, and let macerate for 15 days; than decant the clear essence and filter the remainder. Mix the two liquid and add the essence of musk.

PROCESS OF MANUFACTURE

Treatment Before pasteurization:-

Adequate storage capacity for raw milk is necessary for efficient operation of a plant. Many plants hold the current days receipts in storage tank at 40°F or below, so that once the next days operation has been started no shot downs will be necessary. Delays during the pasteurization process result in bum on of milk in contact with heating surfaces, as well as waste of labour, heat-and refrigeration.

The process steps usually taken before pasteurization are:-

1. Filtering or clarifying,
2. Separating,
3. Standardizing,
4. Vitaminizing,
5. Homogenizing.

1. Filtering or Clarifying:-

The process of filtering is achieved by running raw milk through a cloth filter or filter pad. For cold filtration (50°F or below) the filter is placed in the line loading from the receiving room or the holding tank to the pasteurizing units. For warm filtration (110°F or above) filter is placed between the generation and the final heater. Where large volumes of milk are received it pays to have two filters arranged in parallel order so that the flow or milk can be diverted through the second filter while the first one is opened and the pad or cloth replaced. In this way, operations can continue without interruption.

Separating

Most milk plants separate milk for standardization or the obtain cream for bottling purpose and skim milk for butter milk and cottage cheese. Also, at some seasons of the year, surplus milk received will need to be separated in order to process it into products such as frozen cream, butter, cheese sweetened condensed milk, or dry skim milk which can be stored. The same way be true of milk, returned from sales routes. A separator, therefore, usually is a necessity.

For many years it was customary to heat milk to 85° to 95°Fseparation, because at this temperature the difference, in density between the fat and the skim milk is greatest and results in the most efficient separation of fat from skin milk.

With cold milk separators, efficient separation is possible at a milk temperature as low as 40°F. These separators are of the air tight type and the milk is pumped through them at a controlled rate of flow. The speed of the pump is adjusted for the results desired. If more than 0.1 percent fat is found in the skim coming for the machine, the milk flow should be reduced until not more than that amount of fat is lost.

Where air tight separators (either for cold or warm milk) are used and the milk is pumped through the machine, the separator outlets should be connected directly to the processing vats. In such cases, the pump that feeds the separator will force the cream and the skim milk through the pipe line to the vats.

Separation of cold milk has the advantages of eliminating a heater and also results in less damage to the fat emulsion of the cream.

Milk may be separated after pasteurization by sending it through the separator directly from pasteurizer. Where load regulations permits the cream and the skim milk need not be pasteurized separately but should be cooled promptly no avoid undue holding at the high temperature some loose of cream viscosity may result from this method of handling.

Standardizing

Where local regulations permits, a plant may find it desirable to standardize fluid milk to a desired butter fat content. The standardizing operation must be carried out prior to pasteurization or homogenization in small operations, this is done manually by the removal or addition of cream or skim milk. The standardizing separator may be used for standardization of large volumes of milk in continuous operation.

Vitaminizing

When milk is fortified by the additional of one or more vitamins, the concentrate is usually added to the milk in the storage tank or holding vat. Agitate thoroughly to assure complete mixing before the milk is processed.

Flavourizing

After vitaminizing, the flavours and other chemicals are added to the milk to give different and better tastes. The flavours and chemicals are tested before adding and such flavours are added which have no bad effect on drinking the milk.

Although, a large number of flavouring extract are on the market, vanilla rose, stawberry extract are used so much more commonly than other flavours that a knowledge of their purity is of the greatest importance.

Again in the flavouring process sufficient quality of saffron, cashew nut (in small pieces). almonds pista is added far better taste and increase its nutrition's value.

Pasteurization of Milk

In order to make milk safe for human consumption it is necessary to destroy any harmful bacteria which may be present. By far the most widely used method is one of heat treatment or pasteurization named after its inventor pasteur.

There are two methods of pasteurizing milk, one known of the "flash" process and the other the "holder" process.

In the first method the milk is heated to a temperature of 160 to 165°F for about 1 minute, cooled to about 40°F bottled and placed in refrigerator. In the "holder" process the milk is heated and kept at a temperature of about 140°F for 30 minutes cooled as before and bottled.

Pasteurized milk is less easily digested by infants as enzymes which is contain are destroyed. The second method is preferable in that the milk does not acquire the "cooked" taste and the enzymes are not as reading destroyed as in the "flash" method which uses a higher temperature.

Pasteurization Process

Modern pasteurizing equipment is designed to expose every particles of milk to a definite and carefully controlled time temperature combination, the object being to destroy all pathogenic and most of the lactic acid producing bacteria and to cool the milk immediately to a temperature low enough to retard the growth of the surviving bacteria.

One important aspect of the pasteurizing process is the need to preserve the creaming properties of the milk if cream line milk is one of the products sold by the plant. The depth of the cream layer in the bottle of milk is still regarded by many consumers as the standard of richness or compositional quality of milk.

There are three method of pasteurizing milk and milk products.

1. **Holding Method:** Heating milk to a temperature of 145°F and holding it at this point for 30 m minutes. (For homogenized milk Higher temperature as used).

2. **Short time Method:** Heating milk to a temperature of 161°F and holding it at that level for 15 seconds.

3. **Flash Method:** Heating milk to 220-260°F without holding, it, then dropping the temperature to 160°F and holding the milk at that level for 15 seconds.

Holding Method:-

In vat pasteurization (holding method), where milk is not pre-heated and outside the vat, it is necessary to raise the milk temperature from about 50° to 145°F in the vat. Stirring or agitating the milk is necessary to obtain uniform as well as rapid heating, but if this agitation is not done care fully, churning may result. Rapid heating of the milk, with gentle agitation through the critical range of 50° to 115°F, is necessary in order to avoid partial churning which may result in reduced cream volume, the pressure of buffer granules, and cream plug in both milk and cream.

The efficient operation of avert pasteurizer require a delicate balance between temperature of the heating medium and the amount and kind of agitation. Most vats are hot water in jacket between the outer and inner shells of the vat as the heating medium. Heat is supplied to the water by introduction of stam which is controlled manually or automatically. The temperature of heating water may range form 150 to 170°F.

With too low a water temperature, the milk temperature will be raised too slowly, and with too high a water temperature milk may cook on the heating surfaces. The ability of the agitator to deep all milk moving towards and away from the heating surfaces will affect the spread of heating. With an efficient agitator, hotter water may used. The method of agitation, must produce a maximum heat transfer with a minimum of turbulence. Vats are designed with specific agitators, to operate at certain speeds and to give most efficient operation for a given volume of milk, over loading the vat or increasing the speed of the agitator will cause to trouble and upset the needed balance between volume, temperature and agitation.

During the holding period, vats covers must be kept closed to prevent any cooling of the milk and to eliminate the chances of contamination from the atmosphere. Vat covers should not be opened when there is milk in the vat except when absolutely necessary.

In the process of vat past enurization it is important to number that the actual pasteurizing is accomplished by holding the entire vat of milk at the correct temperature for the proper length of time (145°F for 30 min). The time required to bring the vat up to temperature should not be counted and the value should not be opened to allow the vat the to empty until the full time interval has expired.

PROCUREMENT OF PLANT & MACHINERY

Bansal Technocrats
1/1431/18, Sharda Nagar,
Saharanpur - 247 001 (U.P).
Ph.: 0132-27914

Products: Milk Reception, Storage and Transportaion Tanks, Ghee Making Equipments (Butter Melting Vats, Prestatification Tank, Ghee Boiler, Ghee Settling Tank, Ghee Storage Tank etc.), Paneer and Khova Making Equipments, Cream Storage and Repening Tanks, CIP Unit (Manual and Automatic), Milk Pumps, SS Pneumatically operated valves, SS pipe fittings and control panels etc.

Dairy Equipments

Bansal Technocrats
1/1431/18, Sharda Nagar,
Saharanpur - 247 001 (U.P).
Ph.: 0132-27914

Products: Milk Reception, Storage and Transportation Tanks, Ghee Making Equipments (Butter Melting Vats, Prestatification Tank, Ghee Boiler, Ghee Settling Tank, Ghee Storage Tank etc.), Paneer and Khova Making Equipments, Cream Storage and Repening Tanks, CIP Unit (Manual and Automatic), Milk Pumps, SS Pneumatically operated valves, SS pipe fittings and control panels etc.

Dairy Den (India) Pvt. Ltd.
25, "Madhuban", Ellisbridge,
Ahmedabad - 380 006

Factory:
9-Parasbaug Society
Bh. National Flats
Nr. Tagore Hall
Ahmedabad, Gujarat.
Ph: Off.: (079)461205, 449538, 44816
Fact.: 77690
Fax: 91-443537
Telex: 121-7157DDPL IN

Products: Soft Ice Cream Machines, Thick Ice Cream Machines, Ice Cream Mix Plant, Homogenizers, Batch Freezers, Continuous Freezers, Fruit Feeder, Rippe Variagatore, Candy Machines, Display Cabinets of all kinds, Cream Whipping Machines, Sluch Machine, Ice Cubes, Hotel & Kitchen Equipments, Laundry Equipment, Refrigerated Juice Disperser Brand Names: DAIRY DEN (INDIA) PVT. LTD., DAIRY MAC ENGINEERING PVT. LTD., CARPGIANLISA, ZANUSSI.

HMT Ltd.,
Sree Nidhi Chambers
Senapati Bapat Marg
Pune - 4111016
Ph.: 350040
Fax: (0212) 358565
Telex: 0145-7262

Factory:
H-2, MIDC, Chikalthana
Aurangabad - 10

Products: Pasteuriser, Centrifugal Pump, Butter Making Machine, Butterfly Valves, Plate Heat Exchangers, Oil Purification & Clarification System, Ice Cream Machinery & Turnkey Projects of small & big capacity Dairy.

SUPPLIERS OF RAW MATERIAL

MILK MANUFACTURERS/SUPPLIERS

Andhra Pradesh Dairy Development
Co-operative Federation Limited
G-28, Jangpura Extn.
New Delhi - 110 014.

Karnal Dist. Co-operative Milk Producers Union Limited
G.T. Road Bypass
Post Box. No. 84
Karnal - 132 001
Haryana

Tamilnadu Cooperative Milk Producers' Federation Ltd.,
29 & 30 Industrial Estate
Ambattur, Chennai - 600 098.
Ph.: 044-6258520

Raw material is easily and locally available in the market.

PLANT ECONOMICS

Rated Plant capacity	=	5.00 TON./day FLAVOURED MILK
LAND & BUILDING (Land area required 500 sq. mts.)	Rs.	6,25,000.00

LIST OF PLANT & MACHINERY

1. Milk processing unit complete with cream extraction machines, pasteurization unit, cooling unit etc.
2. Packing unit, complete with filling machine, sealing machine etc.
3. Milk storage tank
4. Other miscellaneous

FIXED CAPITAL

1.	LAND & BUILDING	Rs.	6,25,000.00
2.	PLANT & MACHINERY	Rs.	13,12,000.00
3.	OTHER FIXED ASSETS	Rs.	1,78,000.00
	TOTAL	**Rs.**	**21,15,000.00**

LIST OF RAW MATERIALS

1. Raw Milk
2. Flavouring saffron, cashewnut (four pieces), pista, Almonds, Elaichi etc.
3. Empty Bottles
4. Miscellaneous

NOTE:- In case synthetic flavour are desired than vanilla, rose, strawberry essence may be added.

TOTAL WORKING CAPITAL/MONTH

1.	RAW MATERIAL	Rs.	46,11,000.00
2.	SALARY & WAGES	Rs.	52,750.00
3.	UTILITIES & OVERHEADS	Rs.	41,750.00
	TOTAL	**Rs.**	**47,05,500.00**

TOTAL CAPITAL INVESTMENT

TOTAL FIXED CAPITAL	Rs.	21,15,000.00
TOTAL WORKING CAPITAL FOR 3 MONTHS	Rs.	1,41,16,500.00
TOTAL	**Rs.**	**1,62,31,500.00**

TURN OVER/ANNUM

1. By sale of flavoured milk, 1500 Ton (75,00,000 Bottles of 200 ml each)
2. By sale of 80,000 kgs. of Ghee

TOTAL Rs. 6,21,00,000.00

PROFIT = RECEIPTS - COST OF PRODUCTION
= 6,21,00,000.00 - 5,97,55,795.00
= 23,44,205.00

PROFIT SALES RATIO = Profit/Sales x 100 = 3.77 %

RATE OF RETURN = Operating profit/T.C.I x 100 = 14.44 %

BREAK EVEN POINT (B.E.P) = 61.49 %

17

ICE CREAM OF DIFFERENT FLAVOURS

INTRODUCTION

Ice cream industries in India is of comparatively recent origin. Today ice cream may be considered a luxury food item, although its popularity is increasing rapidly.

Ice cream is defined as a frozen dairy product made by suitable blending and processing of cream and other milk products together with sugar, flavor , stabilizer and incorporation of air by agitating during the freezing process.

Ice cream and related products are generally classified under frozen desserts.

Some of these frozen desserts are :

1. **Plain** - In this ice cream the total colour and flavour added should not be more than 5% of the volume of the unfrozen ice cream.

2. **Chocolate** - Ice cream flavored with coco chocolate.

3. **Fruit & nut** - Ice cream containing fruit and nut with or with out additions fruit flavouring or colour.

Ice cream is a frozen-food dessert prepared from a mixture of dairy ingredients (16-35%), sweeteners (13-20%), stabilizers, emulsifiers, flavoring, and fruits and nuts. Ice cream has 8-20% milk fat and 8-15% nonfat solids with a total of 38.3% (36-43%) total solids. These ingredients can be varied. The dairy ingredients are milk or cream, and milk fat, which is supplied by milk, cream, butter, or butter oil, an well as solids not fat, which is supplied by condensed whole or nonfat milk or dry milk. The quantities of these products are specified by standards. The milk fat provides the characteristic texture and body in ice cream. Sweeteners are a blend of cane or beet sugar and corn syrup solids. The quantity of these vary depending on the sweetness desired and the cost.

Composition of Icecreams

Component	Ice cream	
	Premium[b]	Average
milk fat	16.0	10.5
milk solids, nonfat	9.0	11.0
sucrose	16.0	12.5
corn syrup solids		5.5
stabilizer	0.1	0.3
emulsifier	0.1	
total solids, kg/l,	41.1	39.9
draw from freezer:		
% overrun	65-70	95-100
approx. kg/l,	0.64	0.55

Nutrient Composition per 100 g

Analysis	Vanilla	ice cream
energy, kJ	845	895
fat, %	10.2	12.1
protein, %	4.1	3.7
carbohydrate, %	23.5	23.2
total solids, %	39.0	40.0
calcium, mg	155	138
phosphorus, mg	115	106
sodium, mg	66	61
vitamin A, RE	86.4	101.6
thiamine, mg	0.5	0.04
riboflavin, mg	0.22	0.20
niacin, mg	0.11	0.10
vitamin D, IU	4	5

ICE CREAM INGREDIENTS

Essential for the manufacture of high quality ice cream are good ingredients and balanced so as to produce a satisfactory composition, together with intelligent processing freezing, and hardening of the product.

The wide choice of ingredients available from various sources may be grouped according to source as given below :

a. Dairy ingredients
b. Sweetening ingredients
c. Flavour characterizing ingredients
d. Additional characterizing ingredients
e. Caseinates
f. Other optional Ingredient.

PROCESS OF MANUFACTURE

PREPARATION OF MIX

A very important process involved in the manufacture of ice cream is preparing the mix. Preparing the mix involves assembling the ingredients from storage area to the preparation zone, weighing or metering and mixing ingredients and the pasteurization, homogenization cooling and storage of the mix.

The lowest cost method for preparing mix is the can and batch pasteurization method due to the low cost of equipment involved.

ORDER OF ADDING INGREDIENTS

All liquid ingredients (cream, milk, condensed milk, syrup etc) are placed in the vat and the agitation and heating started at once. The dry ingredients including MSNF, dried eggs, cocoa, sugar, and stabilizer are added while the liquid material is agitated and before the temp. reaches 120°F. If gelatin is the stabilizer used, it is best to add it after it is thoroughly mixed with an equal volume of sugar and before the liquid reaches 120°F. When butter, plastic cream, frozen cream are added they should be cut into fairly small pieces and added in time to allow complete melting before the pasteurizing temp. is reached.

PASTEURIZATION OF MIX

Pasteurization of all mixes is compulsory because this process destroy all pathogenic or disease producing bacteria, there by safe guarding the health of the consumer. Pasteurization requires only slight additional expenses, since the mix is usually heated to facilitate solution, and since the homogenization process can be accomplished best at the pasteurization temperature level.

For maximum benefits the mix probably should be processed 155° to 175°F.

HOMOGENIZATION OF THE MIX

Homogenization is usually accomplished by forcing the mix through a small orifice under suitable conditions of temperature and pressure, using a positive displacement plunger pump to furnish the pressure. The orific consists of a valve and seat in which the two adjacant surfaces are parallel and lapped smooth and is surrounded by an impact ring against which the mix impringes as it leaves the valve. The breakup of fat particles is caused by the shear forces set up in a thin stream of mix traveling at high velocity between the closely adjacent surface of the valve and seat and then by a shattering effect as it imprages on the impact ring upon leaving the valve.

COOLING THE MIX

Cooling the mix immediately after homogenization to 32°-40°F is essential after which it should be held inageing tanks until used. Unless the mix is cooled to a temperature of 40°F or lower it will become very viscous and the ice cream will not melt down smoothly. Also temp. below 40°F retard the growth of bacteria coolers of the surface or cabinet types are generally used for ice cream mix.

AGEING THE MIX

Experimental work shows that appreciable benefits result from an ageing period although little is gaince by ageing longer than 4 hr.

THE FREEZING PROCESS

Freezing the mix is one of the most important operations in the making of ice cream for upon it depends the quality, palatability and yield of the final product. Freezing is done at a temperature generally between -6° to -10°C.

ICE CREAM PREPARATION

Albumen	-	10 oz
Sugar	-	80 oz.
Whole dried milk	-	10 oz.
Indian Gum	-	5 oz.
Vanillin	-	1.5 oz.
or		
Dried Milk	-	50 oz.
Sugar	-	50 oz.
Cream of tartar	-	4.4 oz.
Sodium alginate	-	2 oz.
Vanillin	-	0.06 oz.
Package 4.5 ounce	=	127.5 gms.

Stir contents of the package into 1/2 pint. (one cup) cold milk. Stir until dissolved. Whip 1/2 pint (one cup) chilled whipping cream. Add the dissolved freeze. It to the whipped and mix freeze.

FORMULATION OF ICE-CREAM (READY TO SERVE)

Formulation -I

Milk	-------	5 Cups
Sugar	-------	2 ½ Tablespoon
Custard Powder	-------	1 Teaspoon
Vanilla Essence	-------	1 Teaspoon

COMPLETE PLANT & MACHINERY SUPPLIERS

Dairy Den (India) Pvt. Ltd.
25, "Madhuban", Ellisbridge,
Ahmedabad - 380 006

Factory:
9-Parasbaug Society
Bh. National Flats
Nr. Tagore Hall
Ahmedabad, Gujarat.
Ph: Off.: (079)461205, 449538, 44816
Fact.: 77690
Fax: 91-443537
Telex: 121-7157DDPL IN

Products: Soft Ice Cream Machines, Thick Ice Cream Machines, Ice Cream Mix Plant, Homogenizers, Batch Freezers, Continuous Freezers, Fruit Feeder, Rippe Variagatore, Candy Machines, Display Cabinets of all kinds, Cream Whipping Machines, Sluch Machine, Ice Cubes, Hotel & Kitchen Equipments, Laundry Equipment, Refrigerated Juice Disperser Brand Names: DAIRY DEN (INDIA) PVT. LTD., DAIRY MAC ENGINEERING PVT. LTD., CARPGIANLISA, ZANUSSI.

HMT Ltd.,
Sree Nidhi Chambers
Senapati Bapat Marg
Pune - 4111016
Ph.: 350040
Fax: (0212) 358565
Telex: 0145-7262

Factory:
H-2, MIDC, Chikalthana
Aurangabad - 10

Products: Pasteuriser, Centrifugal Pump, Butter Making Machine, Butterfly Valves, Plate Heat Exchangers, Oil Purification & Clarification System, Ice Cream Machinery & Turnkey Projects of small & big capacity dairy.

RAW MATERIALS SUPPLIERS

Milk Powder & milk fat:-

1. M/s. Dalmia Dairy Industries,
   11, ABC Atmaram House,
   1, Tolstoy Marg,
   New Delhi - 110001.

2. M/s. Food Specialities Ltd., (Nestle)
   M - 5A, Connaught Circus,
   New Delhi - 11 0001.

GUAR GUM:-

1. M/s. Ace International,
   30- B, Taj Building,
   August Kranti Marg,
   1st Floor, Mumbai - 4000 36.

2. M/s. Bhagwati Enterprises,
   E - 375, Marudhar Indl. Area,
   IInd Phase Basni,
   Jodhpur (Rajasthan).

FOOD COLOURS AND FLAVOURS

Arun Chemical Industries
B-35, Mayapuri Ind. Area
Phase-1, New Delhi - 110 064
Tel./Fax: 5131625

PLANT ECONOMICS

Rated Plant capacity = 1000.00 Kgs/day
ICE CREAM OF DIFFERENT FLAVOURS

LAND & BUILDING (Land Area Required 500 sq.mts.)	Rs.	12,75,000.00

LIST OF PLANT & MACHINERY

1. Milk storage tank (SS) with agitator.
2. Mixing tank (SS)
3. Homogenizer
4. Milk heating tank (SS) with electric heating system
5. Brine making tank (M.S. epoxy lined)
6. Ice cream whipping tank (Jacketed) (SS)
7. Ice cream filling machine (Semi automatic type)
8. Brine solution chiller
9. Ice cream refrigeration unit
10. Pipes, pumps, valves, and other requirements
11. Laboratory testing equipments

FIXED CAPITAL

1.	LAND & BUILDING	Rs.	12,75,000.00
2.	PLANT & MACHINERY	Rs.	16,60,000.00
3.	OTHER FIXED ASSETS	Rs.	10,75,000.00
	TOTAL	**Rs.**	**40,10,000.00**

LIST OF RAW MATERIALS

1. Milk Powder
2. Sugar
3. Milk fat
4. Stabilizer
5. Flavour (vanilla), Chocolate Powder and different flavour
6. Colour
7. Cardboard packs

TOTAL WORKING CAPITAL/MONTH

1.	RAW MATERIAL	Rs.	15,51,875.00
2.	SALARY & WAGES	Rs.	61,875.00
3.	UTILITIES & OVERHEADS	Rs.	80,000.00
	TOTAL	**Rs.**	**16,93,750.00**

TOTAL CAPITAL INVESTMENT

TOTAL FIXED CAPITAL	Rs.	40,10,000.00
TOTAL WORKING CAPITAL FOR 3 MONTHS	Rs.	50,81,250.00
TOTAL	**Rs.**	**90,91,250.00**

TURN OVER/ANNUM

1.	By sale of Ice Cream of different flavour 300000 Kgs.	Rs.	2,70,00,000.00

PROFIT = RECEIPTS - COST OF PRODUCTION
= 2,70,00,000.00 - 2,24,98,506.25
= 45,01,493.75

PROFIT SALES RATIO = Profit/Sales x 100 = 16.67 %

RATE OF RETURN = Operating profit/T.C.I x 100 = 49.51 %

BREAK EVEN POINT (B.E.P) = 38.81 %

18

MILK POWDER

INTRODUCTION

Milk Powder is the milk that has been dried or desiccated. This is usually done by heating the milk. The final product contains less than three percent water. Milk powder can be prepared from whole milk. Milk from which fat has been partially removed, or from skim milk.

There are a number of advantages in converting milk into milk powder. Milk contains Eighty-seven percent water and because of this it gets spoilt quickly. It also needs special and bulky containers for transport. On the other hand, milk-powder takes up only one-eight of the space of the original milk. Besides, milk in powder form can keep for a long period as much as six to eight months under tropical conditions.

There are three main types of plant for producing milk powder or dried milk.

i) Roller dryers

ii) Spray dryers

iii) Vacuum roller dryers.

Most of the powder in Great Britain is produced by roller dryers but there is an increasing amount made by the spray process, vacuum roller, plants are not used in Great Britain. Rollers and spray dried powders differ considerably in their appearance and properties.

Roller powder is creamy in colour, granular "crystalline" in appearance, and has characteristic tallowy or "oxidized-fat" odour.

Spray powder is a fine white powder which reconstitute more easily than roller powder on account of the milder heat treatment and smaller size of particle. However, roller powders is of better bacteriological quality as the milk receives a more intensive heating.

COMPOSITION OF DRY MILK POWDER

The composition of dry milk varies according to the composition of the milk of from which it in made. Due to elimination of water in the process of drying, the other constituents are increased in about the some proportions.

COMPOSITION OF DRY MILK & MILK PRODUCT

DRY PRODUCT	WATER	PROTEIN	FAT	LACTOSE	ASH	TOTAL MILK
Whole Milk	4.0	27.20	16.00	36.80	6.00	96.00
Cream	0.66	13.42	65.15	17.86	2.91	99.34
Skim Milk	4.00	37.40	1.00	49.20	8.40	96.00
Sour butter Milk	1.93	36.74	5.87	29.21	7.78	98.07

PROPERTY OF MILK POWDER

The most of important practical property of milk which can be reconstituted into solution or colidal suspension in water, Spray powder usually gives figures of about 99 percent, while roller powders give figures of about 90 percent. It should be noted, however, that the solubility of a powder may be increase considerably neutralization of the milk, since the excess sodium irons bring more protein and phosphate into solution.

Milk for spray powder is not commonly neutralized, but for roller powder milk is frequently neutralized down to a lactic and acidity of 0.12 percent or even less. When considering solubility figures of powders, therefore, consideration must be given to

i) The method of testing

ii) The degree of neutralization

Unfortunately there is no official method of measuring solubility, and slight differences in technique can easily lead to considerable differences in results.

It is often difficult to get agreement between laboratories for this reason.

The amount and nature of the sediment when the two types of powder are reconstituted are highly characteristic and together with the odour and taste usually enable the reconstituted milk to to readily identified.

In concentrates of 50 percent, total solids ageing and crystallization of the lactose may result in from 10 to 90 percent. If fat becoming free on foam drying (extractable) by carbon tetrachloride). This excess can be prevented by heating the concentrate immediately before drying, a free fat value of less than 10 percent, being possible. Free fat can be decrease by increasing homogenization pressure, and it increases with decrease powder particle size. Dispersibility is slightlv decrease by increasing free fat.

COMPOSITION OF MILK-POWDER

The average composition of milk powders:-

	Whole Milk powder percent	Skim Milk powder percent
Water	3.5	3.5
Fat	26.5	1.0
Protein	25.5	52.0
Ash	6.0	8.0

USES OF SKIM-MILK POWDER

The skim milk powder may be used for enriching bread. Chapatis and for making toffees in the following manner:-

Bread:

Skim-milk powder (80 to 100 mesh)	10 parts
American flour (maida)	100 parts

The ingredients are mixed thoroughly and made into bread in the usual manner soaking for a longer time than usual is recommended.

Chapati:

Skim-Milk Powder	20 parts
Wheat flour (atta)	100 parts.

The ingredients are thoroughly mixed and the dough is allowed to & often for a little longer than usual.

Toffee:

Cooked Ghee residue	453 gms.
Sugar	226 to 283 gms.
Cocoa	31 to 46 gms.
Skim milk powder	113 grams.

Mixed sugar syrup (one part of sugar and two parts of water) with cooled ghee residue in an iron Karahi. Cook the mixture on a flow flame stirring all the time till a dough is formed. Next, add cocoa and skim milk powder and go on stirring till a pat is formed spread the pat in a one and a half inch thick longer and allow it to cool and harder. Finally, cut it into cubes and wrap in porchment paper. Such toffee can well for about three months.

USES APPLICATIONS & SCOPE OF DRY POWDER (SOLUBLE & INSOLUBLE)

Dry milk was first produced as infant food, its use has spread into every industry. Manufacturing food products, in which normal milk is used. It is used in the baking industry in candy and ice cream manufacture and prepared pan cake and biscuit flours. The meat industry makes use of dried skim milk and sweet cream butter milk in the preparation of certain type of sausage. In the kitchen of the home corestuarent either dried whole or skim milk in frequently used because of it in convenient housewives have learned that dry milk may give satisfactory results in the preparation of almost any dish in which fluid milk was used previously. The armed fories of the nations at war have found dry milk to be a valuable food product width good keeping quality and compactness.

Dried whole milk skim milk its makes excellent feed for claves, pigs and chickens and European and other advanced countries. The dry milk produced used for animal food ordinarily are of a lower grade, that is they are not quite fine enough in quality for human food.

The lower grades may be such largely because the raw products may not have been carefully chosen or the machinery or processing methods. May not have met the strict standards set up for the best grades of dry products.

Nutritive Value of Dry Milk:

The nutritive value of dry milk is essentially that of the milk before drying. It has been found that except for the ascorbic acid content, most of the vitamin present sufferittle change during. It was also found that there is a loss during drying of less than 10% of the vitamin. A originally present. No less, either during drying or storage was detected in thiamine, riboflavine, niaccin, calcium pan to thenate, biotin and pyridoxine.

MANUFACTURING MILK POWDER ON COMMERCIAL SCALE:

There are two methods of making milk-powder on a large scale one is the roller-drying method and the other is called the spray drying process. In both the cases a large quantity of milk is required.

In India owing to small scale and scattered production and difficulty in collection of milk in the villages, setting up of big milk powder factories as is done in some other countries is a difficult task.

Recently, however, a number of factories have been set up in various parts of the country, with or without foreign collaboration.

PROCESS OF MANUFACTURE

There are mainly two process:

i) Roller drying

ii) Spray drying

Although Roller drying is widely preferred:-

ROLLER DRYING:

The basic type is the just-Hatmaker, and consists of two steam heated rollers about 5 feet long by 2- 1/2 feet in diameter. They have a clearance of about 0.02 inch. Which may vary according to the conditions of processing.

The cylinders are heats by steam at a pressure of 40-70 lb. per square inch, corresponding to temperature of 285°F to 302°F, and revolve inwards at the top. The film of milk which forms is so thin that it cannot be separated off by the steel knife. The smoothness and Straightness of the rollers are factors of the highest importance in obtain in a first-class powder, as failure to removal the entire film cleanly means a burning-on if the film and consequently the appearance brown lumps in the powder. The film falls into a box or channel containing a screw conveyer. It is desirable to cool the powder, as soon as possible in order to make the powder friable and minimize oxidation of the fat. The powder is finally sieved and the satisfactory fraction packed into tins (usually 1/2 kg) or special bags.

Whole milk powder in Great Britain must contain 26 percent fat, which corresponds to a milk of about 3.25 percent fat. If therefore the milk is below this value, which may happen in some parts of the country at some times of the year. It must be standardized of the addition of cream.

The economic aspect is controlled chiefly by the number of operators required for a given output, steam being cheap and the maintenance of the plant low output may be increased by

i) Higher steam pressures

ii) Precondensing.

The freeing of thought now is to increase and work with faster revolving drums. Where condensing equipment is available the milk may be precondensed up to about 18 percent total solids, further concentration may lead to burning on the rollers.

A standard pair of rollers may dry 90 gallons in one hour precondensing may raise this to 120 to 130 gallons per hour.

ii) Spray Drying:

This method consists essentially in directing a spray of hot, precondensed milk into a current of hot air. There are three main types:-

i) Simple spray
ii) Revolving sprinklers
iii) Revolving disc.

Spray drying plant much bulkier than roller drying for given output, and spray powder costs more to produce. The product is, however, so much better, that it can only be a matter of time before nearly all milk powder is produced by the spray process. The confectionery and other industries will doubtless continue to accept roller powder.

The stages in spray drying are essentially the following :

i) Reception
ii) Clarification or filtration
iii) Cooling
iv) Storage
v) Preheating (160° to 190°F)
vi) Precondensing at about 110°F to about 42 percent total sides.
vii) Atomizing in chamber, hot air entering at about 330° and leaning at about 200°F)
viii) Separation of powder
ix) Packing

The modern plant can dry 1,000 gallons per hour, and those part coming into contact with liquid milk treatment and general nature of the spray drying process it is essentially to keep the entire plant in good hygienic for any time. Such part of the plant should be regarded as pasteurizing plant and stripped, cleaned, and sterilized after running for a certain period.

SUPPLIERS OF RAW MATERIALS

M/s. Chittoor Co-Op Milk Supply Union,
Chittoor (A.P.)

M/s. Btikoppake Sugar Factor,
Daralapudi, Visakhapatnam,

M/s. Bhawani Dairy Co.,
Bhawani Tole,
Muzafarpur, Bihar.

Hessian Laminated Multilayer Bags

Packart
22, Upper Anand Parbat
Behind Ramjas Nursery School
New Delhi - 110 005
Ph.: 5723379
Fax: 6850355

RAW MATERIAL SUPPLIERS

MILK MANUFACTURERS/SUPPLIERS

Andhra Pradesh Dairy Development
Co-operative Federation Limited
G-28, Jangpura Extn.
New Delhi - 110 014.

Gujarat Co-operative Milk Marketing Federation Limited
Amul Dairy Road,
Post Box. No. 10
Anand - 388 001 (Gujarat)
Ph.: 23221/23272/23319
Fax: 02692-24950

Karnal Dist. Co-operative Milk Producers Union Limited
G.T. Road Byepass
Post Box. No. 84
Karnal - 132 001
Haryana

Rajasthan State Dairy Development Corporation Limited
15, Raniara Garden
Jaipur (Rajasthan).

Tamilnadu Cooperative Milk Producers' Federation Ltd.,
29 & 30 Industrial Estate
Ambattur, Chennai - 600 098.
Ph.: 044-6258520

SUPPLIERS OF PLANT & MACHINERY

SPRAY DRYERS

1. M/s. Alfa Lavel (India) Ltd.
Mustafa Building
7-A, Sir Phirozeshah Mehta Road
Mumbai - 400001.

Bansal Technocrats
1/1431/18, Sharda Nagar,
Saharanpur - 247 001 (U.P).
Ph.: 0132-27914

Products: Milk Reception, Storage and Transportation Tanks, Ghee Making Equipments (Butter Melting Vats, Prestatification Tank, Ghee Boiler, Ghee Settling Tank, Ghee Storage Tank etc.), Paneer and Khova Making Equipments, Cream Storage and Repening Tanks, CIP Unit (Manual and Automatic), Milk Pumps, SS Pneumatically operated valves, SS pipe fittings and control panels etc.

Dairy Udyog
229-A/230-A
Ghatkopar Ind. Estate
Block-C, L.B.S. Marg
Ghatkopar, Mumbai - 400 086.
Ph.: 5171636/5170938

Folding Cartons for Butter, Cheese, Chocolate & Skimmed Milk Powder, Lined Cartons for Skimmed Milk Powder and Malted Beverages, Wunderpac Bag in Box Packing for Liquid Milk, Condensed Milk, Ice Cream Mix and Frozen Yoghurt Mix

ITC Limited (Packing and Printing Division)
90 Chamiers Road,
Chennai - 600 018 (T.N)
Ph.: 452840

Delhi Off.:
Thapar House
124, Janpath
New Delhi - 110 001
Ph.: 312727

COMPLETE PLANT SUPPLIER

Mojj Engineering Systems Pvt. Ltd.
81-B/15, M.I.D.C., Bhosari
Pune - 411 026
Ph.: 91-212-790360
Fax: 91-212-792836

Delhi Office:
G-4, South Extension Part II,
New Delhi - 110 049.
Ph.: 011-6426632
Fax: 011-6451870

PLANT ECONOMICS

Rated Plant capacity	=	500.00 KG/day MILK POWDER

LAND & BUILDING (Land Area Required 500 sq.mt.)	Rs.	11,75,000.00

LIST OF PLANT & MACHINERY

1. Storage tanks,
2. Feed pump
3. Preheater, jacketed type
4. Precondenser
5. Spray drier with atomizer
6. Condenser
7. Baby Boiler
8. Chilling plant
9. Packing unit
10. Laboratory testing equipments
11. Miscellaneous equipments i.e. Sieves, valves etc.

FIXED CAPITAL

1.	LAND & BUILDING	Rs.	11,75,000.00
2.	PLANT & MACHINERY	Rs.	7,85,000.00
3.	OTHER FIXED ASSETS	Rs.	2,57,000.00
	TOTAL	**Rs.**	**22,17,000.00**

LIST OF RAW MATERIALS

1. Milk
2. Citric Acid
3. Mangnesium oxide
4. Miscellaneous chemicals Nacl CaC03 etc.
5. Tin containers

TOTAL WORKING CAPITAL/MONTH

1.	RAW MATERIAL	Rs.	6,34,650.00
2.	SALARY & WAGES	Rs.	1,14,875.00
3.	UTILITIES & OVERHEADS	Rs.	67,000.00
	TOTAL	**Rs.**	**8,16,525.00**

TOTAL CAPITAL INVESTMENT

TOTAL FIXED CAPITAL	Rs.	22,17,000.00
TOTAL WORKING CAPITAL FOR 3 MONTHS	Rs.	24,49,575.00
TOTAL	**Rs.**	**46,66,575.00**

TURN OVER/ANNUM

1. By sale of 150000 kg of milk powder Rs. 1,27,50,000.

PROFIT = RECEIPTS - COST OF PRODUCTION
= 1,27,50,000.00 - 1,10,93,071.50
= 16,56,928.50

PROFIT SALES RATIO = Profit / Sales x 100 = 13.00 %

RATE OF RETURN = Operating profit / T.C.I x 100 = 35.51 %

BREAK EVEN POINT (B.E.P) = 56.68 %

19

MILK TOFFEE MANUFACTURES

INTRODUCTION

Chocolate is one of the important confectionery item having good demand. It is directly consumed by children young people, old man., old woman and others. It is one of the tasting confectionery products, which is liked by almost all people of all ages.

B.I.S SPECIFICATIONS

IS : 1163 - (1971) - Chocolate
IS : 11924 - (1986) - Chocolate coating
IS : 6762 - (1982) - Drinking chocolate sweetened cocoa powder.
IS : 11730 - (1986) - Glossary of terms for cocoa, chocolate and its products.

FORMULATION

Milk Chocolate:

Fat - free cocoa mass	- 15%
Cacao Butter	- 25%
Sugar	- 40%
Milk Powder	- 20%

English Milk Chocolate:

Protein	- 7.4%
Milk Fat	- 5.5%
Cacao Butter	- 26.3%
Lactose	- 8%
Sucrose	- 43.2%

Chocolate Toffee:

Sugar	- 10 lb.
Corn Syrup	- 10 lb.
Coconut Butter	- 8 oz.
Salt	- 1 table spoonful
Fresh Cream	- 2 mt.
Evaporated milk	- 2 lb.
Butter	- 21 lb.
Butter Chocolate	- 2.5 lb.
Vanilla flavour	- 3 teaspoon full

The sugar , corn syrup, salt , coconut butter and cream are placed in a large copper pan on the stove and stirred until dissolved. When the batch stirred until dissolved. When the batch begins to boil, the evaporated milk is stirred in gradually stirring is continued while the patch is cooking. The caromed plastic is added and the batch is cooked until it forms a medium balls when tested in cold water. The batch is removed to a stand and the chocolate and flavour are added and stirred until completely melted. After adding the marshmallows and mixing well the batch is poured out on a greased slab between iron bars and spread out evenly with a palette knife. It is allowed to cool until it is hard enough to hand. Then it is passed through a sizing machine, cut into square caramels and wrapped as usual. This batch yield 48 pounds product.

MANUFACTURING PROCESS

The majority of chocolate preparations contain sugar. Some preparations, used for special purposes, are unsweetened or contain saccharin as sweetening agent. Chocolate consumed as beverage often contains up to 20 % arrowroot starch or some other farinaceous substance. Chocolate contains more fat than beverage cocoa, and in its manufacture block cocoa is employed as such. In the preparation of products of high quality, cacao butter, obtained as a by-product in cocoa manufacture, is added and the fat content augmented. Due to the high price of cocoa butter, however, cheaper non-greasy digestible fats, having the hard and brittle, or snap properties of cacao butter, and a low m. (not exceeding 37-38°), are sometimes used to replace cacao butter either wholly or in part. Important among such substitutes is Borneo tallow and refined and deodorized sterines from coconut and palm kernel oils. More recently hydrogenated coconut and palm kernel oil are being employed.

Plain chocolate is prepared by incorporating sugar, cacao butter, and flavouring materials with cocoa mass, and grinding the mixture in a mill or melangeur, to a fine particle size. Eating chocolate contains about 50% sugar. Sucrose should be finely ground before incorporation. Vanilla is the principal flavouring agent, though other essential oils, e.g., cinnamon, clove, mace and nutmeg are sometimes used. The ground mass is then refined by passing it repeatedly through water-cooled massive steel rollers to give a smooth velvety mass without grit. More cocoa butter is added and the mixture is conched or subjected to rolling pressure in a granite rectangular box fitted with granite rollers having a to-and fro motion. Conching, which is continued for 12-96 hrs., has the effect of removing moisture, mellowing, and eliminating harshness and acidity. It also helps in securing a homogeneous velvety mixture in which every particle of sugar is uniformly coated with cacao butter and improves the keeping properties (Corsbie-Walsh, 220). The conched mass is transferred to tanks and stirred at 120-130°. This treatment liquefies the fat and ensures it s uniform distribution throughout the material thus minimizing the tendency for fat bloom.

The tempered chocolate is cooled, and moulded into blocks, bars, cakes, and fancy shapes. Refrigerated moulds are used for removing the liberated latent heat, the rate of heat removal being so controlled that the fat sets in a finely crystalline form.

Milk chocolate contains in addition dried milk powder. The proportion of ingredients used by different makers Vary. Chocolates containing block milk are said to have better texture and better keeping quality than those made with dried milk. Freshly prepared condensed milk may also be incorporated. The product obtained is reported to have the characteristic fresh milk flavour.

MANUFACTURING PROCESS

First of all weigh the above ingredients in proper quantity. Then place the condensed milk, corn syrup, inver sugar, molasses and mix homogeneously. Then add coconut butter in cooking kettle equipped with double action mixers. Then heat the kettle by heating system till the batch is melted completely. Then add the granulated sugar and again mix well. Turn the steam in full boil the batch as rapidly as possible to a medium firm ball. Turn off the heat. Add the salt and flavour and mix thoroughly. Then spread the batch into the mould and cool it. When the product toffee is cool and hard bring it and pack in polyethene pouches or wrap in printed polyethene film by hand or by manual machine.

FLOW DIAGRAM FOR THE MANUFACTURE OF TOFFEE

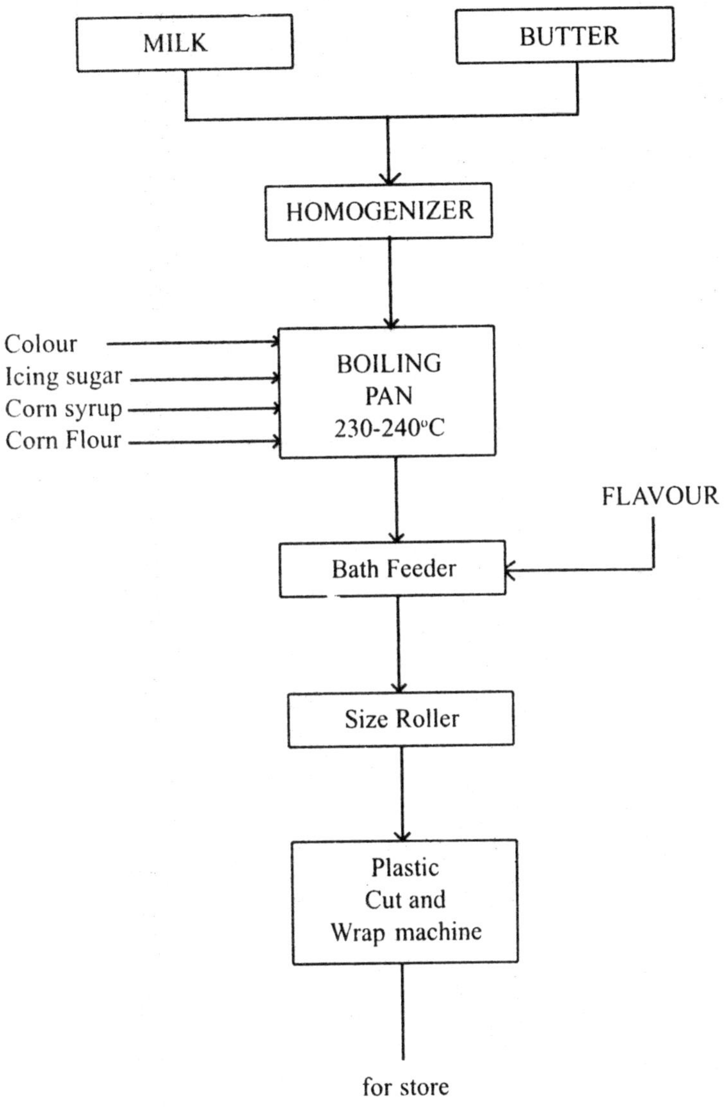

COMPLETE PLANT AND MACHINERY SUPPLIERS

M/s. Somani International Corporation
1510, Maker chambers V,
221, Nariman Point,
Mumbai - 400 021.
Phone : 223543, 223549, 230344,
Telex - 011 - 4050 SIC IN.

M/s. Nagema Chocolate Machinery,
G.D.R.,
C/o. The Standard M/c.Company ,
546, Mount Road,
Teynaplet,
Chennai - 600 018.

M/s. Dhiman Industries,
Dakhni Gate,
Nakodar -141 310
Branch :- 53/19, Old Rajinder Nagar,
New Delhi.

Wrapping Machine

1. M/s. R.G. K. Enterprises
Parekh Industrial Estate
Chandansar Road
Virar (E)
Distt. Thana (M.S).

Homogeniser

1. M/s. United Technologie
B 3/201, Ashokvan Borivali (E)
Mumbai - 66.

SUPPLIERS OF RAW MATERIALS

1. M/s. A.S. Industries,
   A-17, Lawrence Road,
   Industrial Area,
   New Delhi -35

2. M/s. Boota Ram, Prabagh,
   329, Gali Farahtulla Khan,
   Kucha Pandit Lalkuan
   Delhi- 110006.

Milk Powder/Condensed milk:-

1. M/s.Kiran Kotak & Co.,
   414/418 M.J.
   Phule Market,
   Mumbai-400 001.

2. M/s.Elegant Enterprise,
   502, Cotton Exchange Building,
   Kalbadevi,
   Mumbai-400 002.

Food Flavours:-

1. M/s.The Aromati Chemicals & Oil Co.,
   P.O.Box No.1267,
   Chennai - 600 001.

2. M/s.Bharani Chemical Company,
   30, Watkins Street,
   P.B.No.854, Perambur,
   Chennai - 600 011.

Cocoa Butter

1. M/s.Hindustan cocoa (P) Ltd.,
   Cadbury House,
   Bhula-bhai Desai Road,
   Mumbai-26.

2. M/s.Cocoa Products and Beverages Ltd.,
Mount Ponnamalle High Road,
Manapakkam,
Chennai - 600 089.

COMPLETE PLANT SUPPLIERS

Dhiman Systems
Dhiman Group Complex,
Kapurthala Road,
Nakodar - 141 310,
Dist. Jullandhar
Punjab
Ph.: 01821-20707, 20469
Fax: 21007

Brach:
53/19, Old Rajandera Nagar
New Delhi - 110 008

20

MILK PRESERVATION AND MARKETING TO WHOLESALERS (IN POUCH PACKING) BY UHT TECHNIQUE

INTRODUCTION

Milk is an Important human food. It is palatable, easy to digest and highly nutritives. It contains proteins, fat, sugar, minerals and a liberal quantity of different kinds of vitamins.

The importance of milk in human diet especially for children and expectant and nursing matters is vital. To meet the demand of the increasing population milk production in India has to be increased upto about 64 million tonnes by 2000 Ad. It is neither possible nor desirable to increase the cattle and buffalo population to achieve this target. This can only be achieved by stepping up milk production of our bovine population by cross breeding of cows and use of improved cows and buffaloes.

Unlike rich countries like the U.K. and the U.S. dairying in India is a subsidiary occupation of almost all the farmers. More than 60 per cent of the families involved in dairying belong to the small or marginal farmers or even agricultural labourers.

Some private dairies were more or less modern processing facilities were encouraged to make pasteurized butter mainly for the British Army. In the early 1940's one such firm also become the prime supplies to the country's first official urban milk supply scheme "The Bombay Milk Scheme". Under it chilled milk was transported in cans by rails to Mumbai from Anand in Kheda District some 425 km from Mumbai.

The urban dairies were unable to obtain more than a 30 per cent share of their liquid-milk markets.

"Dairy development" had after been treated as if-it were synonymous with building dairy processing plants and there plants frequently got built in the towns where the consumers were, rather than in the milk-sheds where milk was produced and so they had found if difficult to organise rural milk procurement.

With growth of population and charge in pattern of life with urbanization there was a rapid increase in demand for milk and its products particularly in urban areas where these items could not be and were not produced in any large quantity. As a result there was an upsetting in the ancient system of production and consumption of milk and milk products, and there developed an imbalance between the production in the village and supply to fast growing demand centres in congested urban areas.

With various development in milk production methods availability of milk is increasing even though it is not in pace with rise in population.

PROPERTIES OF MILK

1. Milk is a balance diet. It is a complete food in itself. It is very clear from the fact that an infant lives completely on milk and upto the stage of outing teeth.

2. Milk has got friendly germs which help in bactericidal property of human system.

3. Milk contains diastase and galactose which help in digestive system.

4. Milk contains vitamin A, Vitamin B, Vitamin C, Vitamin D, and Vitamine E.

FOOD AND NUTRITIVE VALUE OF MILK

Milk is an almost ideal food. It has high nutritive value. It supplies body-building proteins, bone-forming minerals and health giving vitamins and furnishes energy-giving lactose and milk fat. Besides supplying certain essential fatty acids, it contains the above nutrients in an easily digestible and assimilable form. All these properties makes milk an important food for pregnant mothers, growing children, adolescent, adults, invalids, convalescent and patients alike.

USES OF MILK

1. Milk is used as a food.
2. Used as a complete foot of infant.
3. It is used to prepare curd, butter, ghee cream and ice cream etc.
4. Milk is used in all homes.
5. It is used in hotels and restaurants as milk food preparations and in the preparation of tea and coffee.

BUYING AND COLLECTION OF MILK

A. BUYING

Various methods for buying milk are employed, singly or in combination, as given below:

(a) Payment according to weight or volume (also known as a flat rate). Advantages: (i) saves time; (ii) simple to calculate. Disadvantage: (i) encourages watering or skimming. Payment by weight is preferred to payment by volume as the former is not affected by either foam or specific gravity. (If is popular in the unorganized sector).

(b) Payment according to the fat content of milk (includes, among others, the straight fat method of payment). Advantages: (i) practical; (ii) discourages adulteration with water. Disadvantages: (i) does not prevent removal of skim milk; (ii) does not take into account the solids-not-fat content of milk (practiced by most dairies).

(c) Payment according to the use made of milk. This practice is followed mainly for milk products.

(d) Payment of premiums. Usually confined to market milk. Based on quality of milk as measured by (i) sediment test; (ii) flavour score; (iii) bacterial count or Methylene Blue Reduction Time. (encourages the production of high-grade milk).

(e) Payment according to the cost of production. complicated, although rational.

Note: The urgent need for a sound pricing policy for milk and milk products in this country is being increasingly realized by diary planners today. The problems, no doubt, is complicated, as the price has to be acceptable to the producers, processors and manufacturer, distributors and finally consumers. Further, the approach must be of long-range significance to dairy development.

The minimum standards prescribed by the PFA (1976) rules for cow milk are 3.0 to 4.0 per cent fat and 8.5 to 9.0 per cent solids-not-fat, while those for buffalo milk are 5.0 to 6.0 per cent fat and 9.0 per cent solids-not-fat throughout the country. With a view to encouraging milk production through high yielding indigenous and cross-bred cows, it is necessary to adopt a pricing policy which would provide an adequate incentive for production of cow milk. In this context, the National Dairy Development Board has suggested the two-axis milk pricing policy. Such a policy ensures payment for milk on its compositional quality evaluated rationally on its fat and solids-not-fat components. This would discourage adulteration of buffalo milk and at the same time ensure a common approach to cow and buffalo milks.

However, one difficulty that can be foreseen in this system is the accurate testing of milk at source for its solids-not-fat content. Since the estimation of solids-not-fat in milk is a time-consuming process, research would have to be undertaken to develop a rapid test which could be carried out under field conditions.

The overall pricing policy for milk products should encourage efficiency of production, minimization of costs, quality of the product, etc. Dairy factories should try to create the feeling that the price of producer's milk is not predetermined unilaterally at a fixed rate but varies, rather, with season and quality.

B. COLLECTION

In almost all developed dairying countries, production of milk is confined to rural areas, while demand is mostly urban in nature. Hence milk has to be collected and transported from production points in the milk-shed areas to processing and distribution points in cities.

(a) The common systems for collection (assembling of milk are as follows:-

(i) By co-operative organizations. Formed by individual or collective milking societies, Suits producers best as no profit-making middlemen are involved.

(ii) By contractors. Less return to producers.

(iii) By individual producers. Practical for those situated near processing dairies.

Note: -

(a)'milk-shed' is the geographical area from which a city dairy receives its fluid milk supply. The allocation of definite milk-sheds to individual dairies for the purpose of developing the same is now being considered in India.

(b) Milk collection-cum-chilling centers/depots. Normally attached to city dairies.

Objects. These are: (i) to preserve the quality of raw milk supplies, and (ii) to provide easy transport to the processing dairy.

Location. This is guided by: (i) adequate milk production; (ii) adequate (potable) water supply; (iii) proximity to a good road or railway station; (iv) electric supply, and (v) sewage disposal facilities.

Major items of equipment. (i) Milk weight tank//pan and weighing scale (ii) Drop (dump) tank with cover; (iii) Can washer, (iv) Milk Pump (sanitary type) (v) Surface/plate cooler; (vi) Refrigeration unit (of suitable capacity); (vii) cold room (of suitable capacity); (viii) milk testing unit, etc.

Operational procedures. Essentially this is the same as in a small dairy. On arrival, the milk is graded for acceptance/rejection, weighed, sampled for testing, cooled an stored at a low temperature until dispatch to the processing dairy.

CHILLING AND TRANSPORTATION OF MILK TO PROCESSING STATION

The milk after collection from the people or cooperative society, is immediately chilled to 4.4°C by placing in bulk tank coolers, which is run by a mechanical refrigeration system. It will cool the milk rapidly to a low temp 4.4°C and automatically maintain this temperature during the storage period. Milk can be poured directly from the milking pan into the tank (under Indian Condition). Subsequently milk can be drawn into cans or pumped into a tanker, for dispatch to city dairy.

Advantage: Permits collection of producers' milk on alternate days.

Disadvantage: Relatively expensive in initial equipment.

Milk Chilling Centers: Now that electricity is available even in most Indian villages, these have great scope in this country, largely because of predominantly small and scattered milk production, the number of organized dairy farms in India is rather small. Consequently, the centers can provide the only alternative solution to the collection and chilling of village milk. They can profitably be run by the producers themselves through their co-operative organizations.

Transportation:

(a) Importance. Under Indian Conditions, milk has to be regularly collected and transported twice a day (morning and evening).

(b) Modes of transport. These depend upon the carrying load, the distance of collection and local conditions.

MANUFACTURING PROCESS

COOLING AND STORING MILK:

The careless handling of milk between milking and delivering to the place can cause high bacteria counts to develop in the milk, a mechanical cooler is employed for the purpose. Whole of the milk should be started at 50°F to prevent spoilage. Storage tanks made of stainless steel are employed for storing the raw milk.

FILTRATION:

The cold raw milk is filtered, however, it can be filtered before cooling and storing in tank, but the precaution is to be taken at this stage so that no foreign matters or understand materials may be carried on.

STANDARDIZATION:

Milk is standardized according to ISI specification or according to requirements by wholesaler.

HOMOGENIZATION:

Filtered milk is fed into homogenizer. Homogenization is the process by which the milk is emulsified and are further divided to produce a more stable emulsion that will not separate on standing. The fat is emulsified with liquid part of milk that are at water mostly. Hence to prevent sedimentation of fat in milk that homogenization process is done. But this way high quality homogenized milk is produced.

After feeding the milk into homogenizer, the pressure of the homogenizer is increased about 2500 psi. However, of this pressure does not produce milk that meets the standard, it may be necessary to use a pressure high as 3000 to 3500 LB.

A uniform, steady pressure is necessary to secure satisfactory homogenization. The milk should have a slight, positive pressure. Otherwise air may be drawn into the pistons which causes the needles of the pressure gauge to vibrate. Such a result indicates irregular pressure. Sediment may appear in the operation which is undesirable. To reduce sediment, clarification is done.

CLARIFICATION :

The milk is passed through a clarifier is it leaves the homogenizer. Cold milk clarification is preferred to hot milk. This clarification operation can be perform before homogenization but the complete clarification can be achieved at this stage clarifier can be replaced by cream separator but since the separator bowl is not designed to hold a large amount of sediment and consequently is not efficient for clarifying a large volume of milk. However, this operation can be omitted to get high quality milk.

PASTEURIZATION :

The milk after clarification is passed through a plate heat exchanger for pasteurization. In plate heat exchanger (P.H.E.) the milk is pasteurized by UHT method. This was first developed by A. P. V. Co. in the United Kingdom in 1922. It is modern method of pasteurization of milk and used where large volumes of milk are handled. The UHT pasteuriser gives a continuous flow of milk which is fully pasteurized and free from pathogens.

After complete processing milk is stored in cold upto chilling conditions so that unwanted micro organisms/pathogenic micro Organism can not be developed in the processed milk. It is sacred until delivered for distribution to wholesalers.

Testing:-

The testing of milk is an essential for the quality control purposes however may be done prior to storage under freezing condition.

FLOW DIAGRAM

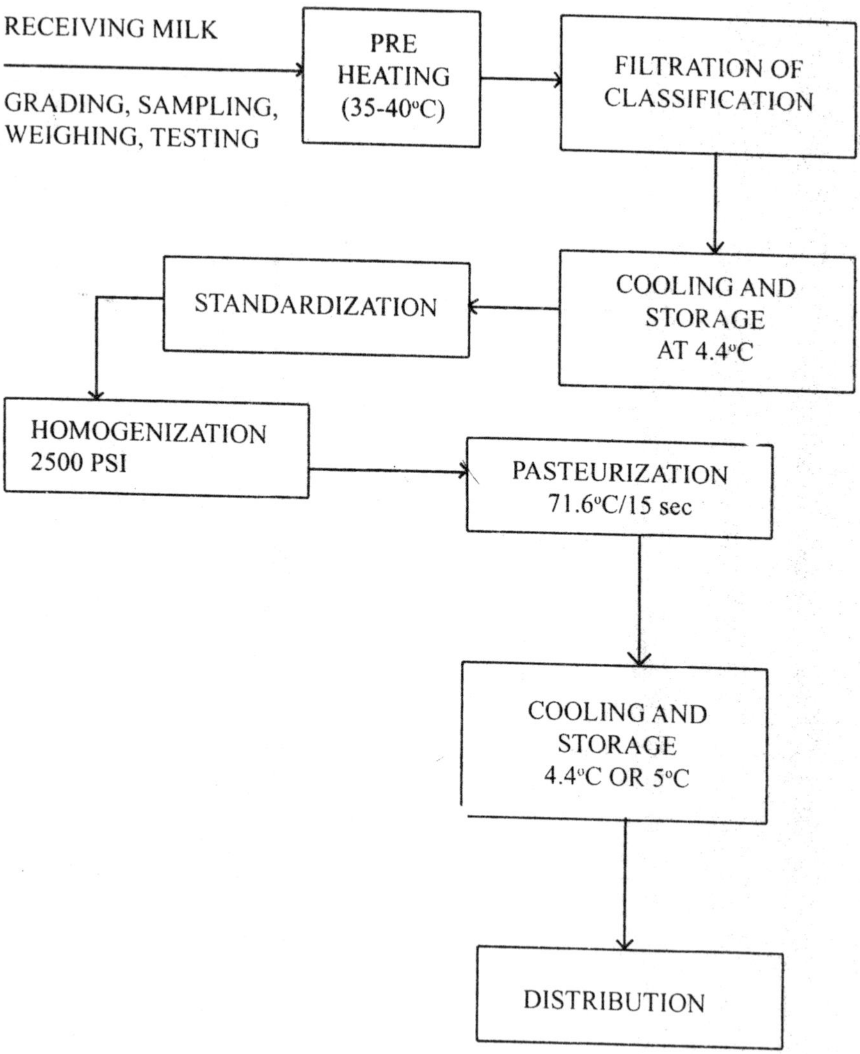

Distribution:-

After Complete processing, the processed milk is checked for proper pasteurization by quality controller. Then the milk at 1 or 2°C is supplied to the wholesalers present at distant places by the tanker or by filling in the big stainless steel cans. Under chilling conditions Temp may rise to 7 to 8°C during transportation.

SUPPLIERS OF RAW MATERIALS

MILK MANUFACTURERS/SUPPLIERS

Andhra Pradesh Dairy Development
Co-operative Federation Limited
G-28, Jangpura Extn.
New Delhi - 110 014.

Gujarat Co-operative Milk Marketing Federation Limited
Amul Dairy Road,
Post Box. No. 10
Anand - 388 001 (Gujarat)
Ph.: 23221/23272/23319
Fax: 02692-24950

Karnal Dist. Co-operative Milk Producers Union Limited
G.T. Road Byepass
Post Box. No. 84
Karnal - 132 001
Haryana

Rajasthan State Dairy Development Corporation Limited
15, Raniara Garden
Jaipur (Rajasthan).

Tamilnadu Cooperative Milk Producers' Federation Ltd.,
29 & 30 Industrial Estate
Ambattur, Chennai - 600 098.
Ph.: 044-6258520

From Villagers.

PLASTIC CRATES

M/s. Needo Mfg. and Trading Corporation
768, Chabi Ganj
Kashmere gate,
Delhi - 110 006.

FLEXIBLE POUCHES

M/s. Paper products Ltd.,
13-14, Ajmeri Gate Extension,
Delhi- 110 006

M/s. Rainbow Plastic Industries,
44/45, Giriraj Industrial Estate,
Mahakali Calves Road,
Andheri, Mumbai-93.

SUPPLIERS OF PLANTS & MACHINERIES

BOILER

Indcon Boilers Limited
D-170, Okhla Ind. Area,
Phase-1, New Delhi - 110 020
Ph.: 6811441/442

PACKAGING MACHINERIES

Nichrome International
46, Dr. B.R. Ambedkar Road
Near Sangam Bridge
Pune - 411 001 (M.S)
Ph.: 0212-622137/622259

Rado Packaging Machines Pvt. Ltd.
C-377, Sector-10
Noida - 201 301 (U.P)
Ph.: 8-555190, 8-533341
Fax: 8-525699

Products: Form Fill and Seal Machines

HOMOGENIZER & PASTEURIZER

M/s. Central Dairy Farm,
Govt. of U.P. Undertaking,
Aligarh (U.P.)

M/s. Filtron Engineers Pvt. Ltd.,
Gokul, Fergusson Road,
Pune - 411 005.
Phone - 51641
Tel : 0145 - 323 TRON IN.

CANS AND CAN WASHING SYSTEM

M/s. Mulakhraj & Co.,
204 Azad Market,
Delhi - 110 006.

M/s. Agricultural Guplements and Brass
Utensils,
Court Road,
Jagadhri - 145 003.

LABORATORY EQUIPMENT

M/s. Bharat Laboratory (Regd),
8, Amrit Kaur Market,
Opp. New Delhi Railway Station,
P.B. No. 180,
New Delhi - 110 001.

M/s. Capital Scientific Industries,
Amul Dairy Road,
Anand - 388 001.

MILK RECEPTION TANKS

M/s. Anup Engineering Ltd.,
The dairy Div. Behind 66 KV.
Electric Sub. Station,
Odhav Road,
Ahmedabad - 380 002.

MILK STORAGE TANKS

M/s. Dany Dairy And Food Engineers
Private Limited,
7/4 km. Stone Dehradun Road,
P.B. No. 115,
Saharanpur - 247 001.

POUCHES (PRINTED/LAMINATED)

Flex Industries Limited
A-107/108, Sector - IV,
Noida - 201 301 (U.P)
Ph.: 85-22558

PASTEURISER

1. M/s. Filtron India Ltd.,
Gokulnagar.
1184/4, Shivajinagar,
F.C. Road,
Pune-411005.

COMPLETE PLANT SUPPLIERS

Bansal Technocrats
1/1431/18, Sharda Nagar,
Saharanpur - 247 001 (U.P).
Ph.: 0132-27914

Products: Milk Reception, Storage and Transportaion Tanks, Ghee Making Equipments (Butter Melting Vats, Prestatification Tank, Ghee Boiler, Ghee Settling Tank, Ghee Storage Tank etc.), Paneer and Khova Making Equipments, Cream Storage and Repening Tanks, CIP Unit (Mannual and Automatic), Milk Pumps, SS Pneumatically operated valves, SS pipe fittings and control pannels etc.

Dairy Den (India) Pvt. Ltd.
25, "Madhuban", Ellisbridge,
Ahmedabad - 380 006

Factory:
9-Parasbaug Society
Bh. Bational Flats
Nr. Tagore Hall
Ahmedabad, Gujarat.
Ph: Off.: (079)461205, 449538, 44816
Fact.: 77690
Fax: 91-443537
Telex: 121-7157DDPL IN

Products: Soft Ice Cream Machines, Thick Ice Cream Machines, Ice Cream Mix Plant, Homogenisors, Batch Freezers, Continuous Freezers, Fruit Feeder, Rippe Variagatore, Candy Machines, Display Cabinets of all kinds, Cream Whipping Machines, Sluch Machine, Ice Cubers, Hotel & Kitchen Equipments, Laundry Equipment, Refrigerated Juice Disperser Brand Names: DAIRY DEN (INDIA) PVT. LTD., DAIRY MAC ENGINEERING PVT. LTD., CARPGIANLISA, ZANUSSI.

HMT Limited,
Sree Nidhi Chambers
Senapati Bapat Marg
Pune - 4111016
Ph.: 350040
Fax: (0212) 358565
Telex: 0145-7262

Factory:
H-2, MIDC, Chikalthana
Aurangabad - 10

Products: Pasteuriser, Centrifugal Pump, Butter Making Machine, Butterfly Valves, Plate Heat Exchangers, Oil Purification & Clarification System, Ice Cream Machinery & Turnkey Projects of small & big capacity Dairy.

LIST OF EQUIPMENT

Sr. No	Qty. No.	Description of Item

EQUIPMENT SCHEDULE:

1. RECEPTION

1.1	1 No.	Can Tippint bar
1.2	1 No.	Gravity Roller Conveyer
1.3	1 No.	Dial type weigh scale complete (0-250 Kg)
1.4	1 No.	Milk Weigh Bowl Cap. 250 Kg.
1.5	1 No.	Milk Dump Tank Cap. 500 lit.
1.6	2 Sets	Milk in line Strainer Cap. 2000 LPH
1.7	1 No.	Milk Transfer pump type FM1AIIIb 3.5 HP
1.8	1 No.	Milk Chiller Cap. 2,000 LPH (35 to 4)
1.9	1 Nos.	Can Scrubber & Can steaming Block
1.10	1 No.	Can Drip Saver
1.11	1 No.	Platform Weigh Scale (0-100 kg,
1.12	1 Nos.	Raw Milk Storage Tank Cap. 5,000 lit
1.13	1 No.	Milk Transfer pump (Tanker unloading Alfa Laval Type FM1AIIIb 3.5 HP

2. MILK PROCESSING:

2.1	1 No.	Alfa Laval Type P13RCF Milk Pasteurization plant complete Cap. 2000 lph
2.2	1 No.	Milk Separator Alfa Laval Type 2181
2.3	4 Nos.	Milk Storage Tank pasteurized standardized Milk Cap. 2,000 lit.
2.4	1 No.	Intermediate Balance Tank with pump Cap. 500 lit & GM1 pump
2.5	1 No.	Ghee Boiler Cap. 500 kg.
2.6	1 Set	Milk Pouch Filling Machine Cap. 2000 pouches/hr. complete with conveyor crate washing system
2.7	2 Nos.	Pump for transfer of milk Alfa Level FM1AIIIb 3.5 HP
2.8	1 No.	SMP Reconstitution unit complete with pump

3. SERVICE EQUIPMENT ELECTRICALS:

1.	1 Set	1 X 150 KVA transformer, including two pole structure, HT & LT panels/breakers i.e Sub-station equipment
2.	1 Set	Motor Control Centers & Remote panels
3.	1 Set	DG Set Cap. 60 KVA & panel

STEAM RAISING EQUIPMENT:

1.	1 Set	Oil Fired Boiler Cap. 500 kg/hr. complete with chimney, water softening plant, oil & water service tanks etc.
2.	1 lot	Related steam, oil pipes & fittings
3.	1 lot	Oil storage tank - one month Capacity complete with loading/ Unloading, pumps & piping

COMPRESSED AIR EQUIPMENT:

1.	1 Set	Air compressor complete with air cooler, After dryer.
2.	1 lot	Comp. Air pipes & fittings.

WATER HANDLING EQUIPMENT:

1.	2 Nos.	Water pumps Cap. 15 M3/hr At 30 MWC
2.	1 lot	Water pipes & fittings based on compact layout

REFRIGERATION PLANT:

1. Refrigeration plant comprising of 2 nos. compressor with drive accessories, condenser, ice bank tank, chilled water pumps as per standard battery limit.

2. Cold Store diffuser, insulation of cold store walls, ceiling & floor for storage of 10,000 lit milk in pouches

3. Chilled water pipes & fittings, insulation & aluminium cladding as per standard practice

4. MISCELLANEOUS EQUIPMENT:

1.	6 Nos.	Steam & Water Mixing battery complete with hose pipe stand etc.
2.	1 lot.	Remote control panels, dust and vermin proof
3.	2 Nos.	Differential Weigh scale for pouch filling area
4.	1 set	Alfa Level type ESP 400 CIP unit.

PLANT ECONOMICS

Rated Plant capacity = 10000.00 LTS./day

MILK PRESERVATION BY UHT TECHNIQUE

LAND & BUILDING Rs. 34,00,000.00

(Land Area Required 4000 sq.mts.)

LIST OF PLANT & MACHINERY

1. Complete Plant & Machinery with sections I,II,III,IV with installation, electrification, erection & commissioning
2. Laboratory equipments.
3. Miscellaneous

FIXED CAPITAL

1.	LAND & BUILDING	Rs.	34,00,000.00
2.	PLANT & MACHINERY	Rs.	58,00,000.01
3.	OTHER FIXED ASSETS	Rs.	15,00,000.00
	TOTAL	**Rs.**	**1,07,00,000.01**

LIST OF RAW MATERIALS

1. Raw milk
2. Chemicals for laboratory & process
3. Pouches

TOTAL WORKING CAPITAL/MONTH

1.	RAW MATERIAL	Rs.	26,31,500.00
2.	SALARY & WAGES	Rs.	1,23,125.00
3.	UTILITIES & OVERHEADS	Rs.	5,00,000.00
	TOTAL	**Rs.**	**32,54,625.00**

TOTAL CAPITAL INVESTMENT

TOTAL FIXED CAPITAL	Rs.	1,07,00,000.01
TOTAL WORKING CAPITAL FOR 3 MONTHS	Rs.	97,63,875.00
TOTAL	**Rs.**	**2,04,63,875.01**

TURN OVER/ANNUM

1. By sale of 72,00,000 pouch of milk (500 mls.)
2. Ghee 68,000 kgs.

TOTAL Rs. 5,06,80,000.00

PROFIT = RECEIPTS - COST OF PRODUCTION
= 5,06,80,000.00 - 4,44,03,997.50
= 62,76,002.50

PROFIT SALES RATIO = Profit/Sales x 100 = 12.38 %

RATE OF RETURN = Operating profit/T.C.I x 100 = 30.67 %

BREAK EVEN POINT (B.E.P) = 57.06 %

21

PANEER

INTRODUCTION

Paneer is the product made from the curd obtained from whole or skimmed milk, with or without added cream, by coagulating the casein and further treatment, of the separated curd by ripening ferments, special molds or seasoning. Cheese has not been the popular item of food in India mainly because animal enzyme rennet is used in its preparation. Preparations such as surti manner, Bandal and Ducca Cheese, within are popular in certain parts are allied to cheese.

Surti paneer is a soft variety of paneer made from buffalo milk using rennet (from the stomach of the goat) as coagulant.

Bandal is soft cheese, similar to the suirt paneer, made from cow milk without the use of rennet.

Soft cheese, known as paneer, is made in punjab and other regions by using berries of " Withania coagulans " as the source of coagulating enzymes for clotting milk.

Cheese in an important dairy product in several countries. There are about 20 distinct varieties of cheese. All kinds of cheese contain approximately the same ingredients but in different quantity.

NATURE OF CHEESE

Cheese consists of a concentration of the constituents of milk, principally fat, casein and insoluble salts, lactose, and albumin are found. To retain these constituents in concentrated from, milk is coagulated either by means of lactic acid produced by bacteria or by the addition of rennet. A portion of water is removed by cooking stirring or draining the cured or by mechanical application of pressure. The cheese may or may not be ripened, but it ripened the nature of the process depends upon the particular variety of cheese.

CLASSIFICATION OF CHEESE

There are probably 20 varieties of cheese and more than 400 names are applied to these varieties all over the world.

1. Hard, and
2. Soft.

Hand cheese may be sub-divided as

a. Very hard.

A_1. Without gas holes like chedder

A_2 With gas holes like swiss

b. Semi hard

b_1 Ripened by molds like roquefort.

b_2 Ripened by bacteria like bricks.

Softs cheese may

i. Ripened by bacteria like limburger

ii. Ripened by mold like camem bert

iii. Unripened cheese, cottage.

Only the cottage type soft cheese (paneer) is produced in India.

COMPOSITION OF PANEER

Variety of (Paneer/Cheese)	Fat %	Protein %	atose and Ash %	Water
Cottage	0.40 to 1.90	12.70-21.00	0.20-1.00	71.40-79.90
Neufachatal	23.00-28.00	18.00-21.00	0.50-1.25	50-55
Swiss (American)	30-34	26-30	3-5	30-34
Cheddar (Green)	30-36.79	20-80-26.11	3.12-7.02	32.69-43.89
Brick	28.34-33.77	20-03-23.29	1.68-4.20	39.61-45.26

The composition of cheese depends upon the variety. All cheese contain the same constituents of milk but in varying proportions. The most variable constituents are fat and water.

A number of factor influence the compositions of cheese, however a typical composition of a selected number of varieties is given above.

USES & APPLICATIONS

Paneers are used throughout the world in a large quantity. Consumptions are of the following types:-

i) Hotel & Restaurant.
ii) Cafeteria.
iii) Air Port Restaurant.
iv) Railway Restaurant.
v) Guest houses.
vi) Domestic cooked vegetables.
vii) Lodging & Boarding places.
viii) Hostel mess.

In nut shell where there is the possibility of cooking food for human consumption; there exist a possibility of using paneers too.

PROPERTIES & NUTRITIONAL VALUE OF PANEER

All kinds of Paneer contain approximately the same ingredients but these vary in amount according to the type of cheese. Cheese in the most concentrated form of nitrogenous foods commonly used. Practically all analysis reports the nitrogenous matter as protein but this is not entirely correct since some of the original milk may not be partially digested or by changed into protein split products during ripening process.

The fat content of cheese varies from almost 30% in plain, uncreamed cottage cheese. Although cheese in a concentrated food, it does not contain all the nutritive essentially of milk, Most of the milk sugar, Milk albumin, and soluble mineral salts, remain in the whey certain special types of cheese, such as mysost and ricotta are made from whey and so contain whey constituents rather than these of normal cheese.

Some special cheese foods, and spreads contain added whey or skim milk solids which supply nutritive ingredients missing is most forms of cheese.

In general cheese made from milk coagulated with rennet is a good source of calcium and phosphorous however, lactic acid varieties especially cottage cheese, usually contain but little of these elements. About 80 % of the calcium and 38 % of the phosphorous of the milk is retained in cheddar cheese, while only 20 % and 37 % respectively is retained by soft cheese as shown earlier, since salt is added to cheese the ash content may not give a correct picture of the original milk mineral presents.

MILK FOR PANEER MANUFACTURE

Cow's milk is used most frequently for the manufacture of cheeses, however, several varieties are made from goats, ships or mare's milk. The quality of milk used for cheese making on a commercial scale is of prime importance. It must be of very best of it desired results are to be obtained. Since most cheese made must pass through a ripening period, the type of bacteria which predominate in the milk may play an important part in the development of the flavour of a given cheese. To ensure satisfactory results, milk to be used for cheese making must be fresh, clean, of low bacterial content, and posses a clean desirable flavour. Any abnormalities in flavour or in odor are to be avoided. A dirty milk or milk containing large number's of bacteria which are found associated with unsanitary methods in the dairy cannot be used in the manufacture of a high quality cheese milk having undergone extensive fermentation in practically useless. Further, more no treatment of milk can be depended upon the improve a low quality milk of the manufacture of cheese.

As it will be noted, all of the cheese mentioned defend in a large ensure upon microorganism for the development of their characteristic flavour, aroma or appearance. The organism may be the principal factors but in nearly every case there is evidence that various enzymes may also take part in the curing process. In every instance there must be an accurate control of conditions of curing to that. Particular type of organism may be follows, otherwise untoward results, will appear.

Cheese is often made from milk which has been subjected some heat treatment but not enough to qualify as pasteurized milk as measured by the phosphate test. Temperatures from 145-150°C and an exposure time of about 15 seconds may be used. This heat exposure destroys many bacteria capable of causing difficulty in cheese making and ripening. The treatment is not enough to destroy all enzymes of milk and some bacteria of value in cheese ripening probably sournine. Cheese made from milk heated in this fashion develops more flavour than those cheese made from pasteurized milk. Such cheese must be aged for 60 days before sale unless it is to be used for manufacturing purposes, when it will be given an additional heat treatment. Cheese made from pasteurized milk may be solid at any time after its manufacture.

EQUIPMENTS REQUIRED

A vat is used to hold the milk and this vat sits inside a second designed to hold water, by controlling the temperature of the water in the outer vat, the temperature of the milk is adjusted to the proper point. The vat should be rectangular in shape, flat bottomed shaping, however, towards the center and the outlet end where the whey is drawn off.

Curd Knives

A set of two cured knives is required with which to cut the cured. The knives consists of blades or wires set in a frame.

Curd Rave

A rare constructed of wood is necessary for the stirring of the cured.

Curd Mill

The curd mill consists of a pieces of apertures equipped to cut slabs of mill curd into the strips.

Cheese Hoops

Cheese hoops built of heavily tinned steel are used for holding the curd in preparation for pressing the curd and shaping the finished cheese.

Cheese Bandages & Circles

The cheese hoops are lined with a cheese bandage which is made of thin woven cotton known as cotton cloth.

Cheese Press

A cheese press by means of which the cheese may be pressed after being placed in the cheese whoops is also required.

Miscellaneous Equipments

In addition to the above equipments, the cheese factory will need considerable equipment such as Babcock tester, Milk testing glassware, and apparatus for acidity testing. More modern factories find equipments for the complete analysis of milk and cheese desirable.

PROCESS OF MANUFACTURE

This type of Paneer is generally made of skim milk. The milk for best result should be pasteurized. The process may be divided into following steps.

1. Selection of Milk.
2. Pasteurization of Milk.
3. Curd formation.
4. Paneer formation.
5. Cutting & packing.

Selection of Milk

The milk is selected as desired under the heading of milk for Paneer. The milk should however, be fresh with no unwanting odour. The milk may be blended as obtained from different sources to cover up the required composition, the milk and portion content. The milk is finally filtered to remove any foreign materials. The milk so obtained is collected and stored.

Pasteurization

This consists of applying heat for the minimum period necessary to destroy microbial contamination, the temperature being big enough to kill them but so high as to affect the chemical and physical characteristics or the nutritive value of milk.

Two methods of pasteurization are in use.

1. The holding and the flash.

2. High temperature short Time (H.T.S.T).

In the holding method, the milk is heated to 140-150°Fheld at that temperature of 30 minutes and rapidly cooled to 50°F. In the H.T.S.T. method, the milk is heated to 160-162°F held at the temperature for 10-12 sec and cooled immediately to 50°F.

First method is more commonly employed in India.

Curd Formation

The pasteurized milk is then set at a temperature of 68-72°F (20- to 22.2°C) and approximately 5 percent of good starter is added. After 8 to 12 hours the milk will coagulate and form a firm cured.

Paneer formation

The curd may be cut with curd Knives as in the case of cheddar cheese, after which it is cooked slowly to 98° to 110°F or 36.7° to 43.3°C). The whey then removed and the curd allowed to drain. (The some factories the curd and the whey are drain into the paneer cloth bags which are hung in a cool room where the whey is permitted to drain of a starter flavour is not desired. The curd may be washed with cold water. The curd then is stirred and salted to taste.

PLANT & MACHINERY SUPPLIERS

Bansal Technocrats
1/1431/18, Sharda Nagar,
Saharanpur - 247 001 (U.P).
Ph.: 0132-27914

Products: Milk Reception, Storage and Transportation Tanks, Ghee Making Equipments (Butter Melting Vats, Prestatification Tank, Ghee Boiler, Ghee Settling Tank, Ghee Storage Tank etc.), Paneer and Khova Making Equipments, Cream Storage and Repining Tanks, CIP Unit (Manual and Automatic), Milk Pumps, SS Pneumatically operated valves, SS pipe fittings and control panels etc.

Dairy Den (India) Pvt. Ltd.
25, "Madhuban", Ellisbridge,
Ahmedabad - 380 006

Factory:
9-Parasbaug Society
Bh. National Flats
Nr. Tagore Hall
Ahmedabad, Gujarat.
Ph: Off.: (079)461205, 449538, 44816
Fact.: 77690
Fax: 91-443537
Telex: 121-7157DDPL IN

Products: Soft Ice Cream Machines, Thick Ice Cream Machines, Ice Cream Mix Plant, Homogenizers, Batch Freezers, Continuous Freezers, Fruit Feeder, Ripped Variagatore, Candy Machines, Display Cabinets of all kinds, Cream Whipping Machines, Slouch Machine, Ice Cubers, Hotel & Kitchen Equipments, Laundry Equipment, Refrigerated Juice Disperser Brand Names: DAIRY DEN (INDIA) PVT. LTD., DAIRY MAC ENGINEERING PVT. LTD., CARPGIANLISA, ZANUSSI.

HMT Ltd.,
Sree Nidhi Chambers
Senapati Bapat Marg
Pune - 4111016
Ph.: 350040
Fax: (0212) 358565
Telex: 0145-7262

Factory:
H-2, MIDC, Chikalthana
Aurangabad - 10

Products: Pasteuriser, Centrifugal Pump, Butter Making Machine, Butterfly Valves, Plate Heat Exchangers, Oil Purification & Clarification System, Ice Cream Machinery & Turnkey Projects of small & big capacity Dairy.

BOILER

Indcon Boilers Limited
D-170, Okhla Ind. Area,
Phase-1, New Delhi - 110 020
Ph.: 6811441/442

COMPLETE PLANT SUPPLIER

Mojj Engineering Systems Pvt. Ltd.
81-B/15, M.I.D.C., Bhosari
Pune - 411 026
Ph.: 91-212-790360
Fax: 91-212-792836

Delhi Office:
G-4, South Extension Part II,
New Delhi - 110 049.
Ph.: 011-6426632
Fax: 011-6451870

RAW MATERIAL SUPPLIERS

MILK MANUFACTURERS/SUPPLIERS

Andhra Pradesh Dairy Development
Co-operative Federation Limited
G-28, Jangpura Extn.
New Delhi - 110 014.

Gujarat Co-operative Milk Marketing Federation Limited
Amul Dairy Road,
Post Box. No. 10
Anand - 388 001 (Gujarat)
Ph.: 23221/23272/23319
Fax: 02692-24950

Karnal Dist. Co-operative Milk Producers Union Limited
G.T. Road Bypass
Post Box. No. 84
Karnal - 132 001
Haryana

Rajasthan State Dairy Development Corporation Limited
15, Raniara Garden
Jaipur (Rajasthan).

Tamilnadu Cooperative Milk Producers' Federation Ltd.,
29 & 30 Industrial Estate
Ambattur, Chennai - 600 098.
Ph.: 044-6258520

PLANT ECONOMICS

Rated Plant capacity	=	500.00 KGS./day PANEER	
LAND & BUILDING (Land area required 400 sq.mts)		Rs.	7,50,000.00

LIST OF PLANT & MACHINERY

1. Storage tanks (Aluminium)
2. Pasteurization Vat
3. Curdling Vessel
4. Paneer Press
5. Cutting Machine
6. Other tanks, Pumps, Valves & miscellaneous handling equipment
7. Mini Boiler

FIXED CAPITAL

1.	LAND & BUILDING	Rs.	7,50,000.00
2.	PLANT & MACHINERY	Rs.	2,08,000.00
3.	OTHER FIXED ASSETS	Rs.	55,000.00
	TOTAL	**Rs.**	**10,13,000.00**

LIST OF RAW MATERIALS

1. Milk
2. Citric Acid
3. Other Various Chemical

TOTAL WORKING CAPITAL/MONTH

1.	RAW MATERIAL	Rs.	4,05,000.00
2.	SALARY & WAGES	Rs.	43,125.00
3.	UTILITIES & OVERHEADS	Rs.	18,000.00
	TOTAL	Rs.	**4,66,125.00**

TOTAL CAPITAL INVESTMENT

TOTAL FIXED CAPITAL	Rs.	10,13,000.00
TOTAL WORKING CAPITAL FOR 3 MONTHS	Rs.	13,98,375.00
TOTAL	**Rs.**	**24,11,375.00**

TURN OVER/ANNUM

1.	By sale of 500 x 300 kgs. of Paneer	Rs.	75,00,000.00

PROFIT = RECEIPTS - COST OF PRODUCTION
= 75,00,000.00 - 61,46,350.50
= 13,53,649.50

PROFIT SALES RATIO = Profit/Sales x 100 = 18.05 %

RATE OF RETURN = Operating profit/T.C.I. x 100 = 56.14 %

BREAK EVEN POINT (B.E.P) = 40.19 %

Manufacturers & Suppliers of Plant and Machineries

Mahesh Eng. Works
Supplying of extracting machinery, oil extractor machines, dryor-de-hydrator oil extractor machines, dairy machinery, butter making machinery, milking machine, bucket milking machine, mobile milking machine, dairy milking equipment, bulk milk cooler, etc.
Address: No. 1, Modi Estate,
Near Mahakali Temple, Dudheswer Road,
Ahmedabad - 380 004, India
Phone: +(91)-(79)-25626688
Fax: +(91)-(79)-25626688
Mobile: +(91)-9825336443
Website: www.milkycreamseparator.com

Master Food Tech
Supply and manufacture of food processing plants, ice cream plant machinery, ice plant machinery, brine chilling plant equipment, deep freezer plant equipment, cold storage plant, mushroom plant, dairy plant and industrial food processing plant.
Address: S. No. 232/2, Pune Nasik Road,
Atlas Compound, Opposite Rupee,
Co.Op.Bank, Bhosari, Pune - 411 039, India
Mobile: +(91)-9822027910

Shreya Engineering Works
Deals in manufacturing and supplying automatic filling machine, liquid fillers, filling machines, ice cream plant and dairy machinery, ice cream cup filling machine, ice cream filling machine, ice cream cup filling machine.
Address: Zone E-3, Shed No. C1/309,
Opposite Old Telephone Exchange,
Vitthal Udyognagar, Anand - 388 121, India
Phone: +(91)-(2692)-232185
Fax: +(91)-(2692)-232185
Mobile: +(91)-9427004851
Website: www.shreyaengineering.co.in

Swaraj Industries, India
Manufacturer and supplier of machinery such as weigh bowl horizontal milk storage tanks, stainless steel horizontal milk storage tanks, weigh bowl dairy tanks, leakage proof dairy tanks and steel dairy tanks.
Address: Gat No. 53, A/ P, Chimbli, Tal.
Khed, Pune - 412 105, India
Mobile: +(91)-9921691005
Website: www.swarajindustries.com

Triveni Engineering
Supplying and manufacturing chemical machinery, dyes machinery, dye intermediate machinery, industrial dyrer, ro system, wet cake dryer, paste dryer, herbal products machinery, food products machinery, nutraceutical machinery, dairy product machinery.
Address: Plot No. 62, Yamuna Estate, GIDC,
Phase- II, Vatva, Ahmedabad - 382 445,
India

Phone: +(91)-(79)-25830411
Fax: +(91)-(79)-25830411
Mobile: +(91)-9825095243/9879476859

Aaryavrat Engineering & Technologies
Engaged in manufacturing and exporting a range of weighing scales, electronic weighing scales and electronic weighing scale platform type. Also supply industrial process machinery, industrial process equipment, dairy equipments etc.
Address: 8 Renuka Royal, Plot No. 52, CTS 6258, Near Master Bakery, Ajmera Colony, Pimpri, Pune - 411 018, India
Fax: +(91)-(20)-30622073
Mobile: +(91)-9923087879/9370787980

Four Brothers Ex-imp Private Limited
Engaged in exporting and manufacturing of food processing machines, bakery machinery, candy machines, dairy equipments, popcorn machines, vermicelli machines, peanut butter making machine and dry fruit cutting machines.
Address: Old No. 123 New No. 255, Linghi Chetty Street, Chennai - 600 001, India
Phone: +(91)-(44)-42163224
Fax: +(91)-(44)-42167724
Mobile: +(91)-9940166232

Maruti Machines Pvt. Ltd.
Supplier of food processing equipments, bakery machinery, biscuit making machines, candy machines, confectionery machines, dairy processing plants, fruit processing equipments, mineral water plants, snack machines and vegetable dehydration plants.
Address: B - 23, Ambica Industrial Estate, Ambica Nagar, Odhav, Ahmedabad - 382 415, India
Phone: +(91)-(79)-22975760/22874026
Fax: +(91)-(79)-22874026
Mobile: +(91)-9879599554/9879798821

SS Engineers & Consultants
Manufacturing and supplying of food processing equipments that includes sterilizers, industrial sterilizers, bottle sterilizers, food sterilizers and dairy equipments. Also offers dairy plant and machinery, food processing equipments and dairy equipments.
Address: D. No. 11-49/2, Morumpudi Junction, Rajahmundry - 533 103, India
Phone: +(91)-(883)-2426845/2426846/2426847
Fax: +(91)-(883)-2430819
Mobile: +(91)-9440868551/9346144644

Laxmi Gas Services
Deals in supplying and manufacturing of bakery equipments, commercial bakery equipments, digital bakery equipment, bakery machinery, dairy equipments and steel dairy equipments.
Address: Mumbai Pune Road, Opposite Formaica Company, Akurdi, Pune - 411 035, India
Phone: +(91)-(20)-27692121
Mobile: +(91)-9822089812/9881370626

Sunrise Process Equipments
Manufacturing and supplying of food processing machinery like dairy tanks, diary storage tanks, food product storage tanks, metal food product storage tanks, steel storage tanks, stainless steel storage tanks and mild steel storage tanks etc.
Address: A-102, Shree Rameshwar Tower, Shimpoli Road Borivali West, Mumbai - 400 092, India
Phone: +(91)-(22)-28993705/28993706/28993707
Fax: +(91)-(22)-28993705
Mobile: +(91)-9821226682

BAAF Engineers Private Limited
Deals in manufacturing and supplying of industrial machinery that includes milk spray drying plants, milk evaporating plants, milk pasteurization plant and dairy milk pasteurization plants.
Address: E-48, Site-B, UPSIDC Surajpur Industrial Area, Dadri Road, Greater Noida - 201 306, India
Phone: +(91)-(120)-2560783
Fax: +(91)-(120)-2560784
Mobile: +(91)-9868565403

Delta Engineering, Pune
Engaged in manufacturing chemical processing machinery like pharmaceutical agitators, chemical agitators, chemical

reactors, industrial reactors along with pressure vessel, heat exchanger, dairy bag filters and stainless steel bin wash.
Address: W- 100, S- Block, MIDC, Bhosari, Pune - 411 026, India
Mobile: +(91)-9850329333

D-Mech Engineers
Deals in manufacturing of industrial machinery, milk pasteurizer, cleaning crate washer, can washer, crate washer, semi automatic can washer, processing can washer, electrical can washer and dairy can washer.
Address: Plot 4, Krishna Nagar, Sector 25, Faridabad - 121 001, India
Phone: +(91)-(129)-2441688/4150884
Fax: +(91)-(129)-4150884
Mobile: +(91)-9891267870/9756205100

AKAR MACHINERY CORPORATION
Manufacturer of paneer-press, cream separator, dairy machinery, deep fat fryer and atta kneading machine.
Address: Plot No. G-105, M.I.D.C. Gokul Shirgaon, Kolhapur - 416234, India
Phone: +(91)-(231)-2672008
Mobile: +(91)-9890207989/9326699999

Ashapuri Engineering Works
Deals in manufacturing and exporting of dairy equipments and dairy machinery parts.
Address: Chhagaji Compound, Opposite Pumping Station, Mehdikuva, Ahmedabad - 380 004, India
Phone: +(91)-(79)-25630715
Mobile: +(91)-9924243099

Milk - Tech Engineers
Engaged in production of dairy machinery like evaporator, pasteurizer, spray dryer, milk pump, khoa making machine, ghee ,aking machine and food processing machinery.
Address: No. 80, 3rd Floor, Lavanya Apartment, 13th Cross, Ganga Nagar, Bengaluru - 560 024, India
Mobile: +(91)-9448694666

Airtemp Refrigeration
Engaged in manufacturing and selling ice cream plant, hotel kitchen equipments, pourlour equipments, dairy machinery and refrigeration eqipments.
Address: No. 4, Kotadiya Estate, Opposite Raj Rani Beda Works, Near Corporation Gardan, Ambica Nagar, Odhav, GID, Ahmedabad - 380 024, India
Phone: +(91)-(79)-22977999
Fax: +(91)-(79)-22748743
Mobile: +(91)-9426014765

Shree Vishwakarma Engineering Corporation
Manufacturing and exporting all kinds of dairy equipments and dairy machinery.
Address: 2001/3, GIDC Vunagar, Vadodara - 388 121, India
Mobile: +(91)-9824019031

AKAR MACHINERY CORPORATION
Manufacturer of paneer-press, cream separator, dairy machinery, deep fat fryer and atta kneading machine.
Address: Plot No. G-105, M.I.D.C. Gokul Shirgaon, Kolhapur - 416234, India
Phone: +(91)-(231)-2672008
Mobile: +(91)-9890207989/9326699999

Eon Trading, LLC Delaware Usa
Exporters of cheese production machinery, dairy machinery and plants.
Address: T20, 3rd Floor, Super Mall, Salunke Vihar wanowrie, Pune - 411 040, India
Phone: +(91)-(20)-26837606
Fax: +(91)-(20)-26837606
Mobile: +(91)-9823468885/9850244437

Sonus International
Engaged in manufacturing of all kinds of food machinery moulds, dairy machinery moulds, chemical machinery moulds, confectionery machinery moulds and distillery machinery moulds.
Address: F-12, Rangoli Complex, Opposite V. S. Hospital, Ashram Road, Ellisbridge, Ahmedabad - 380 006, India
Phone: +(91)-(79)-26578116
Mobile: +(91)-9898181626

Kaival Engineers & Technology Systems
Manufacturers of a range of dairy machinery.

Address: No. 101, Shreeji Complex,
Plot No. 81, G. I. D. C., Makarpura,
Vadodara - 390 010, India
Phone: +(91)-(265)-2359752
Fax: +(91)-(265)-2637423
Mobile: +(91)-9879063551

Sneha Dairy Consultancy
Leading manufacturer of dairy machinery.
Address: Green Avenue, Opposite TGB Restaurant, Adajan, Surat - 395 009, India
Phone: +(91)-(261)-2746240
Fax: +(91)-(261)-2746240
Mobile: +(91)-9825116239

Milk - Tech Engineers
Engaged in production of dairy machinery like evaporator, pasteurizer, spray dryer, milk pump, khoa making machine, ghee ,aking machine and food processing machinery.
Address: No. 80, 3rd Floor, Lavanya Apartment, 13th Cross, Ganga Nagar, Bengaluru - 560 024, India
Mobile: +(91)-9448694666

The National Engineering Co.
Manufacturer and supplier of spice grinding machinery, dairy machinery, noodles making machinery and pulverizer machine.
Address: 22, Netaji Subhas Road, Kolkata - 700 001, India
Phone: +(91)-(33)-22206910
Fax: +(91)-(33)-22104973
Mobile: +(91)-9903976834

S. Y. M. Engineers
Suppliers of dairy machinery especially homogenizers and spares.
Address: W 72, M. I. D. C., Kolhapur - 416 234, India
Phone: +(91)-(231)-2671439

Vivek Engineering Works, Anand
Manufacturer of dairy machinery.
Address: Lambhvel Road, Near Indira Statue, Anand - 388 001, India
Phone: +(91)-(2692)-250663
Mobile: +(91)-9879859577

Nutec Food & Dairy Consulting
Suppliers of dairy machinery.
Address: Road No. 11, East Patel Nagar, Patna - 800 023, India
Mobile: +(91)-9835267011/9334318997

Srikar Refrigeration
Manufacturer of dairy machinery.
Address: No. 7-1-246/45, Balkampet, Hyderabad - 500 016, India
Mobile: +(91)-9394760979/9505457795

Castech (Uk) Limited
Engaged in supply polyurethane mouldings, precision aluminium castings, investment castings, stainless steel investment castings for instrumentation, food processing industry, dairy machinery etc.
Address: Unit 10 Manor Farm Astwood, Bucks - Mk16 9JS, United Kingdom
Phone: +(44)-(1234)-391973
Fax: +(44)-(1234)-391185

N.T. F.-Aalborg A/S
Deals in all kinds of dairy plants and dairy machinery.
Address: Hagensvej-17, Stovring - DK9 530, Denmark
Phone: +(45)-(9837)-3766
Fax: +(45)-(9837)-3751

Caseartecnica Bartoli Srl
Authorized dealer of mixers, dairy machinery and dairy equipments.
Address: 26, V. Bernini, Parma - 43100, Italy
Phone: +(39)-(521)-982381
Fax: +(39)-(0521)-994866

L. P. Kolding A/S
Deals in all types of dairy machinery.
Address: Egtvedvej-2, Kolding - DK6 000, Denmark
Phone: +(45)-(7552)-4177
Fax: +(45)-(7553)-2351

Hojer Orbaek A/S
Deals in all types of dairy plants and dairy machinery.
Address: Langemosevaenget-3-5, Post Box 21, Orbaek - DK5 853, Denmark
Phone: +(45)-(6533)-1566
Fax: +(45)-(6533)-1668

Ingvald
Deals in all kinds of food processing machines like dairy articles, dairy plants, dairy machinery, fish industry machinery and food industry machines.
Address: Jeppe Aakjaers Alle-14,
Post Box-659, Odense
N. V. - DK5 210, Denmark
Phone: +(45)-(0)-66118211
Fax: +(45)-(0)-66118250

A. B. C. Hansen A/S
Dealing in all kinds of dairy plants and dairy machinery.
Address: Mollestensvej-13, Post Box 73,
Randers - DK8 900, Denmark
Phone: +(45)-(8642)-6488
Fax: +(45)-(8641)-3622

Shree Vishwakarma Engineering Corporation
Manufacturing and exporting all kinds of dairy equipments and dairy machinery.
Address: 2001/3, GIDC Vunagar,
Vadodara - 388 121, India
Mobile: +(91)-9824019031

Srikar Refrigeration
Manufacturer of dairy machinery.
Address: No. 7-1-246/45, Balkampet,
Hyderabad - 500 016, India
Mobile: +(91)-9394760979/9505457795

Milk - Tech Engineers
Engaged in production of dairy machinery like evaporator, pasteurizer, spray dryer, milk pump, khoa making machine, ghee ,aking machine and food processing machinery.
Address: No. 80, 3rd Floor, Lavanya
Apartment, 13th Cross, Ganga Nagar,
Bengaluru - 560 024, India
Mobile: +(91)-9448694666

AKAR MACHINERY CORPORATION
Manufacturer of paneer-press, cream separator, dairy machinery, deep fat fryer and atta kneading machine.
Address: Plot No. G-105, M.I.D.C. Gokul
Shirgaon, Kolhapur - 416234, India
Phone: +(91)-(231)-2672008
Mobile: +(91)-9890207989/9326699999

Parikh Udyog
Engaged in manufacturing steel investment castings, alloy steel investment castings, industrial investment castings and stainless steel investment castings for food processing industry, dairy machinery, artificial limbs and packing equipment.
Address: C-14, M I D C Gokul Shirgaon,
Kolhapur - 416234, India
Phone: +(91)-(231)-2672269/2672438
Fax: +(91)-(231)-2672520
Mobile: +(91)-9822044892

S. Y. M. Engineers
Suppliers of dairy machinery especially homogenizers and spares.
Address: W 72, M. I. D. C.,
Kolhapur - 416 234, India
Phone: +(91)-(231)-2671439

Kaival Engineers & Technology Systems
Manufacturers of a range of dairy machinery
Address: No. 101, Shreeji Complex, Plot No. 81, G.I.D.C., Makarpura,
Vadodara - 390 010, India
Phone: +(91)-(265)-2359752
Fax: +(91)-(265)-2637423
Mobile: +(91)-9879063551

The National Engineering Co.
Manufacturer and supplier of spice grinding machinery, dairy machinery, noodles making machinery and pulverizer machine.
Address: 22, Netaji Subhas Road,
Kolkata - 700 001, India
Phone: +(91)-(33)-22206910
Fax: +(91)-(33)-22104973
Mobile: +(91)-9903976834

Eon Trading, LLC Delaware Usa
Exporters of cheese production machinery, dairy machinery and plants.
Address: T20, 3rd Floor, Super Mall,
Salunke Vihar wanowrie,
Pune - 411 040, India
Phone: +(91)-(20)-26837606
Fax: +(91)-(20)-26837606
Mobile: +(91)-9823468885/9850244437

DIRECTORYSECTION

Vivek Engineering Works, Anand
Manufacturer of dairy machinery.
Address: Lambhvel Road, Near Indira Statue, Anand - 388 001, India
Phone: +(91)-(2692)-250663
Mobile: +(91)-9879859577

Keshari Agro & Dairy Consultant
Wholesaler and trader of dairy machinery.
Address: Govrnment. Milk Scheem, Civil Line, Near W C L, Nagpur - 440 001, India
Mobile: +(91)-9890807179

Sneha Dairy Consultancy
Leading manufacturer of dairy machinery.
Address: Green Avenue, Opposite TGB Restaurant, Adajan, Surat - 395 009, India
Phone: +(91)-(261)-2746240
Fax: +(91)-(261)-2746240
Mobile: +(91)-9825116239

Ashapuri Engineering Works
Deals in manufacturing and exporting of dairy equipments and dairy machinery parts.
Address: Chhagaji Compound, Opposite Pumping Station, Mehdikuva, Ahmedabad - 380 004, India
Phone: +(91)-(79)-25630715
Mobile: +(91)-9924243099

Avedemil
Wholesale dealers of dairy machinery.
Address: Z. I. Rn 10, Ruffec - 16700, France
Phone: +(33)-(545)-891148

A. B. C. Hansen A/S
Dealing in all kinds of dairy plants and dairy machinery.
Address: Mollestensvej-13, Post Box 73, Randers - DK8 900, Denmark
Phone: +(45)-(8642)-6488
Fax: +(45)-(8641)-3622

Handing ApS
Deals into all types of dairy plants and dairy machinery.
Address: Nordkranvej-5-9, Lynge - DK3 540, Denmark
Phone: +(45)-(481)-60166
Fax: +(45)-(481)-60165

Scandinavian Production & Processing Company A/S
Deals in all kinds of dairy plants, dairy machinery and ice cream machines.
Address: Sams?vej-30E, Hinnerup - DK8 382, Denmark
Phone: +(45)-(8691)-1499
Fax: +(45)-(8691)-1833

Fullwood Limited
Deals in robotic milking machines and dairy machinery.
Address: Grange Road, Ellesmere - SY129DF, United Kingdom
Phone: +(44)-(1691)-627391
Fax: +(44)-(1691)-627361

Ingvald
Deals in all kinds of food processing machines like dairy articles, dairy plants, dairy machinery, fish industry machinery and food industry machines.
Address: Jeppe Aakjaers Alle-14, Post Box-659, Odense N. V. - DK5 210 Denmark
Phone: +(45)-(0)-66118211
Fax: +(45)-(0)-66118250

L. P. Kolding A/S
Deals in all types of dairy machinery.
Address: Egtvedvej-2, Kolding - DK6 000, Denmark
Phone: +(45)-(7552)-4177
Fax: +(45)-(7553)-2351

Ganesh Engineers, Mumbai
Manufacturer, exporter and supplier of diary machinery spare parts and dairy equipment.
Address: No. 13/14, Jaybharat Industrial Estate, Opposite Virwani, Industrial Estate, Near Wester Express Highway, Goregaon East, Mumbai - 400 063, India
Phone: +(91)-(22)-28740962

Finix India Equipments
Suppliers of dairy equipments and food machinery.
Address: Sect. 7, Plot No. 55, P.c.n.t.d.a. M. I. D. C., Bhosari, Pune - 411 026, India
Phone: +(91)-(20)-66303168/27125155
Fax: +(91)-(20)-27125155

Mahesh Process Equipments Private Limited
Engaged in manufacturing of food processing machinery and dairy equipment.
Address: Plot No. 408, Savli DIDC, Manjusar, Vadodara - 391 775, India
Phone: +(91)-(266)-7264408/3253183
Mobile: +(91)-9377587898

Kims Engineers Private Limited
Manufacturing and exporting dairy processing machinery, food processing machinery and dairy equipment.
Address: Plot No. 39, Phase-II, Kasba Industrial Estate, Kolkata - 700 001, India
Phone: +(91)-(33)-24428622
Fax: +(91)-(33)-24431181

Shree Sai Projects, Saharanpur
Manafacturers and exporters of food processing equipments, dairy equipments like milk silo, bulk milk cooler, amcs, milk storage tanks, ghee boiler, butter churn, spray dryer, evaporators, chemical and distillary plant and machinery.
Address: Trade Centre, Pratap Market, Saharanpur - 247 001, India
Phone: +(91)-(132)-2766355
Fax: +(91)-(132)-2766355
Mobile: +(91)-9258077752

Intoto Marketing
Exporters of all kinds of packaging machineries for dairy, food industries, rotary band sealers etc.
Address: Off. 4, Commerce Centre Paud Road, Kothrud, Pune - 411 038, India
Phone: +(91)-(20)-25412389/25412390
Fax: +(91)-(20)-25461824

E. I. Daggoy Trading Company
Exporter of all type of machineries like soap cutting, embossing, candy plant, pouch machinery, tallow bleaching plant, salt milling, dairy milk plant & machinery, stone crusher machine, wheat silo plant etc.
Address: Mata Ramabai, Ambedkar Nagar, Mumbai - 400 076, India
Phone: +(91)-(22)-25786345
Mobile: +(91)-9820251944

Devi Exim Private Limited
Exporters of food processing machinery such as dairy equipment etc.
Address: 20, Barakhamba Road, New Delhi - 110 001, India
Phone: +(91)-(11)-23314786/23310815
Fax: +(91)-(11)-23315405

Ess Pee Sales Agency, Delhi
Exporters of Dairy Plants,dairy Equipments,Food Processing Machinery,float balance tank, ghee boiler, milk storage tank,soft drink plants, plate heat exchangers, htst pasteurization plant etc.
Address: 71, Kundan Nagar, Laxmi Nagar, Delhi - 110 092, India
Phone: +(91)-(11)-22413437

Suruchi Consultants
Manufacturers of dairy and food industry plants and machineries
Address: A 661, Sector 19, Noida - 201 301, India
Phone: +(91)-(120)-2523845/4320845
Fax: +(91)-(120)-2523845 / 2553033
Mobile: +(91)-9810315831

3A Technik
Merchant trader of food processing machinery and dairy food machines.
Address: Landstrasse 60, Vaduz - 9490, Switzerland
Phone: +(41)-(77)-2534375
Fax: +(41)-(77)-2534375
Mobile: +(41)-772534375

Beigi Enterprises Limited
Sellers of used packaging, processing dairy equipments and machineries.
Address: 1500 Marine Drive, North Vancouver - V7P1T7, Canada
Phone: +(1)-(604)-9041213
Fax: +(1)-(604)-9041213
Mobile: +(1)-604-762-2266

Hammerum Stainless A/s
Dealing in all kinds of dairy equipments and slaughterhouse machinery.
Address: Dunsbjergvej-20, Rudkobing - DK5 900, Denmark
Phone: +(45)-(6333)-1800

DIRECTORYSECTION

Yemen Dairy & Juice Industries Syc
manufacturers of machinery for juice and dairy products.
Address: P. O. Box 333, Hodeidah, Sana Road, Al-Hudaydah - 3337, Yemen
Phone: +(967)-(3)-228801
Fax: +(967)-(3)-228825

Kanters Gilze B. V.
Exporters of milking machinery and dairy cooler tanks.
Address: Lange Wagenstraat 11 A,
Gilze - Nl5126 Ba, The Netherlands
Phone: +(31)-(161)-459797

A. P. V. Canada, Inc.
Manufacturer of all kinds of food processing machinery and dairy processing equipments.
Address:3280, Langstaff Road,
Concord - L4K 4Z8, Canada
Phone: +(1)-(905)-7601852
Fax: +(1)-(905)-7601879

Millerbernd Manufacturing Co.
Engaged in manufacturing and supplying plant machinery, metal fabrication equipment and dairy processing equipment.
Address:622, 6th Street South,
Winsted - 55395-772,
United States Of America
Phone: +(1)-(320)-4852685
Fax: +(1)-(320)-4853900

Agmachine.com Limited
Engaged in supplying of all types of agricultural machinery such as farm equipments, tractors, sowing machinery, grain harvesting machinery, crop drying machinery, chemical spraying machinery, chemical fertilising machinery and dairy farming machine.
Address: 25 Roman Road, Steyning,
Sussex - BN443FN, United Kingdom
Phone: +(44)-(1903)-810263

Jaya Industries, Kolkatta
Suppliers of food processing equipment, dairy equipment, road milk tanker, storage tanks, milk product chillers, milk product pasteurizes, aging tanks, equipment of manufacturing and packing butter/ghee, milk powder conveying systems, milk cans etc.
Address: No. 543, Jessore Road, Kolkata, West Bengal - 700 028, India
Phone: +(91)-(33)-25600361/25513568 Fax: +(91)-(33)-25799337
Mobile: +(91)-9231694285/9433005594
Website: http://www.jaya-industries.com

Nu-tech Dairy Engineers Private Limited
Exporter and manufacturer of industrial machinery such as material handling machinery, bagging machinery, khoya making machinery, post harvest machinery and food processing machinery.
Address: Plot No. 34, H S I I D C Food Park Saha, Ambala - 133 104, India
Phone: +(91)-(171)-2822700
Fax: +(91)-(171)-2822699
Mobile: +(91)-9354706554/9896067779

Yash Pharma Machineries
Deals in exporting and manufacturing of dairy products such as cream manufacturing plants, jacketed cream plants and automatic cream manufacturing plants.
Address: 110, Pushpak Industrial Estate,
Nika Tube Compound, Phase-1, G.I.D.C.,
Vatva, Ahmedabad - 382 445, India
Phone: +(91)-(79)-25895872
Fax: +(91)-(79)-25895872
Mobile: +(91)-9376148872/9426040661

Indian Dairy Equipment Co.
Engaged in manufacturing and supplying of industrial machinery, milking machine with single cluster, power operated industrial machinery and electrical power operated industrial machinery.
Address: No. 364, Azad Market,
Delhi - 110 006, India
Phone: +(91)-(11)-23615823
Fax: +(91)-(11)-23682900
Mobile: +(91)-9313824222

Kadam Dairy Equipments Private Limited
Manufacturer and supplier of food processing plants, food processing machinery, milk cooler, drip saver, can scrubber, cheese making equipment, chillers, milk packing machinery, ice cream plants, ghee boilers, milk storage

tanks and much more.
Address: 612, Vakil Nagar, Erandwana,
Pune - 411004, India
Phone: +(91)-(20)-25448796
Fax: +(91)-(20)-25448796
Mobile: +(91)-9371311709

Gimret & Co.
Manufacturer and suppliers of food processing equipment, food processing machines, food treatment machines, dairy product processing machine, mixing machine, dispersing machine, heating, creaming system and cooling machine.
Address: 403, Rohit House, Tolstoy Marg,
New Delhi - 110 001, India
Phone: +(91)-(11)-43586381/23314422
Fax: +(91)-(11)-23314377

Maxcare Marketing & Technical Services
Manufacturers and exporters of plant machinery for diary and food processing plants
Address: J-188, Saket, New Delhi - 110 017
Phone: +(91)-(11)-29555273/29552464
Fax: +(91)-(11)-29552464
Mobile: +(91)-9810819225

Krishna Dairy Machinery Corporation
Manufacturers of dairy, food processing equipments.
Address: A-23, Haridarshan Park Shopping Centre, Near Shankar Estate, Sureliya Road, Amraiwadi, Ahmedabad - 380 026, India
Fax: +(91)-(79)-25860857
Mobile: +(91)-9426048845

Pray Dairy Machinery Corporation
Manufacturer and dealer of chemical equipment.
Address: No. A/21, Revabhai Estate, Near Ishwarkrupa Kanta, Opposite Shankar Estate, CTM, Amraiwadi,
Ahmedabad - 382 445, India
Mobile: +(91)-9998329938

Thompsons Food Machinery
Exporters of quality used food processing machinery.
Address: Unit K. G., Business Centre,
Dallington, Northampton - NN5 7QS,
United Kingdom
Phone: +(44)-(1604)-655400

Westney International Limited
Dealing in all kinds of agricultural machinery such as cultivators, dairy machinery, disc harrows and fertiliser spreaders.
Address: The Old Granary New Street,
Sudbury - CO101JB, United Kingdom
Phone: +(44)-(1787)-379600
Fax: +(44)-(1787)-372846

Shanghai Pilotech Instrument
Manufacturer of all kinds of milk processing equipments and dairy machines.
Address: Building B No. 521, South Wanpinglu, Wanping Nan Road, Xuhui District, Shanghai - 200 032, China
Phone: +(86)-(21)-51082915
Fax: +(86)-(21)-54243425

Dairy Engineers & Consultants
Manufacturer and exporter of dairy machines and ice cream machines.
Address: No. 601, Satkrut Tower, Parth Sarthi Avenue, Near Shyamal Row House-2, Satellite, Ahmedabad - 380 015, India
Phone: +(91)-(79)-26760252
Mobile: +(91)-9825243624

Remi Process Plant And Machinery R. P. P. M. L
Manufacturer and exporter of emulsifiers, portable agitators, dairy, breweries and top entry agitators.
Address: Remi House, Plot No.11, Cama Industrial Estates Walbhat Road, Goregaon East, Mumbai - 400 063, India
Phone: +(91)-(22)-40589800
Fax: +(91)-(22)-26852335

Rupesh Equipments
Manufacturers of dairy equipment, chemical equipment and food processing equipment.
Address: Plot No. 29, Sector No. 10, P. C. N. T. D. A., Near Times Of India, Bhosari,
Pune - 411 026, India
Phone: +(91)-(20)-25730743/27119972

ALL FOLLOWING PROJECT REPORTS ARE READILY AVAILABLE

AGRO BASED INDUSTRIES

- Coal Briquettes From Agrowaste
- Furfuralfrom Ricehull
- Mushroom Cultivation & Processing (Button)
- Mushroom Growing & Processing With Air Conditioning
- Mushroom Cultivation & Processing Unit Dehydration & Packaging Of Oyster & Paddy Straw Mushrooms
- Organic Manure
- Papaya Cultivation
- Papaya & Tomato Cultivation
- Processing & Utilisation Of Coconut
- Processing Of Sheep Hair To Produce Wool
- White Oats

BAKERY CONFECTIONERY & FOOD PRODUCTS

- Agrolactor Soya Milk
- Automatic Biscuit Naking Plant
- Automatic Bread Making Plant
- Apple Fruit Juice With Canning Bottling
- Ayurvedic Sharbat
- Bakery Unit (Pastries, Bread, Buns, Cake, Toffee Etc.)
- Baking Powder
- Banana & Its By Products
- Banana Powder
- Banana Wafers
- Banana Cultivation
- Beer Industry
- Dehulling Of Jaun For Beer
- Beer & Wine
- Beer, Alcohol, Imfl
- Besen Plant
- Biscuit Plant
- Bread & Biscuit Plant
- Bottling Plant (Country Liquor) From Rectified Spirit
- Bottling Plant (Imfl And Country Liquor)
- Brandy
- Bread Rusks
- Buffalo Meat/Frozen Meat With Slaughter House
- Canned Fruits & Vegetables
- Canning & Preservation Of Meat
- Canning & Preservation Of Vegetables
- Canning Of Mango Pulp & Mango Slices
- Carbonated Beverags
- Cashew Feni
- Cashew Nut (Dried & Fried)
- Cashew Nut Shell Liquid And Kernel
- Cattle Breeding
- Cattle Breeding & Dairy Farm To Produce Milk
- Cattle Feed From Tapioca
- Chewing Ginger & Amloki
- Chewing Gum
- Chilli Sauce
- Chilli Powder
- Chicken Processing With Slaughter House
- Chocolate
- Cider Plant
- Cocoa Powder
- Cocoa Butter & Cocoa Powder
- Coconut Shell Powder
- Coconut Water
- Coconut Sweet (Watery)
- Coconut Milk Powder (Dehydrated)
- Coconut Products & By Products (Integrated Plant)
- Cold Drink
- Curry Powder
- Dairy For Milk Processing (Ghee, Butter & Paneer)
- Dairy Products
- Dairy Products Milk Packaging In Pouch (Ghee, Butter, Etc.
- Dairy Farm To Prduce Milk With Packaging (Cow)
- Dairy Farm To Prduce Milk With Packaging (Bufalloe)
- Dairy Farm & Milk Products
- Dal Moth, Chanachur & Bhujiya
- Dall Mill (Pulse)
- Dehydration Of Fruits & Vegetable
- Dehydration Of Fruits And Vegetables By Vacuum Drying Method
- Desiccated Coconut Powder From Coconuts
- Dehydration & Canning Of Fruits & Vegetables
- Dry Fruit Roasting & Packaging
- Drying Of Red Chillies, Haldi, Dhaniya, Peas & Ground Nut
- Dry Ginger (Ginger Powder)
- Egg Powder
- Fish Canning In Tin & Pouches
- Fish Dehyration (Drying Of Fish)
- Fish Meal
- Fish Processing (Beast Freezing Processes)
- Flavours For Food Industries
- Flour Mill (Roller)
- Frozen Meat
- Food Dehydration (Fruits & Vegetables)
- Fried & Roasted Ground Nut, Grams, Pear Etc.
- Fruit Juice Making & Packaging In Plastic Container
- Fruit Juice In Tetra Pack (Drinks)
- Fruit Juice, Squashes, Sauce & Ketchup, Jam, Jelly, Vinegar Etc.
- Garlic Flakes
- Garlic Powder
- Ghee & Butter
- Ginger (Pulverised)
- Ginger Glazing & Preservation
- Ginger Storage
- Ginger Processing
- Ginger Oil & Ginger Dust
- Ginger Powder (Dry) & Oleoresin
- Grape Dehydration
- Grape Cultivation
- Grape Juice
- Grape Wine
- Groundnut Processing
- Honey Processing & Packaging
- Ice Cream & Ice Candy
- Ice Cube
- Invert Sugar
- Idli Mix, Dosa Mix Sambhar Mix, Vada Mix,Gulab Jamun Mix
- Instant Coffee & Instant Tea
- Instant Noodles
- Instant Soups
- Iodized Salt From Crude Salt
- Jam Chutney Pickles & Squashes
- Katha Manufacturing
- Lecithin (Soya Based)
- Lemon & Its Products
- Macaroni Manufacturing
- Macaroni, Spaghetti, Vermicelli & Noodles
- Maize & Its By Products Malting Plant
- Mango Pappad (Aam Pappad)
- Mango Powder Ripe
- Mango Powder
- Mango Processing & Canning (Mango Pulp)
- Meat Processing (Chicken Mutton)
- Meat Processing (Buffalo)
- Menthol Bold From Menthol Flakes
- Milk Powder
- Milk Powder & Ghee
- Milk Powder, Ghee & Spices
- Milk Preservation & Marketing To Whole Sellers
- Milk Preservation & Marketing To Whole Sellers (In Pouches)
- Milk Toffee Manufactures
- Mineral Water
- Mineral Water In Pouches
- Mini Flour Mill Atta Maida, Suji & Wheat Bran
- Mithai/Halwai (Sweet & Namkeen)
- Mutton Processing
- Pan Masala (Meetha, Sada, Zarda) Making & Packing
- Pan Masala And Pouch Making
- Paneer (Cheese)
- Papad & Bariyan
- Papad Plant
- Pepsicola In Polytubes
- Petha Packaging
- Pickles
- Piggery/Meat/Chicken Processing
- Pine Apple Juice Manufacturing And Canning
- Potato & Onion Powder
- Potato & Onion Flakes
- Potato Chips
- Potato Granules
- Pouch Filling For Saunf Supari Ilaichi Etc.
- Preservation Of Raws Mango Juice
- Processed Cheese & Marine Pdts.